A New Star-Rating System & Other Exciting News from Frommer's!

In our continuing effort to publish the savviest, most up-to-date, and most appealing travel guides available, we've added some great new features.

Frommer's guides now include a new **star-rating system.** Every hotel, restaurant, and attraction is rated from 0 to 3 stars to help you set priorities and organize your time.

We've also added **seven brand-new features** that point you to the great deals, in-the-know advice, and unique experiences that separate travelers from tourists. Throughout the guide look for:

Finds	Special finds—those places only insiders know about
Fun Fact	Fun facts—details that make travelers more informed and their trips more fun
Kids	Best bets for kids—advice for the whole family
Moments	Special moments—those experiences that memories are made of
Overrated	Places or experiences not worth your time or money
Tips	Insider tips—some great ways to save time and money
Value	Great values—where to get the best deals

Here's what the critics say about Frommer's:

"Amazingly easy to use. Very portable, very complete."

—Booklist

"The only mainstream guide to list specific prices. The Walter Cronkite of guidebooks—with all that implies."

—Travel & Leisure

"Complete, concise, and filled with useful information."
—New York Daily News

"Hotel information is close to encyclopedic."
—Des Moines Sunday Register

"Detailed, accurate, and easy-to-read information for all price ranges."
—Glamour Magazine

Other Great Guides for Your Trip:

Frommer's Canada

Frommer's Nova Scotia, New Brunswick, and Prince Edward Island

Frommer's Montréal & Quebec City

Frommer's Ottawa

Halifax

1st Edition

by Carol Matthews

John Wiley & Sons Canada, Ltd.

About the Author

Carol Matthews loves to write about locations in North America and Europe, but finds spots closer to home, in Nova Scotia, Canada, equally appealing. She has been published in anthologies, magazines and newspapers, and contributes to Internet travel sites.

Published by:

John Wiley & Sons Canada, Ltd.

22 Worcester Road
Etobicoke, ON M9W 1L1

National Library of Canada Cataloguing in Publication

Matthews, Carol
  Frommer's Halifax / Carol Matthews. — 1st ed.

Includes index.

ISBN 0–470–83222–3

1. Halifax (N.S.)—Guidebooks. I. Title.

FC2346.18.M38 2003   917.16'225044   C2003–900260–8
F1039.5.H17M37 2003

Executive Editor: Joan Whitman
Editor: Melanie Rutledge
Publishing Services Director: Karen Bryan
Cartographer: Mapping Specialists, Ltd.
Cover design by Kyle Gell
Front cover photo by Barrett & MacKay Photography
Back cover photo by J. A. Kraulis / Masterfile
Text layout by IBEX Graphic Communications Inc.

Special Sales

For reseller information, including discounts and premium sales, please call our sales department: Tel.: 416-646-7992. For press review copies, author interviews, or other publicity information, please contact our marketing department: Tel.: 416-646-4584; Fax.: 416-236-4448.

1 2 3 4 5 TRI 06 05 04 03 02

Manufactured in Canada

Contents

List of Maps

Acknowledgments

Many thanks to Jean Clulee, Margan Dawson, Andrea Dawson Gosine, and especially my husband, Brian Matthews, for their research assistance, and my family for their help, patience, and support.

—Carol Matthews

An Invitation to the Reader

In researching this book, we discovered many wonderful places—hotels, restaurants, shops. And more. We're sure you'll find others. Please tell us about them, so we can share the information with your fellow travelers in upcoming editions. If you were disappointed with a recommendation, we'd love to know that too. Please write to:

Frommer's Halifax, 1st Edition
John Wiley & Sons Canada, Ltd. • 22 Worcester Road • Etobicoke, ON M9W 1L1

An Additional Note

Please be advised that travel information is subject to change at any time—and this is especially true of prices. We therefore suggest that you write or call ahead for confirmation when making your travel plans. The authors, editors, and publishers cannot be held responsible for the experiences of readers while traveling. Your safety is important to us, however, so we encourage you to stay alert and be aware of your surroundings. Keep a close eye on cameras, purses and wallets, all favorite targets of thieves and pickpockets.

New! Frommer's Star Ratings & Icons

Every hotel, restaurant and attraction listing in this guide has been ranked for quality, value, service, amenities, and special features using a star-rating scale. In country, state, and regional guides, we also rate towns and regions to help you narrow down your choices and budget your time accordingly. Hotels and restaurants in the Very Expensive and Expensive categories are rated on a scale of one (highly recommended) to three stars (exceptional). Those in the Moderate and Inexpensive categories rate from zero (recommended) to two stars (very highly recommended). Attractions, towns, and regions are rated according to the following scale: zero stars (recommended), one star (highly recommended), two stars (very highly recommended), and three stars (must-see).

In addition to the rating system, we also use seven icons to highlight insider information, useful tips, special bargains, hidden gems, memorable experiences, kid-friendly venues, places to avoid, and other useful information:

(Finds   (Fun Fact   (Kids   (Moments   (Overrated   (Tips   (Value

The following abbreviations are used for credit cards:

AE	American Express	DISC	Discover	V	Visa
DC	Diners Club	MC	MasterCard		

FROMMERS.COM

Now that you have the guidebook to a great trip, visit our website at **www.frommers.com** for travel information on nearly 2,000 destinations. With features updated regularly, we give you instant access to the most current trip-planning information available. At Frommers.com, you'll also find the best prices on air fares, accommodations, and car rentals—you can even book travel online though our travel booking partners. At Frommers.com you'll find the following:

- Daily Newsletter highlighting the best travel deals
- Hot Spot of the Month/Vacation Sweepstakes & Travel Photo Contest
- More than 200 Travel Message Boards
- Outspoken Newsletters and Feature Articles on travel bargains, vacation ideas, tips & resources, and more!

The Best of Halifax

Halifax is the major cultural, business, and education center of Canada's three Atlantic provinces, and of this it is rightly proud. The city is home to annual music and film festivals, as well as to theater and symphony. The highly regarded Art Gallery of Nova Scotia not only boasts an impressive permanent collection that keeps pace with other public art institutions in Montreal and Toronto, but increasingly plays host to internationally touring exhibitions—and it's often the only Canadian stop on the tour. If you include pubs, bars, and the like in your definition of culture, rumor has it that Halifax has more per capita than any other city in North America.

The city's economy is pumping away, these days. The educated workforce with high-tech know-how attracts investment from the information technology industry. Gas and oil discovered just off the coast is bringing business to the city as well. Halifax has what can only be described as a youthful buzz, since thousands of university students from North America and abroad call the city home for eight months of the year, attending one of six post-secondary institutions.

It's not all roses, however. Halifax Harbour is still polluted, lack of sufficient parking—particularly downtown—continues to be a headache, and bicycle routes aren't being developed fast enough for ecology-conscious commuters.

History is a big part of Halifax. You encounter it wherever you go. From the noonday gun that's fired daily (for nearly 350 years!) from Halifax Citadel National Historic Site, to the buildings of Privateers Wharf, where booty stolen from enemy ships during the American Revolution and the War of 1812 was auctioned to the highest bidder. Haligonians are surrounded by their history: in the buildings where they work, on the streets, and in the harbor that encircles their peninsula. Canadian Confederation was promoted and protested in Province House. Victims of the *Titanic* disaster are buried in the graveyards. Allied navies in two world wars were serviced from the harbor. International political leaders came to discuss economic strategies at a G–7 Summit.

In Halifax, the only topic more heatedly discussed than politics is the weather. Will it be an early spring, a wet summer, or a cold fall? Will it snow or rain? Will it snow *and* rain? Will it be a mild hurricane season (Halifax traditionally receives the tail end of hurricanes moving up the Eastern seaboard between August and October), or will the city experience another season like the one that brought Hurricane Edna, in 1954: In her wake, she left flooded basements, roofless buildings, and shipwrecks. Nobody checks the weather announcements more often than Haligonians, because nowhere else does the weather change more often—even during the same day.

Between their history and their weather, Haligonians have generally become a philosophical bunch. That doesn't mean they aren't activists and entrepreneurs and people who get hot-tempered at times, but there's a dose of pragmatism in how they live their lives. They seem to understand that the only permanence in life is change, so they'd better take advantage of the here and now. Which is why Halifax knows how to party. Nothing formal, you understand, just good music, good food and drink, and good friends to share it with after a long day or week.

If this sounds more like a small town than a big city, Halifax seems proud to be that way. It's not interested in becoming another Toronto or Montreal; on the contrary, Haligonians appreciate their home—where motorists stop for pedestrians crossing the street (even if they cross where they're not legally supposed to!), where grounded airplane passengers are hosted in people's homes, and where passing strangers strolling the downtown streets at night encounter each other not so much with anxiety as with acceptance.

1 Frommer's Favorite Halifax Experiences

- **The Noon Gun on Citadel Hill.** You'll experience this regardless of where you are in the city, and, frankly, a good distance away from the Citadel might be your preference. Nevertheless, if you happen to be visiting Halifax Citadel National Historic Site near noontime, be sure to watch the soldiers load the cannon and fire it off. Cover your ears, of course. See chapter 6.

- **The Tour of Alexander Keith's Brewery.** You don't have to be a beer nut to get a kick out of this tour at the legendary and much-lauded brewery. Tour guides—complete in period apparel from the 1800s—lead you through the engaging history of the brewery's signature beer, Keith's India Pale Ale, dropping in bits of insight into Alexander Keith himself. After catching a glimpse of the piece of paper that contains the original recipe for the India Pale Ale, you continue on to view the vats where the beer is brewed today. The tour winds up in the on-site pub (what brewery would be complete without one?), which offers entertainment. This excellent tour is further fueled by generous samples of Mr. Keith's product. See chapter 6.

- **A Ferry Ride across the Harbor to Dartmouth.** For less than C$5 (US$3.50) return, you can get out on the water and take in the best view of the city. Board the ferry to Alderney Gate at the Halifax terminal, on Water Street. Depending on the time of day, you may be joined by a host of Haligonians (locals) during morning and evening rush hours, or you may find yourself practically alone during the middle of the day or early evening. Either way, sit back and admire the Halifax skyline. Bring along your camera. If you're lucky—and your ferry operator is so disposed—you might glide close to one of the many frigates and commercial cruise ships that visit the port. Visit a while in Dartmouth; there's lots to see and do. Round trip time is less than 45 minutes. See chapter 6.

- **The Halifax Public Gardens.** It goes without saying that visitors should spend some time in the Public Gardens. Stroll through 17 acres of fragrant flowers and shady trees, make wishes in an ornate water fountain, watch newlyweds have their photos taken, and lounge on a park bench and feed the ducks. You'll be glad you took the time. See chapter 7.

- **Point Pleasant Park in a Snowstorm.** Well, not a raging snowstorm, but the kind where giant flakes drift slowly to the ground, and the world is more quiet than silent. At such times, a walk through the park is a magical experience, an opportunity for romance or reflection. Bring along some sunflower seeds (unsalted) to feed the chickadees that will likely as not land on your outstretched hand if you stand still long enough. See chapter 7.

- **After Dark on the Waterfront.** You may have been here during the day. Maybe you ate lunch here, or hurried down to one of the piers to catch a boat tour, or ambled along the promenade watching the buskers. But what about at night? What about after the sun goes down, when the waterfront is lit with thousands of lights from the surrounding buildings and boats? Have you seen the white lights of the A. Murray MacKay or Angus L. Macdonald bridges arching over the harbor, with the red taillights of automobiles drawing lines behind them, or the flashing lights of advertising billboards as they make beautiful mirrored pictures on the water? (Even rampant commercialism can be pretty, sometimes.) At night, the historic buildings that line the waterfront take on a special feel and harken back to another time. You sense that you could turn any corner and meet a lady in a fine dress with hoop skirts, or a privateer counting his gold coins. See chapter 9.

- **A Walk across the Angus L. Macdonald Bridge.** Do something many residents haven't and follow the walking lane over the Macdonald Bridge. Best times are a calm day or an especially warm summer night. The bridge is slightly less than a kilometer (⅔ mile) in length, so, depending on your walking speed and the amount of time you spend admir-

ing the view, the trip over and back should take you about an hour. I wouldn't recommend this, however, if you're afraid of heights. See chapter 6.

- **Shakespeare by the Sea.** Talk about melodramatic. Take in a production of *Hamlet* at Point Pleasant Park. The tragedy is played out amid fog and ruins, and sends genuine shivers up your spine. If you visit on July 1, Canada Day, go see *A Midsummer Night's Dream* on the Seawalk Stage at Casino Nova Scotia. The Casino is located at the harbor, right on the water—perfect for the closing scene. The play gets under way at 4am (really!) so that the actual sunrise on the harbor coincides with sunrise in the play. See chapter 9.

- **The Nova Scotia International Tattoo.** This event will appeal to adults and kids alike. And anyone who gets inspired by marching bands will be euphoric. I've seen the Military Tattoo in Scotland, and, except for the one at the Edinburgh Castle, this one is better. The Tattoo is one of the world's largest indoor shows, with over 2,000 entertainers—awe-inspiring just for the numbers alone. The actual spectacle is a combination of international bands, pipes and drums, dancers, gymnasts, competitions, comedy, and military displays. See chapter 6.

- **The Atlantic Jazz Festival.** Held each July, this nine-day festival attracts professional jazz musicians (and a few famous ones too) from around the world. There are a variety of events throughout the festival, but the best of the best is the Jazz Encounters Series, where local and international jazz musicians get together and improvise. See chapter 6.

• **The Atlantic Film Festival.** Held annually in September, this festival attracts professional filmmakers and actors from across the country and around the world. Along with the variety and quality of films for public viewing, there are lots of receptions and parties, and opportunities to spot famous faces. See chapter 6.

• **New Year's Eve at the Grand Parade.** Thousands gather to party and bring in the New Year at the Grand Parade. Dress warmly and bring someone to cuddle with, while you listen to the bands and entertainers until it's time to count down the seconds to midnight. The event is free, and every year different entertainers headline. See chapter 6.

Tips   The Best of Halifax Online

Check out these websites to get a taste of what Halifax has to offer, and to jump-start your trip planning.

• **The Coast (www.thecoast.ns.ca):** Visit this site for up-to-date listings of events and entertainment in Halifax. Click on The Guide.

• **Halifax Tourism, Culture & Heritage (www.halifaxinfo.com):** The official city tourism site offers an overview of the city plus information on festivals and nightlife.

• **Nova Scotia Department of Tourism & Culture (www.explore. gov.ns.ca):** Look under the site-map bar at the top of the page to obtain information about Halifax.

---

2 The Best Hotel Bets

For detailed reviews of all these accommodations, see chapter 4.

• **Best Historic Hotel:** When you can boast royalty on your hotel register, and your lineage is traced directly to the legendary Canadian Pacific Hotel chain, chances are there's lots of history stored behind those walls. While the **Westin Nova Scotian,** 1181 Hollis St. (© **800/228-3000;** www.westin.ns.ca) may not be the oldest hotel in Halifax, it has the most interesting history. See p. 62.

• **Best for Business Travelers:** In business, as in real estate, it's all about location, location, location, and **The Prince George,** 1725 Market St. (© **800/565-1567;** www.princegeorgehotel.com), has

it in spades. The hotel is directly adjacent and connected to the World Trade & Convention Centre, and connected via the Downtown Link (a covered walkway) to most of the downtown office towers and businesses. The hotel itself has a full slate of amenities geared toward business travelers, and when it comes time for a break, the waterfront, with restaurants, entertainment, and attractions, is only a few blocks away. See p. 63.

• **Best for Families:** Although it's a little more expensive, I recommend the **Cambridge Suites Hotel,** 1583 Brunswick St. (© **888/417-8483;** www.cambridgesuiteshalifax.com). The suite provides more space in both the bedroom and lounge area, plus there's a kitchenette where families can fix inexpensive meals and snacks. It's a convenient option for parents as well, since suites are outfitted for business and the hotel is located in the downtown core. See p. 64.

- **Best Value: The Citadel Halifax Hotel,** 1960 Brunswick St. (© **800/565-7162;** www.citadel-halifax.com), has quite reasonable rates and is close to downtown attractions. The hotel was renovated in 2002, so you don't have to feel like you're staying in second-class digs to save some money. See p. 64.
- **Best Luxury Hotel:** Hands down, this distinction goes to the **Westin Nova Scotian,** 1181 Hollis St. (© **800-228-3000;** www.westin. ns.ca) From the friendly, welcoming staff at the front desk, to the harbor-facing suites with two bathrooms, to the famous Westin "Heavenly Beds" with feather duvets, you'll feel duly pampered. There's a free shuttle to downtown locations so you don't have to take your car and contend with nightmarish parking conditions. See p. 62.

- **Best Views:** Whether you're looking for a great harbor view or a glimpse of the odd celebrity, the **Casino Nova Scotia Hotel,** 1919 Upper Water St. (© **866/ 425-4329;** www.casinonovascotia hotel.com) is your best bet, as long as you ask for a room with a harbor view. From your window, watch the sailboats and the ferries during the day, and the lights on the Macdonald Bridge that light up the harbor at night. Step outside your room and descend to the lobby, where you might see the star of the latest Hollywood movie being filmed in Halifax, or one of the headliners at the casino next door. See p. 62.
- **Best Lobby:** There are others that are bigger, but the most impressive lobby is that of the **Lord Nelson Hotel & Suites,** 1515 South Park St. (© **800/565-2020;** www.lord nelsonhotel.com). Its sweeping foyer with wood-paneled walls, broad staircases, and second-floor balcony makes you pause, catch your breath, and admire. See p. 66.

3 The Best Bed-and-Breakfasts & Inns

For detailed reviews of all these properties, see chapter 4.

- **Most Friendly:** Not only does Elizabeth O'Carroll charm you with her Irish hospitality, but her West Highland terrier, Dugal, wants to be your friend too. **The Pebble B&B,** 1839 Armview Terrace (© **902/423-3369;** www.the pebble.ca), has lots more to offer too, including quality linens, luxurious bathrooms, and a great view of the North West Arm. See p. 72.

- **Most Romantic:** Everyone has their own definition of romantic, but if yours includes canopied beds, antique furnishings, historic ambience, and an intimate, outdoor courtyard where you can enjoy evening cocktails by the fountain, then the **Halliburton House Inn,** 5184 Morris St. (© **902/420-0658;** www.hallibur ton.ns.ca) is your answer. See p. 66.
- **Most Unique:** It may be the Gothic-style antiques that do it for you. Or the beautiful stained-

glass windows. Or the sumptuous red sitting room. Or maybe you'll be won over when you contemplate the group of illustrious folk who've stayed here in the past: Oscar Wilde, George Vanderbilt, and P. T. Barnum, to name a few. Whatever strikes your particular fancy, the **Waverley Inn,** 1266 Barrington St. (℗ **800/565-9346;** www.waverleyinn.com) is a great topic for conversation. Did I mention that it might be haunted? See p. 67.

- **Best for Pets:** If you want to bring your furry friend along on your Halifax trip, **Virginia Kinfolk B&B,** 1722 Robie St. (℗ **902/ 423-6687;** www.members.aol. com/vakinfolkz) will welcome your pets as long as you give them prior

notice. There's no extra charge, and there are no size restrictions. And you won't have to feel guilty about leaving your buddy at home. See p. 72.

- **Best All-Rounder:** You'll enjoy spending at least one night in this lovely circa-1915 home that is the **Pepperberry Bed & Breakfast,** 2688 Dutch Village Rd. (℗ **877/ 246-3244;** www.pepperberryinn. com). Hosts Jim and Elizabeth Trites really make you feel at home. There's an expansive deck for lounging, and a cozy living room for reading. You'll know it's not really home come breakfast time, though—the service and menu are wonderful. See p. 69.

4 The Best Dining Bets

For detailed reviews of all these restaurants, see chapter 5.

- **Best Cafe:** It has friendly, speedy service, delicious home-baked goodies, cool smoothies, and killer cappuccino, to name just a few strong points. **Steve-O-Reno's,** 1536 Brunswick St. (℗ **902/429-3034**), is the best cafe in the city. See p. 93.

- **Best Chinese:** Authentic Chinese dishes cooked by brothers Patrick and Ling Wong make the **Great Wall,** 1649 Bedford Row (℗ **902/422-6153**) a hit. Its downtown location close to the waterfront doesn't hurt either. See p. 89.

- **Best Decor:** From the lovely chandelier in the ladies' washroom to the intimate tables located in private corners and alcoves, the **Economy Shoe Shop,** 1663 Argyle St. (℗ **902/423-7463**), brims with imaginative flair and a truly unique sense of design. See p. 89.

- **Best Desserts:** Everybody in Halifax knows that **La Cave,** 5244 Blowers St. (℗ **902/429-3551**), has the best cheesecake in town. There are more than 24 flavors to choose from, and they taste as good as they look—which is divine. See p. 84.

- **Best Greek:** You'll enjoy **Opa! Greek Taverna,** 1565 Argyle St. (℗ **902/492-7999**), for the traditional Greek food and ambience. It's popular with local businesspeople at lunch, and draws the university crowd at night. The statues and paintings give it an added Mediterranean feel. See p. 87.

- **Best Italian:** It's a toss-up between **da Maurizio,** 1496 Lower Water St. (℗ **902/423-0859**), and **Il Mercato,** 5475 Spring Garden Rd. (℗ **902/422-2866**), which isn't surprising, since they're owned by the same people. Both restaurants serve delicious Northern Italian cuisine, so it really comes down to ambience: If you prefer fine dining, choose da Maurizio, with its linen tablecloths and extensive wine list. For a more casual, upbeat location, go with Il Mercato. Be forewarned, though—Il Mercato, unlike its big sister, doesn't accept reservations. See pp. 77, 92.

- **Best Ice Cream:** It's made on the premises and is the creamiest in the city. **Dio Mio Gelato Desserts Café,** 5670 Spring Garden Rd. (© **902/492-3467**), makes real Italian-style ice cream. It's even low in fat Does it get any better? See p. 93.

- **Best Pizza:** Although some reviewers have panned it—writing something to the effect that pizza is basically just bread, tomato sauce, and cheese, and in Halifax, it tastes like it—I'm recommending the much-more-than-ordinary pizza served up at **Il Mercato,** 5475 Spring Garden Rd. (© **902/ 422-2866**). Their thin crusts are the base for a selection of delicious toppings combined in unusual but entirely successful ways. See p. 92.

- **Best Classic Seafood:** This is a tough call, since almost three-quarters of the restaurants in Halifax serve seafood. For purists, I recommend the tried-and-true **Five Fishermen,** 1740 Argyle St. (© **902/422-4421**). They've been serving seafood for 25 years, and while it may not be the latest hot spot in the city, there's something to be said for all those years of experience. The seafood is consistently delicious. See p. 85.

- **Best Nouveau Seafood:** For those who like their seafood with a little more pizzazz, perhaps some lobster and champagne pasta or a combination of scallops, haddock, and shrimp in a creamy sauce would fit the bill. **McKelvie's Restaurant & Bar,** 1680 Lower Water St. (© **902/421-616**), home to "delishes fishes dishes," is located in a renovated century-old firehall. See p. 80.

- **Best Steak:** In a city known for seafood, it's great to enjoy an expertly cooked, tender steak every now and then. If you just can't stand the thought of another clam chowder–themed dinner, head over to **Ryan Duffy's Steak & Seafood,** 5640 Spring Garden Rd. (© **902/421-1116**). The choice-grade steaks are cut and weighed at your table—a spectacle in itself. See p. 92.

- **Best View of the Harbor:** You can head to the upstairs dining room and gaze out over the harbor, or stick to the bar downstairs at dock level, or even enjoy a burger and fries on the outside patio when it's warm enough. Either way, **Salty's On The Waterfront,** 1869 Upper Water St., Historic Properties Pier (© **902/423-6818**), has the best view for harbor-watching. See p. 81.

- **Best Wine List:** I'm giving this to **da Maurizio,** 1496 Lower Water St. (© **902/423-0859**). They offer a huge selection of wines from around the world, and the staff knows what they're talking about, from bottle to bottle to bottle. See p. 77.

5 The Best of Halifax for Families

- **Best Attractions:** Depending on the weather and the season, and your child's inclination, Halifax has several attractions that are sure to please. For the inquisitive hands-on type—and what child isn't—visit the **Discovery Centre,** 1593 Barrington St. (© **902/492-4422**). Science is entertaining and fun at the center's almost 100 interactive exhibits and activities, which will interest mom and dad as well as the kids. If you need to burn off some energy, hike up Citadel Hill and visit the **Halifax Citadel National Historic Site,** Sackville St. (© **902/426-5080**). Who can resist a real-life fort to play in? An underground garrison cell and storage rooms are fun to explore. And a video explains the uniqueness of the fort and why the star shape is so significant for defense. During the summer, soldiers, dressed in the tartan kilts, feathered bonnets, and bright red coats of the 78th Highlanders Regiment, perform precision drills and firing demonstrations that will impress the whole family. In the background, pipers and drummers play the same Scottish music that was heard on the hill in 1869. Older children will especially enjoy watching the soldiers fire the noon gun. For a rollicking ride through the city, board the **Harbour Hopper Tour (902/490-8687).** Along with an animated tour of historic Halifax, everyone will enjoy the splashdown into the harbor on an amphibious vehicle that moves from land to water, and the great views of the city from that perspective. See chapter 6.

- **Best Accommodation:** Let's face it, sometimes family members just need a little space of their own when traveling together. **The Cambridge Suites Hotel,** 1583 Brunswick St. (© **888/417-8483;** www.cambridgesuiteshalifax.com, gives you that space. All suites have kitchenettes—an added bonus for those times when eating out isn't convenient or appealing

for whatever reason. Another bonus: the great location, close to Citadel Hill, Spring Garden Road, and downtown attractions. See chapter 4.

- **Best Outdoors:** Need some room to run and play? The **Halifax Common** has plenty of grassy, wide-open spaces. If you want to stroll acres of beautiful gardens and feed the ducks, visit the **Halifax Public Gardens.** The **Waterfront Boardwalk** gives you 3km (2 miles) of harbor ship-watching, with lots of interesting shops, restaurants, and attractions to stop in and explore along the way. For a special treat, there's **Point Pleasant Park,** which offers walking trails, ruins of forts, and a great view of the harbor. See chapter 6.

- **Best Events:** What better way to introduce your children to *Hamlet* than outside among the mists and ruins of Point Pleasant Park. **Shakespeare by the Sea** offers summer visitors the unique opportunity to view this and other productions in an outdoor setting. In early July, Halifax hosts the **Nova Scotia International Tattoo** with marching bands, dancing, and amazing military performances. In August, the **Halifax International Busker Festival** fills the waterfront area with entertainment by dozens of street performers. See chapter 6.

- **Most Fun Dining:** There's a rambling old building on the waterfront that will be a hit with the whole family. **The Waterfront Warehouse,** 1549 Lower Water St. (© **902/425-7610**), has good food, and lots of interesting items to amuse the kids—such as the dory hanging from the ceiling. When it comes time for mom and dad to enjoy their coffee, the kids can hang out and watch a video in

Hilary's Fish Shack, a child-size replica of a fishing shanty. See chapter 5.

- **Best Shopping: Woozles Bookstore,** 1533 Birmingham St. (© **902/423-7626**) is a joy for kids 16 and under. If you need to do some family shopping for clothes or personal items, your best bet is the **Halifax Shopping Centre & Annex,** 7001 Mumford Rd. (© **902/453-1752**) with over 150 stores. Strollers, wheelchairs, and walkers are complimentary, and there are special parking spaces for expectant mothers or families with young children. Each of the two mall levels has a special baby changing and feeding area near the washrooms, and there's a playroom for children ages 3 to 7.

2

Planning Your Trip to Halifax

Vacations can be loads of fun—or one big disaster. Often a little planning is all it takes to make the difference between a so-so trip and a real hit. Halifax has lots to offer whether you're single, a couple, or a family; whether you're traveling on business or strictly for pleasure—you just need to know where to look.

1 Visitor Information & Entry Requirements

To get your trip preparations under way, you may wish to contact tourism offices in Halifax or elsewhere in Nova Scotia. You'll also want to apply for a passport or visa, if you require one or both to visit Canada. Contact the **Halifax Tourism, Culture & Heritage International Visitors Center,** 1595 Barrington St., Halifax, NS B3J 1Z7 (© **800/565-0000** or 902/490-5946; www.halifaxinfo.com).

VISITOR INFORMATION
FROM NORTH AMERICA
The recommended first stop for everyone who arrives in Halifax is one of two visitor information centers. **The Visitor Information Centre** at the **Halifax International Airport** (© **800/565-0000** or 902/873-1223; www.novascotia.com) is located in the central area of the building, halfway between the departure and arrivals desks. It's open 7 days a week, from 9am to 9pm, with the exception of December 25. The **International Visitor's Centre,** 1595 Barrington St., Halifax, NS B3J 1Z7 (© **800/565-0000** or 902/490-5946; www.novascotia.com), is open in May and June daily from 8:30am to 7pm, in July and August daily from 8:30am to 8pm, and

from September to the end of April, Monday to Friday from 8:30am to 4:30pm. There's a **third information center** on the Halifax waterfront, conveniently located for those strolling the boardwalk. It's at 1655 Lower Water St., Halifax, NS B3J 1S2 (© **800/565-0000** or 902/424-4248; www.novascotia.com), behind the Maritime Museum of the Atlantic, next to the World War II corvette tied up at the Sackville Landing. This visitor information center is usually open from July to mid-October daily from 8am to 8pm, and from mid-October to July daily from 8:30am to 4:30pm. Call for confirmation, as the hours were being reviewed at press time. The staff at all three visitor information centers can help out with specific facts on Halifax and the surrounding area, providing this service in English, French, or German. They will also assist with booking local tours and purchasing tickets to events. The Barrington Street location has kiosks with videos on each of Nova Scotia's eight **Scenic Travelways** (the Nova Scotia Department of Tourism & Culture has divided the province into eight geographical regions for traveling), as well as printed literature and maps. You can book your accommodations at any visitor information center, or ahead of time by contacting **Check In** (℃ **800/565-0000** or 902/425-5781; www.checkin novascotia.com), a computerized **reservation and information service.**

If you're arriving in Halifax by car, you may want to check out one of the municipal information centers located on the outskirts of the city: The **Dartmouth Visitor Information Center,** 2 Ochterloney St. Dartmouth, NS, B2Y 4W1 (℃ **902/490-4443**) is located in the ferry terminal at **Alderney Landing.** It's open from mid-May to the end of October, daily from 9am to 9pm. Staff can assist you with directions and provide printed brochures on Halifax and other areas of the province. The **Bedford Visitor Information Center** (℃ **902/490-9111**) is located along the Bedford Highway, Route 2, next to the Hammonds Plains Road ramp, Route 213. Look for a small, square building on the opposite side of the road from the water, with a MOIRS sign at the top. It's open from mid-May until the end of September, daily from 9am to 6pm.

For information about the province of Nova Scotia as a whole, get in touch with the **Nova Scotia Department of Tourism and Culture,** PO Box 456, Halifax, NS B3J 2R5 (toll-free in North America ℃ **800/565-0000,** outside of North America ℃ **902/425-5781;** http://explore.gov.ns.ca). Ask for the *Nova Scotia Complete Guide for Doers and Dreamers.*

Information on Canada in general is available from the **Canadian Tourism Commission,** 55 Metcalfe St., Suite 600, Ottawa, ON K1P 6L5 (℃ **613/946-1000;** www.travelcanada. ca). They provide general information for visitors from all over the world, and more customized information for visitors from the U.S., Germany, Italy, the Netherlands, Great Britain, Australia, New Zealand, Korea, Japan, and Taiwan.

Visitors from the United States can obtain information about Canada from one of the several **Canadian Consul General's offices** located throughout the U.S. You can also visit the U.S. Embassy in Ottawa website at **www.usembassycanada.gov.**

(*Tips* **Passport Savvy**

Allow plenty of time before your trip to apply for a passport; processing normally takes 3 weeks but can take longer during busy periods (especially spring). And keep in mind that if you need a passport in a hurry, you'll pay a higher processing fee. When traveling, safeguard your passport in an inconspicuous, inaccessible place such as a money belt, and keep a copy of the critical pages along with your passport number in a separate place. If you lose your passport, visit the nearest consulate of your native country as soon as possible for a replacement.

FROM ABROAD
Visitors traveling from abroad can obtain information from the following locations:

- **Australia: The Canadian High Commission,** Commonwealth Ave., Canberra, ACT 2600

(℃ **02/6270-4000;** www.info export.gc.ca/ie-en/Office.jsp? oid=168).
- **New Zealand: The Canadian High Commission,** 3rd Floor, 61 Molesworth St., Thorndon, Wellington (℃ **644/473-9577;**

www.dfait-maeci.gc.ca/new zealand/).

- **South Africa: The Canadian High Commission,** 1103 Arcadia St., Hatfield 0083, Pretoria (℗ **012/422-3000;** www.dfait-maeci.gc.ca/southafrica/).
- **The United Kingdom and Ireland: The Canadian High Commission,** 1 Grosvenor Square, London W1K 4AB (℗ **0207/ 258-6600;** www.dfait-maeci.gc. ca/london/).

ENTRY REQUIREMENTS
DOCUMENTS

Canada requires that travelers from Europe carry a valid passport, a return ticket, and sufficient funds to support themselves and their dependents during their stay in Canada. European visitors to Canada who also wish to visit the United States must possess valid passports to be admitted; residents of Portugal are also required to have a visa.

United States residents visiting Canada do not require a passport or visa to enter, however they must have identification to establish citizenship, such as a birth certificate, and at least one identification card with photo. Permanent U.S. residents who are not U.S. citizens must carry their alien registration cards (green cards). Visitors from the United States who are temporary residents of that country must carry a passport and may also require a visa, depending on their country of citizenship.

Travelers from other countries may require a visa to enter or travel through Canada. International travelers who wish to find out more about Canadian customs regulations should visit the **Canada Customs and Revenue Agency** website, at **www.ccra-adrc.gc. ca,** or contact a Canadian consulate in their own country. Entry visas must be obtained from the country of origin before arriving in Canada.

Travelers bringing children under age 19 should carry identification similar to their own for each child, plus a letter of permission from the parents of any accompanying children of whom they do not have legal custody. Divorced parents with shared custody rights should carry legal documents establishing their status. Unaccompanied children should carry a letter of permission from either their parents or a legal guardian.

If you are driving into Canada, you will require your car's registration papers along with your other required papers.

PASSPORTS
For Residents of Canada: Passport applications are available at travel agencies throughout Canada or from the central **Passport Office,** Department of Foreign Affairs and International Trade, Ottawa, ON K1A 0G3 (℗ **800/567-6868;** www.dfait-maeci. gc.ca/passport).

For Residents of the United States: Whether you're applying in person or by mail, you can download passport applications from the U.S. State Department website at **http:// travel.state.gov.** For general information, call the **National Passport Agency** (℗ **202/647-0518**). To find your regional passport office, either check the U.S. State Department website or call the **National Passport Information Center** (℗ **900/225- 5674**); the fee is 55¢ per minute for automated information and $1.50 per minute for operator-assisted calls.

For Residents of the United Kingdom: To pick up an application for a standard 10-year passport (5-year passport for children under 16), visit your nearest passport office, major post office, or travel agency, or contact the **United Kingdom Passport Service** at

(C) 0870/521-0410 or search its website at www.ukpa.gov.uk.

For Residents of Ireland: You can apply for a 10-year passport at the **Passport Office,** Setanta Centre, Molesworth Street, Dublin 2 ((C) 01/ 671-1633; www.irlgov.ie/iveagh). Those under age 18 and over 65 must apply for a 12€ 3-year passport. You can also apply at 1A South Mall, Cork ((C) 021/272-525) or at most main post offices.

For Residents of Australia: You can pick up an application from your local post office or any branch of Passports Australia, but you must schedule an interview at the passport office to present your application materials. Call the **Australian Passport Information Service** at (C) 131-232, or visit the government website at www.passports.gov.au.

CUSTOMS
WHAT YOU CAN BRING INTO CANADA
Most items required for your personal use will be accepted, including food, fishing tackle, fuel, sports equipment, musical instruments, computers, and cameras. Weapons are not allowed, including firearms, mace, or any spray that can be used for self-defense purposes. Certain handguns and all automatic weapons are classed as prohibited firearms and are banned from entering Canada. Under special circumstances, certain handguns and long guns may be allowed for use in competitions or for hunting. *Note:* The Canadian government is reviewing possible changes to the rules for the importation of firearms, so be sure to check with a customs office prior to your visit. Or log on to **www.ccra-adrc.gc.ca.** You may bring gifts for friends or family worth up to C$60 (US$40) each without paying duty, provided they are not tobacco or alcohol. Visitors over age 19 can bring 1.14 liters (38.5 oz.)

of liquor or wine and 24 containers at 355 milliliters (12 oz.) each of beer without paying duty, and up to 200 cigarettes, 50 cigars, and 200g (7 oz.) of loose tobacco, before duty is required. Prescription drugs must be clearly identified and should be carried in the original packaging with a label that specifies both what they are, and that they are being used under prescription. A copy of your prescription and your doctor's telephone number makes it even easier. If you use syringes, you will require written evidence of why you need them.

Pets can enter Canada with their owners as long as you provide a valid rabies vaccination certificate. Seeing-eye dogs are allowed into Canada without restriction, and Canadian law allows them to accompany their owners into restaurants, hotels, and other establishments.

Regulations concerning **plants** are stringent. As a rule, it's advisable not to bring any live plants, bulbs, seeds, or other propagative material with you into Canada.

For more detailed information on what you can bring along for your stay in Canada, contact the **Canada Customs and Revenue Agency's (CCRA) 24-hour Automated Customs Information Service** at (C) 800/461-9999 (within Canada) or (C) 204/983-3500 (in the U.S.). Because of increased vigilance at border crossings, you can expect longer lineups. To obtain current information on the amount of time you may expect to wait at the time of your crossing, visit the CCRA website, at **www.ccra-adrc.gc.ca.**

WHAT YOU CAN TAKE HOME
Whatever your home country, make sure you register such items as cameras, laptop computers, and cellphones with your home customs service before you leave. This ensures that you will not be charged duty on these items when you return.

The items you can take home from Canada vary depending on the regulations of your home country. Visitors from the United States should be aware that border-crossing regulations are much more stringent since the September 11, 2001 terrorist attacks, so allow extra time. Contact the **U.S. Customs Service,** 1300 Pennsylvania Ave., NW, Washington, DC 20229 (*©* 877/287-8867; www.customs. ustreas.gov) for more information. From the website, you can print out a copy of *Know Before You Go,* a brochure that outlines what and how much you can bring home. For more information on border crossing wait times, visit **www.customs.ustreas.gov/ travel/travel.htm.** Returning U.S. citizens who have been away for at least 48 hours are allowed to bring back, once every 30 days, $400 worth of merchandise duty-free. You'll be charged a flat rate of 4% duty on the next $1,000 worth of purchases. Be sure to have your receipts handy. On mailed gifts, the duty-free limit is $100. You cannot bring fresh foodstuffs into the United States; tinned foods, however, are allowed.

Citizens of Australia can obtain information by contacting the **Australian Customs Service Information Center,** GPO Box 8, Sydney NSW 2001 (*©* 300/363-263; www. customs.gov.au). The duty-free allowance in **Australia** is A$400 or, for those under 18, A$200. Citizens can bring in 250 cigarettes or 250g (9 oz.) of loose tobacco, and 1.125 liters (38 oz.) of alcohol. If you're returning with valuables you already own, such as foreign-made cameras, you should file form B263. A helpful brochure available from Australian consulates or customs offices is *Know Before You Go.*

The duty-free allowance for **New Zealand** is NZ$700. Citizens over age 17 can bring in 200 cigarettes, 50 cigars, or 250g (9 oz.) of tobacco (or a mixture of all three if their combined weight doesn't exceed 250g/ 9 oz.); plus 4.5 liters (150 oz.) of wine and beer, or 1.125 liters (38 oz.) of liquor. New Zealand currency does not carry import or export restrictions. Fill out a **certificate of export,** listing the valuables you are taking out of the country; that way, you can bring them back without paying duty. Most questions are answered in a free pamphlet available at New Zealand consulates and customs offices: *New Zealand Customs Guide for Travellers, Notice no. 4.* For more information, contact **New Zealand Customs,** The Customhouse, 17–21 Whitmore St., Box 2218, Wellington (*©* 04/473-6099 or 0800/428-786; www.customs. govt.nz).

Citizens visiting from South Africa can obtain information by contacting the Office of the Commissioner, Lehae La Sars, 299 Bronkhorst St., Nieuw Muckleneuk 0181 (*©* 27 12/ 422-4000; www.sars.gov.za).

U.K. citizens returning from a non-EU country have a customs allowance of 200 cigarettes; 50 cigars; 250g (9 oz.) of smoking tobacco; 2 liters of still table wine; 1 liter (34 oz.) of spirits or strong liqueurs (over 22% volume); 2 liters (68 oz.) of fortified wine, sparkling wine, or other liqueurs; 60 milliliters (2 oz.) of perfume; 250 milliliters (8.5 oz.) of toilet water; and £145 worth of all other goods, including gifts and souvenirs. Children ages 16 and under are not eligible for the tobacco or alcohol allowance. For more information, contact **HM Customs & Excise** at *©* 0845/010-9000 (from outside the U.K., 020/8929-0152), or consult their website at **www.hmce.gov.uk.**

To make your customs declaration easier, keep receipts from all your purchases in one place, and carry your purchases in a separate suitcase or box.

Destination Halifax: Red Alert Checklist

• Are there any **special requirements** for your destination? Vaccinations? Special visas, passports, or IDs? Detailed road maps? Bug repellents? Appropriate attire?

• Do any theater, restaurant, or travel reservations need to be booked in advance?

• Did you make sure your favorite attraction is open? Call ahead for opening and closing times. Get in touch with the **Halifax Tourism, Culture & Heritage International Visitor's Centre**, 1595 Barrington St., Halifax, NS B3J 1Z7 (✆ **800/565-0000** or 902/490-5946; www.halifaxinfo.com).

• If you purchased traveler's checks, have you recorded the check numbers, and stored the documentation separately from the checks?

• Did you pack your camera and an extra set of camera batteries, and purchase enough film? If you packed film in your checked baggage, did you invest in protective pouches to shield film from airport X-rays?

• Do you have a safe, accessible place to store money?

• Did you bring your ID cards that could entitle you to discounts such as CAA/AAA and AARP cards, student IDs, and so on?

• Did you bring emergency drug prescriptions and extra glasses or contact lenses?

• Did you find out your daily ATM withdrawal limit?

• Do you have your credit card PINs? Is there a daily withdrawal limit on credit card cash advances?

• If you have an E-ticket do you have documentation?

• Did you leave a copy of your itinerary with someone at home?

• Do you have the measurements for people for whom you plan to buy clothes while on your trip?

2 Money

CURRENCY

The currency system in Canada uses dollars and cents, similar to the U.S. system. Coins include the 1¢ (penny), 5¢ (nickel), 10¢ (dime), 25¢ (quarter), $1 (loonie), and $2 (toonie). One hundred cents equals $1. The paper currency comes in different colors and different designs. Most common are the $5 bill (blue), $10 bill (purple), and $20 bill (green). There are also the $50 bill (red) and $100 bill (brown).

EXCHANGE RATE

Recently, the Canadian dollar has been fluctuating around 64¢ in U.S.

dollars, give or take a few points. Given that prices of many goods are roughly on par with those in the U.S., the favorable exchange makes travel in Canada a bargain.

The British pound has also been very strong compared to the Canadian dollar. At press time the exchange rate was UK£1=C$2.49.

You will always obtain the best exchange rate at a recognized financial institution, bank, trust company, or currency exchange. If you choose to exchange your money at stores, hotels, or restaurants, look for the FAIR EXCHANGE sign, which guarantees

The Canadian Dollar, the U.S. Dollar & the British Pound

The prices in this guide are given first in Canadian dollars, then in U.S. dollars. Amounts over $5 have been rounded to the nearest dollar. At the time of writing, C$1 was worth about US$0.64, which means your C$125-per-night hotel room will cost only US$80 and your C$8 breakfast about US$5. The British pound is worth approximately 2½ times the value of the Canadian dollar. When you convert £100 to Canadian dollars, you will receive C$249. Exchange rates do fluctuate, so be sure to check with your local bank for up-to-date rates. Here's a quick sampling of conversions:

C $	U.S. $	U.K. £	U.S. $	C $	U.K. £
1	0.64	0.40	1	1.57	0.64
5	3.20	2.00	5	7.85	3.20
10	6.40	4.00	10	15.70	6.40
20	12.80	8.00	20	31.40	12.80
50	32.00	20.00	50	78.50	32.00
80	51.20	32.00	80	125.60	51.20
100	64.00	40.00	100	157.00	64.00

an exchange rate within 5% of the current bank rate. Remember also that change received from any purchase will be in Canadian dollars.

SALES TAX

The sales tax in Nova Scotia is called the **Harmonized Sales Tax (HST)** and is charged at 15%. (This is comprised of the 7% federal goods and services tax and the 8% provincial sales tax.) Keep all of your receipts, as you may be able to claim a refund for some or all of this tax (see "Taxes" under "Fast Facts: Halifax" in chapter 3).

It's a good idea to exchange at least some money—just enough to cover airport incidentals and transportation to your hotel—before you leave home, so you can avoid lines at airport ATMs (automated teller machines). **American Express cardholders** can order foreign currency over the phone at *©* **800/807-6233.**

It's best to exchange currency or traveler's checks at a bank or an ATM—not a currency exchange, hotel, or shop.

ATMS

ATMs (automated teller machines) are linked to a network that most likely includes your bank at home. **Cirrus** (*©* 800/424-7787; www.mastercard. com) and **PLUS** (*©* 800/843-7587; www.visa.com) are the two most popular networks in Canada. Call or check online for ATM locations at your destination. Be sure you know your personal identification number (PIN) before you leave home, and be sure to find out your daily withdrawal limit before you depart. You can also get cash advances on your credit card at an ATM. Keep in mind that credit card companies try to protect themselves from theft by limiting the funds someone can withdraw away from home. It's therefore best to call your credit card company before you leave and let it know where you're going and how much you plan to spend. You'll get the best exchange rate if you withdraw money from an ATM, but keep in mind that many banks impose a fee every time a card is used at an ATM. On top of this, the bank from which you withdraw cash may charge its own fee.

TRAVELER'S CHECKS

Traveler's checks are something of an anachronism from the days before the ATM made cash accessible at any time. Traveler's checks used to be the only sound alternative to traveling with dangerously large amounts of cash. They were as reliable as currency, but, unlike cash, could be replaced if lost or stolen.

These days, traveler's checks seem less necessary because most cities have 24-hour ATMs that allow you to withdraw small amounts of cash as needed. However, keep in mind that you will likely be charged an ATM withdrawal fee if the bank is not your own, so if you're withdrawing money every day, you might be better off with traveler's checks—provided that you don't mind showing identification every time you want to cash one.

You can get traveler's checks at almost any bank. **American Express** offers denominations of $20, $50, $100, $500, and (for cardholders only) $1,000. You'll pay a service charge ranging from 1% to 4%. You can also get American Express traveler's checks over the phone by calling ✆ **800/221-7282;** cardholders with Amex Gold and Platinum cards who use this number are exempt from the 1% fee.

If your wallet is lost or stolen, contact your issuing company to obtain cash advances or replacement cards:

- **American Express** (✆ **800/869-3016;** www.americanexpress.com),
- **MasterCard** (✆ **800/307-7309;** www.mastercard.com),
- **Visa** (✆ **800/847-2911;** www.visa.com).

What Things Cost in Halifax	C$	U.S.$	U.K.£
Shuttle from airport to downtown hotel	12.00	7.57	4.85
Newspaper	1.25	.80	.50
Local telephone call	.25	.16	.10
Movie ticket (adult single, Sunday to Thursday)	6.75	4.26	2.73
Movie ticket (adult single, Friday and Saturday)	10.00	6.31	4.04
Theater ticket	35.00	24.00	14.00
Taxi fare, typical 5-km (3-mile) ride	4.00	2.52	1.62
Toll for bridge crossing	.75	.75	.75
Bus ticket (adult single)	1.65	1.04	.67
Ferry to Dartmouth	1.65	1.04	.67
Two-course lunch for one (moderate)*	20.00	12.60	8.00
Three-course dinner for one (moderate)*	40.00	25.00	16.00
Parking meter downtown, per hour	1.00	.63	.40
All-day parking lot, downtown	15.00	9.47	6.06
Museum entrance fee	3.00	1.89	1.21
Roll of Kodak film, 24-exposure print	6.00	3.79	2.42
Cup of coffee	1.00	.63	.40
Bottle of juice	2.00	1.26	.80
Large takeout pizza	15.00	9.47	6.06

*Includes tax, tip, but not wine.

Tips   Small Change

When you change money, ask for some small bills or loose change. Petty cash will come in handy for tipping and public transportation. Consider keeping the change separate from your larger bills, so it's readily accessible. If you take this precaution, you'll be less of a target for theft.

3 When to Go

Halifax summers are short (June, July, August), and many of the special events in the city are held during these three traditional vacation months. While there's a lot to see and do, including outdoor festivals and special programs for children, it's also the busiest time for hotels and restaurants, parks, and other public areas, and parking spots are at a premium. If your schedule allows, you might want to consider visiting at another time of the year. **Spring** usually arrives in mid-April, along with the maple syrup festivals, hiking, and spring bird migrations. **Autumn** in Halifax is stunning, as the "city of trees" turns from cool green to blazing reds, oranges, and yellows. A stroll in one of the city's many parks and green areas is enthralling—and free! Autumn is also the season for the acclaimed **Atlantic Theatre Festival** (see chapter 6). Both spring and fall can have

warm afternoons followed by cold nights, so bring clothes you can layer. Winter in Halifax is not a typical time to visit, but there are lots of bargains to be found at hotels and bed-and-breakfasts, and a full slate of live theater, symphony concerts, and fresh seafood to enjoy.

CLIMATE

Halifax borders the Atlantic Ocean and enjoys a temperate climate—not too hot in the summer and not too cold in the winter. Fog is common in the spring, and snowfalls often finish off as rain showers. However, Halifax weather can change on a moment's notice—and often does—with fog, warm sunshine, and rain making appearances on the same summer day. Be aware that winter storms can blow in from the Atlantic Ocean without warning, causing icy roads and flight cancellations.

Halifax's Average Temperatures (°C/°F) and Precipitation (mm/in.)

	Jan	Feb	Mar	Apr	May	June	July	Aug	Sept	Oct	Nov	Dec
High	0/32	0/32	3/26	8/46	14/58	19/65	22/72	23/74	19/66	13/56	8/46	3/37
Low	−8/21	−8/21	−4/23	0/32	5/41	10/50	14/58	15/59	11/51	6/43	1/34	−5/23
Prec.	112/4	76/3	106/4	112/4	119/5	108/4	104/4	98/4	107/4	134/5	147/6	132/5

HOLIDAYS

Halifax celebrates Canada's 11 national holidays: New Year's Day (January 1), Good Friday and Easter Monday (March or April), Victoria Day (first Monday after May 20), Canada Day (July 1), Natal Day/Civic Holiday (first Monday in August), Labour Day

(first Monday in September), Thanksgiving Day (second Monday in October), Christmas Day (December 25), and Boxing Day (December 26). Most banks, post offices, schools, and government organizations are closed on these days. The remainder of the business and entertainment communities

Eastern Canada

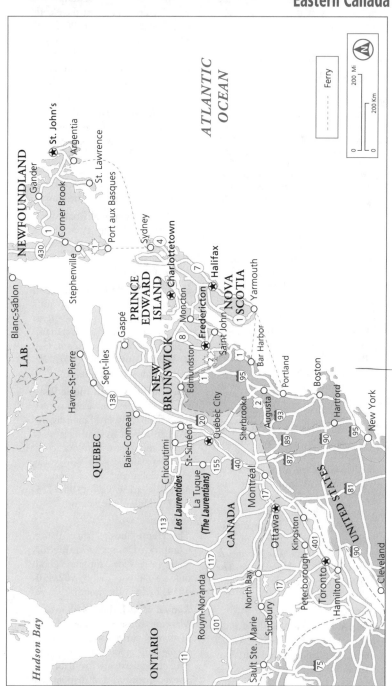

may be closed on some or all of the holidays, so it's smart to double-check before you go.

HALIFAX CALENDAR OF EVENTS

Halifax is a city that likes to make merry. Whether it's music or history or culture or food, Haligonians can always find a festival to celebrate it. Confirm locations and times by contacting the **Halifax Civic Events & Festivals Information Line** (© 902/490-6776, press 2) or visit the City of Halifax tourism website at **www.halifaxinfo.com**. **The Halifax Metro Center** is the venue for many sports and entertainment events. The box office is reachable at © 902/421-8000, or visit its website at www.halifax metrocenter.com. There are also plenty of goings-on just outside the Halifax area. Contact the **Nova Scotia Department of Tourism & Culture** (© 800/565-0000; www.novascotia.com) for details.

January

New Year's Day Levees, various locations throughout Halifax. Levees are a great opportunity for citizens and visitors alike to greet local officials while enjoying light refreshments and entertainment. The lieutenant governor of Nova Scotia hosts a levee at his residence; the mayor of Halifax is host at City Hall; and the Roman Catholic archbishop is host at St. Mary's Basilica Glebe, to name just a few. Call the civic information line (© 902/490-6776, press 2), or visit **www.halifaxinfo.com** for details. Also look for information in local newspapers prior to the events. Check out *The Chronicle Herald* (www.herald.ns.ca), or *The Daily News* (www.canada.com/halifax/). January 1.

February

African Heritage Month, various locations throughout Halifax. A celebration of the history and culture of African Canadians, many of whose ancestors migrated to Nova Scotia from the United States after the War of 1812 and the American Civil War. For details, contact the **North End Branch Library** (© 902/490-5723) or visit the Black History Month Association website, at www.chebucto.ns.ca/Heritage/BHMA. Throughout the month.

Halifax Kennel Club All Breed Championship Dog Shows & Obedience Trials, Exhibition Park. Entertaining and educational whether you're a dog owner or simply a dog lover. Call © 902/876-2456 or 902/477-0311 for information. Middle of the month.

Halifax International Boat Show, Exhibition Park. This event hosts a wide variety of boats and products for boat enthusiasts. Call © 888/454-7469. Middle of the month.

Halifax Winterfest, waterfront and surrounding areas. A week of family activities, including sporting events and dining. There's also entertainment specifically for children. Call © 902/423-6044 or 902/429-6164. Middle of the month.

Nova Scotia Kiwanis Music Festival, Dalhousie Arts Centre, Dalhousie University. Held annually, this event attracts all ages and all levels of competitors from across Nova Scotia. Includes competitions in voice, piano, violin, and school bands, to name just a few. Call © 902/423-6147. Middle of the month.

March

The Home Show, Halifax Forum Complex. Dozens of exhibitors showcase new ideas for homes, both indoors and out. Call © 902/490-4614. Early in the month.

Annual Model Maker's Showcase, Maritime Museum of the Atlantic, Halifax. A variety of Tall Ship and theme ship models are on display. The modelers are available to answer questions and demonstrate techniques. Call ✆ **902/424-7490.** Late in the month.

Springtime Craft & Antique Festival, Exhibition Park, 200 Prospect Rd. Between 75 and 100 exhibitors from the Atlantic region and across Canada display antique, food, and craft products. Crafts are all handmade of high quality. Call ✆ **902/876-8221.** Late March/early April.

May

Atlantic Book Week & Festival, various locations throughout Halifax. This is an annual celebration of books and authors from Atlantic Canada. It features readings, workshops, children's activities, and tours. Call ✆ **902-423-8116;** www.writers.ns.ca. Late in the month.

June

War Canoe Challenge, Lake Banook, Dartmouth. Corporate and community teams compete in a series of war canoe races to raise funds for the Izaak Walton Killam Children's Hospital, in Halifax. There's also live entertainment, sports contests, children's activities, and a giant barbecue. Call ✆ **902/496-7059.** Middle of the month.

50+ Expo (pronounced "50-plus"), Exhibition Park. Displays, food, live entertainment, and giveaways for seniors. Call ✆ **902/429-5808** or 902/424-5407; www.50plusexpo.ns.ca. Late in the month.

Bedford Days, DeWolfe Park, Bedford. This festival takes place over several days and includes music, fireworks, a kid's night, a youth night, a lobster dinner, even a beer festival. Call ✆ **902/490-4740** or 902/490-6776. Late in the month.

Mayflower Ball, World Trade and Convention Centre. This is a ballroom and Latin dancing competition. Brush up on your moves as you watch, or just watch, period.

Call ✆ **902-455-1924.** Late in the month.

Multicultural Festival, Events Plaza, Dartmouth waterfront. Sample food and enjoy entertainment presented by various cultural societies in the Halifax region. Call ✆ **902/423-6534.** Late in the month.

July

Canada Day Celebrations, various locations throughout Halifax. Apart from the official ceremony on Citadel Hill, other highlights include pancake breakfasts, the Nova Scotia International Tattoo, Canada Day Parade (many of the international bands and military organizations that perform in the annual Tattoo march in the parade), a family picnic at the Halifax Commons, and fireworks over Halifax Harbour. Call ✆ **902/490-4092** or 902/490-4729; www.region.halifax.ns.ca/canadaday/index.htm. July 1.

Nova Scotia International Tattoo, Halifax Metro Centre. A 2-hour spectacular that involves more than 2,000 Canadian and international military and civilian performers. Second only to the Tattoo in Scotland (some say better!). For information on dates and times, call ✆ **902/420-1114.** To purchase tickets, call ✆ **902/451-1221.** First week of the month.

Music in the Gazebo, Halifax Public Gardens. Come and enjoy a series of free concerts. There's a different band each week. Call ✆ **902/479-1312.** Sunday afternoons.

Atlantic Jazz Festival, various locations throughout Halifax. This is an international festival of live music including jazz, blues, and "world beat," featuring hundreds of artists from around the world. Call ✆ **902/492-2225.** Early in the month.

Halifax Highland Games and Scottish Festival, Wanderers

Grounds, corner of Sackville and Summer sts., Halifax. Got any Scottish blood in you? Come and enjoy Highland dancing, pipe bands, Scottish country dancing, and fiddling. There are also crafts for sale and programs that let you explore your Scottish genealogy. Call © **902/ 469-2023;** www.halifaxhighland games.com. Early in the month.

Halifax Dragon Boat Festival, Lake Banook, Dartmouth. Entrants participate in both recreational and competitive categories as they race in these giant boats of Chinese design. Fun to watch. Call © **902/ 425-5450.** Middle of the month.

Labatt Blue 24-hour Relay, St. Mary's University. Over 4,000 people converge on the St. Mary's University campus for 24 hours of activities, fun, and friendly competition to support the Abilities Foundation of Nova Scotia. Money is raised to help kids, teens, and adults with physical disabilities. Call © **902/453-6000;** www.abilities foundation.ns.ca. Middle of the month.

Pride Week Parade and Activities. Downtown and various locations throughout Halifax. Whether you're out or not, come out to these events and enjoy yourself. Activities include dinners, dances, and barbecues. © **902/455-8417;** http://halifax pride.org. Middle of the month.

Provincial Rose Show, Museum of Natural History. This is a juried show for amateur gardeners. You're welcome to come take a look—and a smell! Call © **902/423-4458.** Middle of the month.

August

Halifax/Dartmouth Natal Day Celebrations. Join Haligonians as they take to the streets to celebrate the city's birthday. Events include parades, road races, and concerts.

Call © **902/490-6773** or 902/ 490-6776; www.natalday.ca. Early in the month.

Halifax International Busker Festival, downtown Halifax. Hundreds of street performers, including musicians, acrobats, comedians, and dancers, entertain onlookers throughout the city's downtown. Call © **902/429-3910.** Early to middle of the month.

Clam Harbour Beach Sandcastle Contest, Clam Harbour Beach. (Cross the A. Murray MacKay Bridge to Dartmouth and follow Highway 7 east. Approximately a 1-hour drive from downtown Halifax.) It's worth the trip to enjoy a day of sand sculptures, food, and fun. Recommended if you have children. Call © **902/845-2093.** Middle of the month.

Atlantic Fringe Festival, various locations throughout Halifax. Experience leading-edge performance art, including musicals, drama, stand-up comedy, and mime. Call © **902/435-4837.** Late August to early September.

September

Nova Scotia International Air Show, Shearwater. This is the largest combined air show, Armed Forces Day, aerospace exhibition, and lifestyle exhibition in Canada. Call © **902/465-2725.** Early in the month.

Atlantic Film Festival, various locations throughout Halifax. A weeklong, juried festival with films from all four Atlantic provinces, the rest of Canada, and from regions and countries bordering the North Atlantic Rim. Call © **902/422- 3456.** Middle of the month.

Nova Scotia International Tuna Tournament, Halifax waterfront. Teams from around the world come to Halifax to compete. This is a fund-raiser for the Izaak Walton Killam Children's Hospital in Halifax. Call ✆ **902/499-0909.** Middle of the month.

Terry Fox Run, Point Pleasant Park. This is a fund-raiser for cancer research in memory of Terry Fox, an ardent fund-raiser and activist who was himself claimed by the disease in 1981, but not before he'd run 5,373km (3,339 miles) across Canada in a bid to raise money for other cancer patients and research. His effort is all the more impressive because he did so with one leg amputated above the knee. The 1- to 10-km (⅔- to 6.2-mile) memorial run is a non-competitive event, and you don't even have to run. You can walk, bike, or skateboard—as long as you cover ground! Call ✆ **888/836-9786** or 902/423-8131. Middle of the month.

The Word on the Pier (formerly The Word on the Street), Pier 21. This is a giant annual book and magazine fair offering a variety of family-oriented activities. Call ✆ **902/ 423-7399.** Late in the month.

October

Maritime Fall Fair, Exhibition Park. A 10-day agricultural fair with traditional attractions such as livestock, a fruit and vegetable exhibit, horse and cattle competitions, a petting zoo, and a carnival midway. Especially fun for children. Call ✆ **902/876-8214;** www.maritimefallfair.com. Middle of the month.

November

Christmas at the Forum, Halifax Forum. This is Canada's largest festival of its kind, with over 450 craftspeople, artists, antique dealers, and food exhibitors in attendance. Call ✆ **902/532-7798.** Early in the month.

Port of Wines Festival, World Trade and Convention Centre. Enjoy this celebration of wine, food pairings, and oenophile-inspired decor, featuring over 250 wines from around the world. Call ✆ **902/450-5936.** Early in the month.

Annual Holiday Parade of Lights, downtown Halifax. Sponsored by the Downtown Halifax Business Commission, the parade begins on Barrington Street and includes floats, majorettes, and marching bands. Call ✆ **902/423-6658** or 902/490-6776. Middle of the month.

Annual Christmas Tree Lighting Ceremony, Halifax City Hall. Join Haligonians in lighting their 40-foot (12-m) Christmas tree at the Grand Parade in front of City Hall. Grab a cup of eggnog and enjoy the entertainment. The school choirs that perform are a special treat. Call ✆ **902-490-6776.** Late in the month.

Dalplex Christmas Craft Market, 6260 South St, Halifax. Another great shopping opportunity; this is a juried show, with more than 180 booths. Call ✆ **902/494-2558.** Late in the month.

Nova Scotia Designer Craft Council Christmas Craft Market, World Trade and Convention Centre. This delightful exhibition features fine art and crafts from Atlantic Canada. A great opportunity to do some holiday shopping. Call ✆ **902/423-3837.** Late in the month.

December

Halifax Explosion Memorial Service. Fort Needham Memorial Park. A laying of wreaths and a moment of silence to commemorate the tragic explosion that took place in Halifax Harbour in 1917. Call ✆ **902/490-4740.** December 7.

Breakfast Television Grand Parade New Year's Eve Countdown. If you're in Halifax for the holidays, come out and enjoy this live concert, with spectacular fireworks at midnight. Remember to bundle up! Call ℂ **902/490-6776.** December 31.

4 Health, Insurance & Safety

MEDICAL

Residents of Canada receive medical coverage through their provincial governments, and are protected when traveling within Canada by their home province's health insurance plan, for a limited time period. Check with your provincial agency for specific details. Purchasing additional travel insurance is a good idea, though, for various reasons. See "Insurance" below for more information.

Visitors from outside Canada should purchase out-of-country travel insurance for the duration of their stay in Halifax. Check your existing policy for travel insurance covering medical emergencies. Remember that many hospitals require nonresidents to pay for expenses up front, which will later be reimbursed through your policy.

Halifax is the medical center of the Atlantic provinces, and therefore has ready access to a variety of specialists. The city's medical complex is made up of several formerly independent hospitals, now known as the **Queen Elizabeth II Health Sciences Centre** (or QEII) (ℂ **902/473-2700;** www. qe2-hsc.ns.ca). See chapter 3 for a map showing the exact location of the QEII and other hospitals in Halifax.

For minor health problems, see a pharmacist at any of the dozens of pharmacies/drug stores in the city. Many pharmacies have extended hours; **Shoppers Drug Mart** has several locations that are open daily until midnight. If you require routine medical assistance, call the **QEII General Information** number, at ℂ **902/473-2700.** For emergencies call ℂ **911.**

See "Doctors" and "Drugstores" under "Fast Facts: Halifax" in chapter 3.

If you suffer from a chronic illness, consult your doctor before your departure. For conditions such as epilepsy, diabetes, or heart problems, wear a **MedicAlert Identification Tag** (ℂ **800/825-3785;** www.medicalert. org), which will immediately alert doctors to your condition and give them access to your records through MedicAlert's 24-hour hotline.

Carry **prescription medications** in their original containers and pack them in your carry-on luggage. Bring along copies of your prescriptions in case you lose your pills or run out.

Don't forget sunglasses and an extra pair of contact lenses or prescription glasses.

INSURANCE

Travel insurance provides benefits and services to cover a variety of travel concerns: What if you need to cancel your trip? What if you lose your luggage, become ill, or need to be evacuated before the date of your departure? Along with covering the expense of these emergencies, travel insurance purchases peace of mind, so that you can relax and enjoy your trip. Ask your travel agent about comprehensive travel policies that cover a combination of travel-related needs, including health coverage, emergency assistance, theft and loss, and flight or tour cancellation. Remember that many regular insurance policies include travel insurance as part of their coverage, so be sure to check your existing policies before you decide to purchase another. Check your credit card services as well: some Gold and Platinum cards provide this type of coverage. Contact the financial service provider where you obtained your card for more information:

- **American Express** (© **800/869-3016;** (www.americanexpress.com),
- **MasterCard** (© **800/307-7309;** www.mastercard.com),
- **Visa** (© **800/847-2911;** www.visa.com).

Car rental insurance may also be included in an existing insurance policy, or by your credit card service. In addition, home-owners' insurance may cover theft and loss when you travel. Contact your insurance company to confirm this.

SAFETY

Halifax, and Atlantic Canada in general, is considered a safe region. Residents and visitors alike feel comfortable strolling the streets and waterfront at night, or walking alone by day. As a cosmopolitan, university center, Halifax is open to different nationalities and lifestyles. Even so, use your common sense: Lock your hotel room and car doors, don't walk alone late at night, and be alert to your surroundings.

5 Tips for Travelers with Special Needs

FOR TRAVELERS WITH DISABILITIES

Travelers with disabilities of any type can contact the **Nova Scotia League for Equal Opportunities,** 2786 Agricola St., Suite 208, Halifax, NS B3K 4E1 (© **902/455-6942;** nsleo@ns.sympatico.ca) with inquiries regarding transportation services, access to recreational facilities, and other services in Halifax.

Both the *Halifax Visitors Guide* and the *Nova Scotia Guide for Doers and Dreamers* (available by contacting the **International Visitor's Centre** (© **800/565-000;** www.halifaxinfo.com) note accommodations that are adapted for special needs. It is wise to make reservations before you arrive, however, because such facilities are usually limited.

The **Halifax Metro Transit** has recently upgraded its bus service to include **Accessible Low Floor (ALF)** buses. The benefits include no-step entry and exit, bus floors that lower to curb level, extra-wide door entrances, ramps for quick and safe wheelchair access, and provision for securing up to two wheelchairs while in transit. Look for the **International Symbol of Accessibility** (a stylized wheelchair design) at Metro Transit bus stops and on all four sides of designated buses. ALF buses operate regularly scheduled bus service on routes 3 (Manors), 7 (Robie/Gottingen), and 54 (Montebello). The cost per trip is C$1.65 (US$1.10) for adults, C$1.15 (US76¢) for seniors and children 15 and under, free for children 4 and under. Exact change is required. For more information on the ALF buses, call **Halifax Metro Transit,** at © **902/490-4000.** *Note:* Passengers must be able to board the bus, deposit their fare, and depart independently. They must also be able to position their wheelchair so that it will be secured properly. Halifax Metro Transit also provides a door-to-door wheelchair-accessible bus service, **Access-A-Bus,** for people whose disabilities prevent them from using the regular Metro Transit services, ALF buses, or other modes of transportation. Registration is required to use the service and can take four to six weeks; however, you're welcome to call **Halifax Metro Transit** (© **902/490-6681**) to obtain a registration form prior to your visit. Better yet, save time by visiting their website and downloading the registration form. Log on to **www.region.halifax.ns.ca/ metrotransit.** The cost per trip is C$1.65 (US$1.10) for adults, C$1.15 (US76¢) for seniors and children 15 and under, free for children 4 and under. Exact change is required.

FOR FAMILIES

Halifax is usually a safe and family-friendly city. Malls, museums, parks, and playgrounds abound and are often within walking distance of one another.

Museums and universities offer special programs and workshops for children and students during vacation periods. In Halifax, this includes the months of July and August, approximately two weeks surrounding the Christmas holiday, and a weeklong break in March.

Despite the variety of activities for kids and parents, however, accommodations in Halifax can become expensive for families who want to stay in the downtown core—where most of the attractions are located. Try to book at a hotel where children can stay or eat for free when accompanied by a parent. If you require babysitting services, most hotels have a referral service they can offer you. A few hotels provide organized activities on site. If your family includes a pet, many of the downtown hotels will accommodate them. The more expensive hotels might even feed or walk Fido for you if you ask, but they don't advertise this service.

Refer to the detailed reviews in chapter 4 for specific information on which hotels provide free accommodation for children staying with parents, access to babysitting and organized activities for children, or assistance with pets.

You can find good family-oriented vacation advice on the Internet from sites such as the **Family Travel Net-**work (www.familytravelnetwork.com); **Traveling Internationally with Your Kids** (www.travelwithyourkids.com), a comprehensive site offering sound advice for long-distance and international travel with children; and the **Busy Person's Guide to Travel with Children** (http://wz.com/travel/TravelingWithChildren.html), offering a "45-second newsletter" where experts weigh in on the best websites and resources with tips for traveling with children.

FOR GAY & LESBIAN TRAVELERS

Unlike many other Canadian cities, where "gay villages" are delineated, Halifax's gay population is integrated. For information on events and activities, order a free copy of the *Pride Guide Directory,* from **Pride Guide Publishing,** 3–1563 Walnut St., Halifax, NS B3H 3S1 (© **902/423-6999;** prideguide@hfx.eastlink.ca), or visit **Gay-Mart's Guide to Halifax** online at www.gaymart.com/travel/ca/ns/halifax.html.

FOR SENIORS

Halifax is built on a hill. While attractions, accommodations, and restaurants are located within walking distance of one another, that walking often includes going uphill. During the summer months of June, July, and August, the city has made getting around downtown Halifax much easier by introducing *fred* **(Free Rides Everywhere Downtown),** a special bus that runs from June to September, daily from 11am to 6pm. Although *fred* is available to anyone, it is especially useful for seniors. To obtain a copy of *fred*'s schedule, contact the **Halifax Metro Transit Service** (© **902/423-6658;** www.downtownhalifax.ns.ca) or look for one of the 18 *fred* bus stops around the downtown, including the one at the **International**

Visitor's Centre, 1595 Barrington St., the **Lord Nelson Hotel,** at 1515 South Park St., the **Maritime Museum of the Atlantic,** at 1675 Lower Water St., and **Pier 21,** at 1055 Marginal Rd.

When you present a photo ID that shows your date of birth, you may be eligible for discounts at Halifax retail outlets, restaurants, and hotels. Special events are organized for seniors, including the **50+ Expo,** held each year in June. For information contact the **50+ Expo** (℃ **902/429-5808** or ℃ 902/424-5407; www.50plusexpo. ns.ca).

If you aren't a member already, you may wish to investigate joining **CARP** (formerly the Canadian Association of Retired Persons, now Canada's Association for the Fifty-Plus), Suite 130427, Queen St. E., Toronto, ON M5C 2M6, (℃ **416/363-8748;** www. 50plus/CARP). Members get discounts on hotels, airfares, and car rentals. CARP offers members a wide range of benefits, including *Fifty Plus* magazine and a monthly newsletter. Anyone over 50 can join.

Members of **AARP** (the American Association of Retired Persons) 601 E St. NW, Washington, DC 20049 (℃ **800/424-3410** or 202/434-2277; www.aarp.org), also get discounts on

hotels, airfares, and car rentals. AARP membership includes *Modern Maturity* magazine and a monthly newsletter. Anyone over 50 can join.

FOR STUDENTS
Halifax is a university town, and is home to thousands of local, national, and international university students. There are free concerts, all-night movie festivals, youth-oriented eateries, and enough of Halifax's own Alexander Keith's India Pale Ale for everyone. If you're keen to save money, stay at the university residences during the summer break, or check out the hostels or the YMCA.

As a high school or university student, you can obtain a variety of discounts by registering for an **International Student Identity Card (ISIC).** Find out more about what the card offers by checking out **www.isic. org.** Contact **Travel CUTS** (℃ **800/ 667-2887** or 416/614-2887; www. travelcuts.com) to obtain your card.

To find out which movies are showing, visit **Cinema Clock,** www.cinema clock.com/clock/sco/Halifax.html. For concert listings, contact the **Halifax Metro Centre,** 5284 Duke St., Halifax, NS B3J 3L2 (℃ **902/451- 1202;** www.halifaxmetrocentre.com).

6 Getting There

BY PLANE
WITHIN CANADA
You'll arrive at the **Halifax International Airport** (airport code YHZ), 1 Bell Boulevard, Enfield, NS B2T 1K2 (℃ **902/873-4422;** www.hiaa.ca). To check arrival and departure times for all flights, visit **www.hiaa.ca/todays flights/index.htm.**

Air Canada (℃ **888/247-2262;** www.aircanada.ca) operates nonstop flights to Halifax from many Canadian cities including Vancouver,

Regina, Winnipeg, Ottawa, Toronto, and Montreal. Other major airlines servicing Halifax include **Air Canada Jazz** (℃ **888/247-2262;** www.flyjazz. com), a regional carrier for Air Canada; **Air Canada Tango** (℃ **800/315- 1390;** www.flytango.com), a no-frills air travel alternative complementing Air Canada's full-service operations; **Air St. Pierre** (℃ **800/565-5188** or 902/873-3566; http://209.205.50. 254/AspWeb/index.html); **Air Transat** (℃ **800/872-6728** or 902/873-3140;

Nova Scotia

www.airtransatholidays.com); **CanJet**
(© 800/809-7777; www.canjet.com);
JETSGO (© 866/440-0441; www.
jetsgo.net); **Provincial Airlines Ltd.**
(© 800/563-2800 or 902/873-3575;
www.provincialairlines.ca), a regional
carrier in Atlantic Canada; **Skyservice
Airlines Inc.** (© 800/701-9448 or
902/873-3311; www.skyserviceair
lines.com); and **WestJet Airlines**
(© 888/937-8538 or 800/538-5696;
www.westjet.com).

FROM THE U.S.

Air Canada operates direct flights to
Halifax from Los Angeles, San Francisco, Las Vegas, Spokane, Phoenix,
Houston, and Chicago. Other major
airlines servicing Halifax include **Continental Express Airlines** (© 800/
525-0280 or 902/873-3295; www.
continental.com); **Delta Airlines**
(© 800/221-1212; www.delta.com);
and **Pan American Airlines** (© 800/
FLY-PANAM; www.flypanam.com).

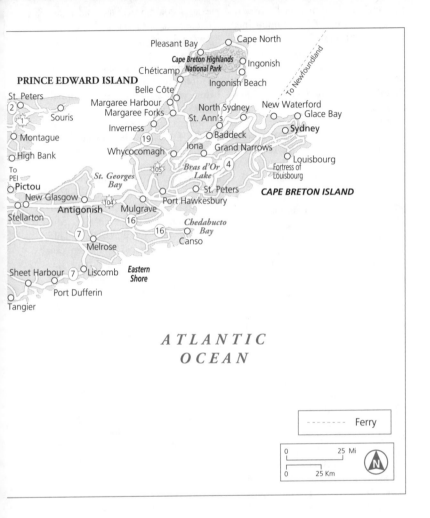

FROM ABROAD

Air Canada flies direct to Halifax from London and Frankfurt. Many international airlines offer nonstop service to Vancouver.

GETTING INTO TOWN FROM THE AIRPORT

The Halifax International Airport is located in Enfield, 35km (21 miles) northeast of downtown Halifax. Whether you travel by bus or car, it will take about 40 minutes along Highway 102 to get to Halifax proper from the airport. Transportation from the airport to the city is available via limousine or taxi, via shuttle, or by renting a car.

LIMOUSINE OR TAXI Both of these services are available curbside in the **Domestic Arrivals area** for all arriving flights. A one-way trip to Halifax city center costs C$43.00 (US$29) in a limo, C$41(US$28) by cab. Limousine companies servicing the Halifax International Airport include **A World Class Limousine, Inc.** (© 800/565-2777 or 902/864-4004; www.aworldclasslimousine.ns.ca); **Executive Limousine** (© 800/868-1880 or 902/456-1176); and **Wood's Limousine Service** (© 888/720-5466 or 902/864-8283; www.woodslimo.com). Taxi companies include **Aero Cab** (© 902/864-3333) and **A Sunshine Share-A-Cab** (© 800/565-8669 or 902/429-5555; www.atyp.com/asunshinecab).

SHUTTLE Air Bus Shuttle (© 902/873-2091) operates an airport-to-city service, delivering passengers to various hotels in Halifax. The booth is located curbside in the **Domestic Arrivals area.** A one-way ticket costs C$12 (US$7.50); a return ticket costs C$20 (U.S.$12.60). Children 9 and under ride free.

CAR RENTAL Rent a car at the airport from one of six companies. Pickup is less than a 5-minute walk outside from the airport arrivals area. Car rental companies include **Alamo Rent A Car (Canada) Inc.** (© 800/522-9696 or 902/873-3149; www.alamo.com); **AvisCar Inc.** (© 800/879-2847 (Canada) or 800/331-1212 (US) or 902/873-3522; www.avis.com); **Budget Rent-A-Car** (© 800/268-8900 or 902/492-7551; www.budget.com); **Dollar Rent-A-Car** (© 800800-4000 or 902/429-1892; www.dollar.com); **Fleet Car Rental Ltd. (Thrifty)** (© 800/367-2277 or 902/873-3527; www.thrifty.com); **Hertz Canada Limited** (© 800/263-0600 or 902/873-2273; www.hertz.com); and **National Car Rental Systems (Tilden)** (© 800/387-4747 or 902/873-3505; www.nationalcar.com).

BE PREPARED

In the wake of the terrorist attacks of September 11, 2001, the airline industry implemented sweeping security measures in airports. Expect a lengthier check-in process and possible delays. Because check-in takes longer and lines can be long, be sure to **arrive at the airport at least an hour early for domestic flights and two hours before your scheduled international flight** to ensure that you don't miss it. Be sure to carry a government-issued photo ID (national, provincial, or local), such as a driver's license. You may need to show this at various checkpoints. With an E-ticket (electronic ticket), you may be asked to show your printed receipt or confirmation of purchase and even the credit card with which you purchased it. This varies from airline to airline, so call ahead to make sure you have the proper documentation. And be sure that **your ID is up-to-date:** an expired driver's license, for example, may keep you from boarding the plane altogether. You can also expedite the boarding process by **knowing what you can carry on—and what you can't**—in advance. Travelers in Canada are now limited to one carry-on bag, plus one personal bag (such as a purse or a briefcase). And keep in mind that **only ticketed passengers will be allowed beyond the checkpoints,** except for those with specific medical or parental needs.

FLYING FOR LESS: TIPS FOR GETTING THE BEST AIRFARE

Travelers who need to purchase tickets at the last minute, change their itinerary at a moment's notice, or get home for the weekend often get stuck paying the premium rate. Here are some ways to keep your airfare costs down.

- Passengers who can book their ticket **far in advance,** who can **stay over Saturday night,** or who **fly midweek** or at **less-trafficked hours** will pay a fraction of the full fare. If your schedule is flexible, say so, and ask if you can secure a cheaper fare by staying an extra day, traveling on a Tuesday, Wednesday, or Thursday, or flying after 7pm. *Note:* The lowest-priced fares are often nonrefundable, require advance purchase of 1 to 3 weeks and a certain length of stay, and carry stiff penalties for changing dates of travel.

- You can also save on airfares by keeping an eye out for **promotional specials** or **fare wars,** when airlines lower prices on their most popular routes, with the competition often following suit. You rarely see fare wars offered during peak travel times, but if you can travel in the off season, you may snag a bargain.
- Search **the Internet** for cheap fares (see "Planning Your Trip Online").
- **Consolidators,** also known as bucket shops, are a good place to find low fares. Consolidators buy seats in bulk from the airlines and then sell them back to the public at prices usually below even the airlines' discounted rates. Their small ads usually run in Sunday newspaper travel sections. *Note:* Bucket-shop tickets are usually nonrefundable or rigged with stiff cancellation penalties, often as high as 50% to 75% of the ticket price. Reliable consolidators include **Council Travel** (© **800/ 226-8624;** www.counciltravel. com) and **STA Travel** (© **800/ 781-4040;** www.sta.travel.com). Both cater especially to young travelers, but their bargain-basement prices are available to everyone. **The TravelHub** (© **888/ AIR-FARE;** www.travelhub.com) represents nearly 1,000 travel agencies, many of whom offer consolidator and discount fares. **TFI Tours International** (© **800/**

745-8000 or 212/736-1140; www.lowestairprice.com) serves as a clearinghouse for unused seats. **1-800-FLY-CHEAP** (www.1800 flycheap.com) is another reliable firm.

- Join **frequent-flier clubs.** Accrue enough miles, and you'll be rewarded with free flights and elite status. It's free, and you'll get the best choice of seats, faster response to phone inquiries, and prompter service if your luggage is stolen, your flight is canceled or delayed, or if you want to change your seat.

LONG-HAUL FLIGHTS: HOW TO STAY COMFORTABLE

Flights of long duration test even the hardiest of travelers. And anyone who has traveled in coach or economy class in recent years can attest to the frustrating reality of cramped seating—which makes it hard to sleep or even relax during long flights. With a little advance planning, however, you can make an otherwise unpleasant experience almost bearable.

- For more legroom, ask for a seat in an emergency-exit row or bulkhead. To do so, you'll have to check in early—airline personnel do not book exit-row seats over the phone because they need to see that exit-row occupants are able-bodied and willing to follow emergency procedures if necessary.
- To have two seats for yourself, try for an aisle seat in a center section toward the back of coach. If you're traveling with a companion, book an aisle and a window seat. Middle seats are usually booked last, so chances are good you'll end up with three seats to yourselves. And in the case that a third passenger is assigned the middle seat, he or she will probably be more than happy to trade for a window or an aisle.

- To sleep, avoid the last row or the row in front of the emergency exit, as these seats are the least likely to recline. Avoid seats near high-traffic toilet areas. You also may want to reserve a window seat so that you can rest your head and avoid being bumped in the aisle.
- Be sure to get up, walk around, and stretch whenever you can to keep your blood flowing.
- Wear comfortable, low-heeled shoes and dress in loose-fitting layers that you can remove as cabin temperature fluctuates. Don't under-dress: Airline cabins are notoriously chilly and blankets may be unavailable. Wear breathable natural fabrics instead of synthetics.

- Drink lots of water before, during, and after your flight to combat the lack of humidity in airplane cabins—which can be drier than the Sahara Desert. Bring a bottle of water on board.
- If you're flying with kids, don't forget toys, books, extra bottles, pacifiers, diapers—and chewing gum to help them relieve ear pressure buildup during ascent and descent. Let children pack their own backpacks with favorite toys.
- Try to acclimatize yourself to the local time as quickly as possible. Stay up as long as you can the first day, then try to wake up at a normal hour ("normal" for where you are visiting) the next morning.

Tips Cancelled Plans

If your flight is cancelled, don't book a new fare at the ticket counter. Find the nearest phone and call the airline directly to reschedule. You'll be relaxing while other passengers are still standing in line.

BY TRAIN

VIA Rail (© 888/842-7245 in Canada, 800/561-3949 in the U.S.; www.viarail.com) brings visitors from Canada's central and western provinces to Halifax, connecting with Amtrak (© 800/872-7245; www.amtrak.com) services in many cities along the way. The trip from Montreal to Halifax takes approximately 20 hours. The Halifax train station, 1161 Hollis St., (© 800/561-3952 or 902/494-7900; www.viarail.ca) is located behind the Westin Nova Scotian Hotel, via Marginal Road. While the station's location is considered downtown, it is at least a 15-minute walk to most attractions and other hotels.

BY BUS

Acadian Lines (© 902-454-9321; www.smtbus.com) and DRL Coach Lines (© 877/450-1987 or ref: 902/450-1987; www.drlgroup.com) provide bus service to Halifax via connections with SMT Eastern (© 800/567/5151; www.smtbus.com) from New Brunswick, Voyager (© 800/668-4438; www.voyageur.com) from Quebec and Ontario, and Greyhound (© 800/229-9424; www.greyhound.com) from the United States.

Several shuttle bus services run between Halifax and Sydney, the Annapolis Valley, and the South Shore in Nova Scotia; between Halifax and Prince Edward Island; and between Halifax and Moncton, New Brunswick. Contact the International Visitor's Centre for shuttle bus service numbers, 1595 Barrington St. (© 902/490-5946; www.halifaxinfo.com).

Approximate Driving Times to Halifax from Cities in Canada and the U.S.

- Albany, NY: 16.5 hours
- Bangor, ME: 9 hours
- Boston, MA 13.5 hours
- Charlottetown, PEI: 3 hours
- Fredericton, NB: 5.5 hours
- Montreal, QC: 14.5 hours
- St. John's, NF: 15.5 hours
- Toronto, ON: 24 hours

BY CAR

Halifax is situated on a small peninsula, which is located on the southern side of the larger peninsula of Nova Scotia, which is located on the eastern side of Canada. Which is to say that it's a long drive from anywhere west of Montreal, or southwest of Boston.

The **Trans-Canada Highway** links Vancouver to Halifax, and the 6,000km (4,000 miles) in between. Crossing provincial borders is not a problem; the province's flag and a welcome sign are usually the only formalities you encounter.

Tips **They Don't Have a Warrant, But that Doesn't Mean They Can't Search You**

Canada and United States customs officials have the right to search your vehicle when you arrive in or depart Canada by car. Although it's not a regular occurrence, be sure to allow yourself extra time at border crossings.

BY FERRY

You can travel to Nova Scotia, and Halifax, by extension, by car ferry from New Brunswick, Prince Edward Island, Newfoundland and Labrador, and from Maine.

FROM NEW BRUNSWICK

If you're coming from New Brunswick, you can take a ferry from **Saint John to Digby, Nova Scotia. Bay Ferries Ltd.,** (© **888/249-7245** or 902/245-2116; www.nfl-bay.com) operates daily, year round except for December 25, October to June, with two sailings per day, at midnight and 11am; June through September, with two and three sailings per day, at 4am,

noon, and 5:45pm. A one-way fare for a vehicle and two adults is C$115 (US$77). Digby is approximately 200km (120 miles) from Halifax, and will take just over 2 hours to drive.

FROM PRINCE EDWARD ISLAND

From Prince Edward Island, take the ferry from **Wood Island to Caribou, Nova Scotia. Northumberland Ferries Ltd.** (© **888/249-7245;** www. nfl-bay.com) makes this run at least five times a day from May 1 to mid-December, and during the peak season (July 15 to September 3) the ferry leaves at 8:30am, 10am, noon, 1:30pm, 3pm, 4:30pm, 6:30pm, and 8pm. A round-trip fare for a vehicle and passengers is C$49 (US$33). It takes less than 2 hours to drive from Caribou to Halifax (170km, 105 miles).

FROM NEWFOUNDLAND & LABRADOR

From Newfoundland, take the ferry from either **Argentia or Port aux Basques to North Sydney, Nova Scotia.** The shortest crossing is from Port aux Basques.

Marine Atlantic (© 800/341-7981; www.marine-atlantic.ca) operates this service from mid-June to the end of September, and there are up to four crossings per day, which take approximately 5½ to 6 hours. The remainder of the year there are two to three crossings per day, and while the trip takes the same number of hours during the day as in the summer, the night crossings take approximately 7 hours. For an automobile and two adults, a one-way fare comes to C$115 (US$77). Cabins can be rented.

The Argentia to North Sydney crossings only run from mid-June to the end of September, on Mondays, Thursdays, and Saturdays. The trip takes approximately 14 hours. For an automobile and two adults, a one-way fare costs C$270 (US$180). Cabins can be rented.

FROM MAINE

The easiest access to Halifax from the United States is through the state of Maine. Since Nova Scotia and the U.S. have no common border, you must go through the province of New Brunswick to Nova Scotia—a 5-hour drive (500km/300 miles), plus another 2-hour drive to Halifax. Or you can take a ferry from **Portland or Bar Harbor** during the summer, and save hours of driving. (Many people opt to travel one way here and the other way home.) The ferries dock in Yarmouth, Nova Scotia, which is 300km (180 miles) southwest of Halifax.

FROM PORTLAND TO YARMOUTH

The overnight trip takes 11 hours aboard the *Scotia Prince Ferry* (**Scotia Prince Cruises**) (© 800/341-7540; www.scotiaprince.com). The season runs from May to October, daily, leaving from Portland at 8pm Eastern Standard Time.

From April 29 to June 20, and October 1 to 26, the one-way fare is C$105 (US$70) for adults, C$53 (US$53) for children 5 to 14, free for children 4 and under. If you're bringing your vehicle with you, the cost is C$135 (US$90) for vehicles under 2m (7 feet) in height, C$53 (US$35) for motorcycles, and C$15 (US$10) for bicycles.

From June 21 to September 30, the one-way fare is C$135 (US$90) for adults, C$69 (US$46) for children 5 to 14, free for children 4 under. The cost for vehicles under 2m (7 feet) in height is C$110 (US$73), C$83 (US$55) for motorcycles, and C$30 (US$20) for bicycles.

Note: A 10% discount applies when you book round-trip passage. Trips between Yarmouth and Portland are cheaper and do not include a cabin as they are day trips and leave Yarmouth at 9am Atlantic Time.

FROM BAR HARBOR TO YARMOUTH

This is a 3-hour voyage on a high-speed catamaran ferry known as *The Cat* (Bay Ferries Ltd., © 888/249-7245; www.catferry.com). The ferry saves you more than 1,000km (600 miles) of driving. Even though it's a short trip, you can still visit the casino on board or purchase food from the cafeteria.

From May 16 to October 15, there are daily, 8am EST crossings from Bar Harbor. From June 22 to September 2, there is an additional crossing departing at 4pm. Between September 3 and September 28, there is one crossing on each of Tuesday, Thursday, Friday, and Saturday, departing at 4pm.

From May 16 to June 26, and September 29 to October 15, the one-way fare is C$68 (US$45) for adults, C$60 (US$40) for seniors, C$30 (US$20) for children 6 to 17, free for children 5 and under. If you're bringing your vehicle with you, the cost is C$323 (US$215) for a family of up to 6 people (2 adults and 4 dependents) in a vehicle up to 6m (20 feet) in length, C$83 (US$55) for motorcycles, and C$15 (US$10) for bicycles. Larger vehicles are charged according to length and height. Check the website or call for details (*C* **888/249-7245;** www.catferry.com). You must also pay the U.S. arrival/departure tax of C$4.50 (US$3) per person.

From June 27 to September 28, the one-way fare is C$83 (US$55) for adults, C$75 (US$50) for seniors, C$38 (US$25) for children 6 to 17, free for children 5 and under. If you're bringing your vehicle with you, the cost is C$383 (US$255) for a family of up to 6 people (2 adults and 4 dependents) in a vehicle up to 6m (20 feet) in length, C$90 (US$60) for motorcycles, and C$15 (US$10) for bicycles. Larger vehicles are charged according to length and height. Check the website or call for details (*C* **888/249-7245;** www.catferry. com). You must also pay the U.S. arrival/departure tax of C$4.50 (US$3) per person.

All of these entry points will have travel information and can provide you with a road map of the province. Remember if you are traveling by car to bring your registration and insurance papers with you. Expect to encounter at least some road construction during the summer months—the only time Nova Scotia weather permits road repair—and allow some time for side trips off the main highways to enjoy the beauty of the province.

BY SEA

Halifax boasts the second largest natural harbor in the world, and the city's history and livelihood are inexorably linked to the harbor and the ocean. Halifax is a port of call for cruise lines operating on the North American East Coast routes and transatlantic itineraries. About 100 cruise ships visit Halifax each year, including **Princess** (*C* 800/775-62377; www.princess. com), **Holland America** (*C* 877/724-5425; www.hollandamerica.com), **Royal Caribbean International** (*C* 800/398-9819; www.royal caribbean), and **Carnival Cruise Lines** (*C* 888/227-64825; www. carnival.com).

If you are sailing your own vessel, you can tie up on the Halifax waterfront at one of several wharves. For information and berthing inquiries, contact the **Waterfront Development Corporation** (*C* **902/422-0341;** www.wdclhalifax.com/berthing.html), or one of the yacht clubs in the area:

- **The Armdale Yacht Club,** PO Box 22105, Bayers Road Postal Outlet, 7071 Bayers Rd. Halifax, NS B3L 4T7 (*C* **902/477-4617;** www.armdaleyachtclub.ns.ca).
- **The Bedford Basin Yacht Club,** 73 Shore Dr. Bedford, NS B4A 2C7 (*C* **902/835-3729;** www. bbyc.ns.ca).
- **The Royal Nova Scotia Yacht Squadron,** 376 Purcells's Cove Rd. Halifax, NS B3P 1C7 (*C* **902/ 477-5653;** www.rnsys.com).
- **Waegwoltic Club,** 6549 Coburg Rd. Halifax, NS B3H 2A6 (*C* **902/429-2822;** www.waeg woltic.ca).

Remember that non-Canadian pleasure crafts must register at the **Canada Customs office,** 1583 Hollis St., PO Box 520, Halifax, NS B3J 2R7 (*C* **800/461-9999** within Canada or

902/426-2071; www.ccra-adrc.gc.ca/customs/menu-e.html) upon first arrival in Canada to file an **inward report.** The vessel is given a **cruising permit,** which covers the boat while it is in Canadian waters. You return the permit to Canada Customs and Revenue Agency when you depart.

7 Planning Your Trip Online

Sites such as **Frommers.com, Travelocity.com, Expedia.com,** and **Orbitz.com** allow consumers to comparison shop for airfares, access special bargains, book flights, and reserve hotel rooms and rental cars. Keep in mind that because several airlines are no longer willing to pay commissions on tickets sold by online travel agencies, these agencies may either add a C$16 (US$10) surcharge to your bill if you book on that carrier—or neglect to offer those carriers' schedules. And be sure to call the airline directly before you surf the Web to see if you can do better before booking online.

Remember, booking a trip online is only convenient if you are familiar with the territory. If the Internet is not one of your regular information sources, stick to the trusted route and consult with a travel agent. On the other hand, planning your trip online can add even more excitement to the voyage. Visiting accommodation sites before booking can show you exactly what they have to offer, and in full color, too. Booking plane tickets and car rentals online can save you money, but you have to shop around. You can obtain last-minute specials on weekend deals or Internet-only fares, but this type of special sometimes means you have to be prepared to travel on two or three days' notice. You can receive regular e-mail announcements of airline specials by signing up on their websites. Or you can access websites that contain comprehensive lists of last-minute specials from a variety of airlines and companies. Check out **Webflyer** (www.webflyer.com), **Smarter Living** (www.smarterliving.com), or **OneTravel.com** (www.onetravel.com).

⌐Tips Stop the Conversion Madness!

Make sure you know which currency you are using when you book your flights, accommodations, or rentals. If you are dealing with a variety of countries—a combination of U.S. airlines and Canadian hotels, for example—convert the costs to the same currency to compare prices. Use the currency that you are most familiar with. For online conversion tables, visit **www.convertit.com** or **www.onlineconversion.com**.

POINT AND CLICK YOUR WAY TO A GREAT TRIP

Following is a list of sites that we've found helpful. Keep in mind that with the speed of change on the Internet, better sites may be created and current sites may disappear between the time you purchase this book and have the opportunity to sit down and read it.

To search by destination, dates or cost, visit:

- **Expedia:** www.expedia.com,
- **ITN** (American Express): www.itn.net,

- **Travelocity:** www.travelocity.com,
- **Yahoo!:** www.travelyahoo.com.

For general travel tips and information, visit:

- **Planet Rider:** www.planetrider. com,
- **Free Travel Tips:** www.freetravel tips.com.

To find spots around the world where you can check your e-mail while you travel, visit:

- **Cybercafes:** www.cybercafes.com,
- **Net Café Guide:** www.netcafe guide.com/mapindex.htm.

To check the street layouts of cities, visit **MapQuest,** at www.mapquest. com. To make sure you will be able to obtain some last-minute cash, check out the ATM locators at **Visa** (www.visa.com) and **MasterCard** (www.mastercard.com). Special interest/special needs travelers can visit the **Independent Traveler's Resource Center** (www.independenttraveler. com), and click on "Special Interests," about halfway down the page.

 ## Frommers.com: The Complete Travel Resource

For an excellent travel-planning resource, we highly recommend **Frommers. com** (www.frommers.com). We're a little biased, of course, but we guarantee that you'll find the travel tips, reviews, monthly vacation giveaways, and online-booking capabilities thoroughly indispensable. Among the special features are our popular **Message Boards**, where Frommer's readers post queries and share advice (sometimes our authors even show up to answer questions); **Frommers.com Newsletter,** for the latest travel bargains and inside travel secrets; and Frommer's **Destinations Section,** where you'll get expert travel tips, hotel and dining recommendations, and advice on the sights to see for more than 2,500 destinations around the globe. When your research is done, the **Online Reservation System** (www.frommers.com/booktravelnow) takes you to Frommer's favorite sites for booking your vacation at affordable prices.

FINAL THOUGHTS

While the Internet can provide you with unlimited information, it can also overload surfers with so many facts and so much data that it's hard to make a decision. Remember too that it can only answer the questions you ask. If you forget or overlook something, there's no one there to remind you. In addition, though Internet sites can help you design your vacation, once you're on your way there's no one there to give alternatives or institute plan B. Some sites can't handle specialized designations, such as seniors, travel or youth discounts, and if you run into difficulty it might be troublesome or even impossible to get an online agency to straighten out your problem. *Note:* Make sure there's a paper trail of all your online transactions.

Online Traveler's Toolbox

Veteran travelers usually carry some essential items to make their trips easier. Following is a selection of online tools to bookmark and use:

- **Halifax Events** (www.halifaxmetrocentre.com), the website of the Halifax Metro Centre, the city's main entertainment and sporting venue. Log on for information on upcoming concerts and hockey games.

- **The Coast** (www.thecoast.ns.ca), for information on music, film, stage, and other events happening throughout Halifax. Click on The Guide.

- **Visa ATM Locator** (www.visa.com), for locations of Plus ATMs worldwide, or **MasterCard ATM Locator** (www.mastercard.com), for locations of Cirrus ATMs worldwide.

- **The Weather Network** (www.theweathernetwork.com). Gives weather forecasts for all areas of Canada and around the world.

- **Mapquest** (www.mapquest.com). This best of the mapping sites lets you choose a specific address or destination, and in seconds it will return a map and detailed directions.

- **Cybercafes.com** (www.cybercafes.com) or **Net Café Guide** (www.net cafeguide.com/mapindex.htm). Locate Internet cafes at hundreds of locations around the globe. Catch up on your e-mail and log on to the Web for a few dollars per hour.

- **Universal Currency Converter** (www.xe.com/ucc). See what your dollar or pound is worth in more than 100 other countries.

Getting to Know Halifax

Halifax's rich history is reflected in the various attributions it's enjoyed over time. The very first was *Chebucto*, the Mi'kmaq word for "biggest harbor." Then came City of Trees, City of Firsts, Birthplace of British Canada, Birthplace of Canadian Democracy, Warden of the North (from a poem by Rudyard Kipling), and the Smart City.

The Mi'kmaq weren't far wrong. Halifax boasts the second largest natural harbor in the world, and that harbor has helped to define the city since its beginnings in 1749. Founded as a British naval and military base, Halifax is still home to Canada's navy. The magnificent harbor and the city's geographic location made it a strategic base of operations for Britain in the Seven Years War, the War of American Independence, the Napoleonic Wars, the War of 1812, and for Canada during the World Wars. These same features made it a natural center for international trade and commerce.

Halifax earned the title Birthplace of Canadian Democracy when the first Elective Assembly held in a British colony met on October 2, 1758. This assembly represented the present-day provinces of Nova Scotia, New Brunswick, and Prince Edward Island. In 1908, Sir Sandford Fleming, who lived in Halifax during the 1880s, when he was engineer-in-chief of construction of the Intercolonial Railway, which operated between the Maritimes and Quebec, established a summer retreat on Halifax's North West Arm, known as the Dingle. Fleming later donated a section of his land for a park, on condition that Halifax build a tower to commemorate this first Elective Assembly held in the overseas British Empire. The tower was completed in 1912 and dedicated by His Royal Highness, the Duke of Connaught, Governor General of Canada (son of Queen Victoria). At the opening ceremonies on August 4, 1912, the Duke dubbed the new Memorial Tower "The Statue of Liberty of Canada."

And then there are those trees. There are close to 500 acres (200 hectares) of parkland on the Halifax peninsula. It's no wonder Haligonians were up-in-arms when the Brown Spruce Longhorn Beetle was discovered in Point Pleasant Park in 1999. The beetle is not native to the area and probably arrived via cargo ships visiting the harbor from Europe some years earlier. When the city decided to cut down 10,000 trees to limit the movement of the beetles, Haligonians fought for a federal court injunction to stop cutting. This ruling was later overturned, but the city lowered the number of trees it intended to remove. The beetles are not dangerous to the public, but have the potential to harm the logging industry. At press time, the controversy is still playing out.

1 Orientation

VISITOR INFORMATION

The **International Visitor's Centre,** 1595 Barrington St., Halifax, NS B3J 1Z7 (© **800/565-0000** or 902/490-5946; www.halifaxinfo.com) is located on the corner of Barrington and Sackville streets, in the shadow of Citadel Hill. The staff is knowledgeable and friendly, and can help you book tours and make reservations. There is a hoard of printed material available, along with individual kiosks and videos of travel routes to help you plan day and overnight trips to other parts of Nova Scotia. The center is open in May and June daily from 8:30am to 7pm, in July and August daily from 8:30am to 8pm, and September to the end of April, Monday to Friday from 8:30am to 4:30pm.

Another **visitor information center** is located on the Halifax waterfront, at 1655 Lower Water St., Halifax, NS, B3J 1S2 (© **800/565-0000** or 902/424-4248; www.novascotia.com). Set back behind the Maritime Museum of the Atlantic and next to the historic HMCS *Sackville* (a World War II convoy escort corvette), this center is convenient for visitors exploring the downtown and waterfront areas on foot. It's open from July to mid-October daily from 8am to 8pm, and November to June daily from 8:30am to 4:30pm. Call for confirmation of these hours, as they were being reviewed at press time.

USEFUL PUBLICATIONS The *Greater Halifax Visitors Guide* is published annually and provides information on museums, galleries, and historical sites, along with up-to-date events and highlights. The guide also provides data on accommodations, restaurants, shopping, and a listing of tours, guides, and charters. The province publishes the annual *Nova Scotia Complete Guide for Doers and Dreamers.* These guides are available at the **International Visitor's Centre** (© **800/565-0000** or 902/490-5946; www.halifaxinfo.com) and all other visitor centers in the Halifax area.

Another helpful publication is *Where Halifax,* a free booklet published monthly that provides information on shopping, dining, and entertainment. It's available at most hotels and restaurants, or online at **www.wherehalifax.com**.

Moments A Citadel View

Standing on the ramparts of the **Citadel Hill National Historic Site,** overlooking Halifax and the harbor beyond, take a few minutes to imagine all the events—fortunate and unfortunate, as with any history—that this fortress has witnessed. Look down at **Brunswick Street,** below, and listen for the marching of the English soldiers. Turn south and imagine dozens of **Tall Ships** making their way up the harbor. Look north and settle your gaze on the **A. Murray MacKay Bridge** that spans the harbor between Halifax and Dartmouth. Imagine the screech of metal meeting metal, the flying debris, the screams of terror: This was where the Halifax Explosion occurred in 1917. Look at the **Bedford Basin,** to the north beyond the bridge. During World War II, it harbored hundreds of merchant marine vessels loaded with supplies for Britain, and the Navy corvettes that accompanied them across the Northern Atlantic. Imagine the riot in the streets when victory in Europe, and the end of the war, was announced in 1945. Picture the excitement and security measures set up for the **G–7 Summit** of world leaders in 1995. The Citadel has seen it all.

NEWSPAPERS & MAGAZINES   Halifax daily newspapers include the privately owned *Halifax Herald,* the *Mail Star,* and the Hollinger/Southam-owned *Daily News.* Find **arts and heritage information** in the Sunday issue of the *Herald.* Entertainment and live performances are listed in the "What's Up" section in the Thursday issue. *The Coast* is a free weekly tabloid that carries news about Halifax and its people, as well as information on dining, arts, and other events—all with an attitude. The information and entertainment bible of the under-25 crowd, this paper is a no-holds-barred review of Halifax city life.

Fun Fact   **Breathe Easy in Halifax**

After much discussion, Halifax has phased in a ban on the use of outdoor pesticides, insecticides, and herbicides for the maintenance of trees and shrubs and other ornamental plants and turf, which applies to all residential and municipal properties in the Halifax Regional Municipality.

CITY LAYOUT

Halifax began life in 1749 as a British fort, and the imposing, star-shaped **Citadel,** perched on the hill overlooking the harbor, still dominates the city. (Its official name is the **Halifax Citadel National Historic Site.**) The firing of the noonday gun from the Citadel is a Halifax tradition, often startling visitors strolling the nearby streets. Because of its hilltop position, the Citadel provides a wonderful view of the city below. Looking east, toward the harbor, there are nine blocks of streets tumbling through the **downtown** to the **waterfront.** Lively and beautiful, the waterfront has been restored in recent years and is once again the center of downtown activity. Unfortunately, the harbor itself has received no such renewal, and is polluted with sewage from private and commercial establishments. Across the harbor is **Dartmouth,** also known as the City of Lakes, and now part of the larger amalgamated Halifax Regional Municipality. To the north is an area dubbed, not surprisingly, the **North End.** This area was flattened in the explosion of 1917, when two munitions ships collided in Halifax Harbour. It was rebuilt almost immediately (see "Neighborhoods" later in this chapter). Also to the north are the Angus L. Macdonald and the A. Murray MacKay bridges that span the harbor. Further north is the outlying community of **Bedford,** and the inner section of the harbor, known as the **Bedford Basin.** The **South End** lies to the south, home to **Point Pleasant Park,** St. Mary's University, and a variety of historic residences. To the west is the **North West Arm**—a beautiful piece of water bordered by yacht clubs, parks, residential areas, and forest.

MAIN STREETS AND ARTERIES   Keep a few Halifax thoroughfares in mind as you explore the city. There's **Robie Street,** which runs from the North End, near the MacKay Bridge, all the way to the South End, ending a few blocks from Point Pleasant Park. **Barrington Street** runs roughly parallel to Robie, also from the North End, at the MacKay Bridge, through downtown Halifax to the South End, near the piers. **Quinpool Road** runs perpendicular to Robie and Barrington streets, east to west, through a shopping and dining district, to the **Halifax Commons.** From the Commons, follow **Cogswell Street** to **Lower**

Halifax Neighborhoods

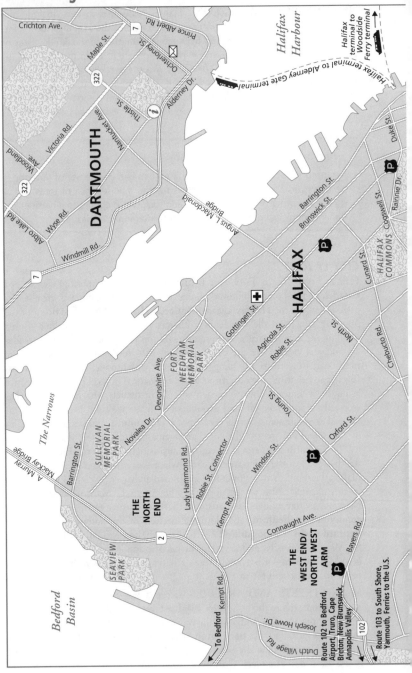

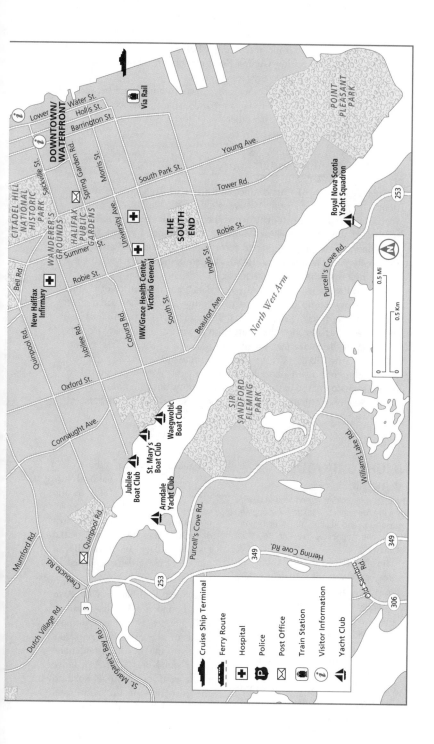

Cruise Ship Terminal
Ferry Route
Hospital
Police
Post Office
Train Station
Visitor Information
Yacht Club

DOWNTOWN/
WATERFRONT

CITADEL HILL
NATIONAL
HISTORIC
PARK

WANDERER'S
GROUNDS

HALIFAX
PUBLIC
GARDENS

THE
SOUTH
END

New Halifax
Infirmary

IWK/Grace Health Center,
Victoria General

Jubilee
Boat Club

St. Mary's
Boat Club

Waegwoltic
Boat Club

Armdale
Yacht Club

SIR
SANDFORD
FLEMING
PARK

POINT
PLEASANT
PARK

Royal Nova Scotia
Yacht Squadron

North West Arm

Via Rail

Water St.
Hollis St.
Barrington St.
Young Ave.
South Park St.
Tower Rd.
Spring Garden Rd.
Morris St.
Sackville St.
University Ave.
Summer St.
Robie St.
Inglis St.
Robie St.
South St.
Coburg Rd.
Beaufort Ave.
Bell Rd.
Jubilee Rd.
Quinpool Rd.
Oxford St.
Connaught Ave.
Quinpool Rd.
Mumford Rd.
Chebucto Rd.
Dutch Village Rd.
St. Margaret's Bay Rd.
Purcell's Cove Rd.
Herring Cove Rd.
Williams Lake Rd.
Old Sambro Rd.

0.5 Mi
0.5 Km

253
349
3
306

43

Water Street and the waterfront area, or follow **Bell Road** to the Halifax Citadel National Historic Site. **Spring Garden Road** is a vibrant shopping and dining district, popular with the university crowd.

Many of the city's accommodations and attractions are located between the Citadel and Halifax Harbour (see chapter 4 and chapter 6, respectively). Most are within walking distance of each other.

⌒ Fun Fact　**What Is the H.R.M.?**
_____

The amalgamation of four distinct and historical areas in and around Halifax took place on April 1, 1996. **Halifax**, the capital city of Nova Scotia; **Dartmouth**, its sister city across the harbor; **Bedford**, a quiet bedroom community; and **Halifax County**, a rural area of farming, fishing, and commerce, came together to form one large municipal entity, the **Halifax Regional Municipality (HRM)**. Though unified, they nevertheless retain their own characters and quirks.

Dartmouth, known as "the City of Lakes," has its own colorful and proud history dating to 1750, not to mention a somewhat competitve attitude towards its big sister Halifax. Bedford, with a population of just over 14,000, has a strong community spirit and identity stemming from its founding in the mid-1700s. When the rural area of Halifax County was folded into the HRM, it was stunned. How could dirt roads and rural mail delivery be considered part of a city? The county even petitioned to become amalgamated with another rural county, but to no avail. So the Halifax Regional Municipality proves a complex marriage of independent spirits.

NEIGHBORHOODS IN BRIEF

The following districts in and around downtown are top spots to explore for shopping, sightseeing, and dining. You'll find more details and suggested walking tours in chapter 7.

The North End　Spanning an area covering approximately 4.8sq. km (3sq. miles), the North End is bounded by Cogswell and Cunard streets to the south, Robie and Windsor streets to the west, the Bedford Basin to the north, and Barrington Street and the harbor to the east. The North End has the oldest naval dockyard in North America, and is home to important public and domestic buildings dating back to the 18th century. Canada's federal government has

designated one of these, St. George's Church, a national historic site, built in 1800 in the formal Roman architectural style, now known as Palladian. This area of Halifax was also the site of the historic village of **Africville,** a unique black settlement settled in the 1700s.

The West End/North West Arm　The boundaries of this area are Robie Street as far as Quinpool Road to the east; Kearney Lake Road to the north; Bicentennial Drive and North West Arm Drive to the west; and Quinpool Road (to the east side of the Arm) and Williams Lake Road (to the west side of the Arm) to the south. Until about 80 years ago, this area was

Africville

In the late 1700s and early 1800s, men and women fleeing slavery in the United States followed the "Underground Railroad" to Halifax and settled on the shores of the Bedford Basin. The community became known as Africville. Although the population never numbered more than 400 from the time of its founding until well into the 1920s, the people owned their land, worked at various jobs, and fished and raised crops. Life in Africville centered around the church, and family and friends provided support for one another. While the majority of Halifax's black population did not live in Africville, it was home to those who wanted to live in privacy, relatively free from the prejudices of the predominantly white population. For over 150 years, Halifax ignored the rights of the inhabitants of Africville, using the nearby land first for a prison, then an infectious disease hospital, and finally, in the 1950s, for an open city dump and incinerator. Nor did the city provide adequate fire and police protection for the community, which resulted in illegal activities.

A series of renewal projects undertaken by the city in the 1960s forced the inhabitants of Africville to move to another location, where they were promised better housing, and social and economic opportunities. However, as they settled elsewhere, they realized they had lost the heart of their community life, their circle of support, and their sense of belonging. Meanwhile, the city was bulldozing the site of Africville into oblivion. It's now a little-used green area called Seaview Park. There is a monument, however, dedicated to the spirit of Africville. You can find out more about Africville at the **Black Cultural Centre for Nova Scotia**, 1149 Main St., Dartmouth, NS B2Z 1A8 (✆ **800/465-0767** or 902/434-6223; www.bccns.com). (See the section on a side trip to Dartmouth in chapter 10.)

Books of interest include *The Spirit of Africville,* published by Formac Publishing, and *Africville: The Life and Death of a Canadian Black Community,* published by Canadian Scholar's Press.

mainly farmland. The municipal airport was located here during the 1930s and 1940s, and residential development exploded from about 1950 on. Its proximity to the downtown business district and easy access to major urban traffic arteries make it one of the more popular areas to live. It also has vibrant shopping areas on the southern and western fringes. Also located in this section of Halifax are the Armdale Yacht Club and Sir Sandford Fleming Park. A gift from Sir Sandford in 1908, this 95-acre (38-hectare) park is better known to older Haligonians as the "Dingle," an Irish-Gaelic name that means "a forested cove."

The South End This area has always been considered the elite part of Halifax. It's **home to three universities** (one of them, the **University of King's College,** is the oldest in Canada; the other two are **Dalhousie University** and **St. Mary's University**), the Queen Elizabeth II Health Sciences Centre's fleet of hospitals, the 195-acre (78-hectare) **Point Pleasant Park,** and politely boasts some of the loveliest, largest,

> **Fun Fact** **Sir Sandford Fleming (1827–1915)**
>
> Sir Sandford Fleming is a famous Halifax figure: Born in Scotland in 1827, he emigrated to British North America in 1845, when he was 18. He made several groundbreaking discoveries in his lifetime. When he was just 21 years old, for example, he designed a prototype for an in-line skate. Upon testing it, he pronounced it "altogether satisfactory." He also designed Canada's first adhesive postage stamp, the Three-Penny Beaver, in 1851, conceived of a coast-to-coast rairoad for British North America, in 1858 (which he later helped to construct), and invented Universal Standard Time, a system that divides the globe into 24 equal time zones (enacted in 1884). Sir Sandford Fleming was knighted by Queen Victoria in 1897. He died in Halifax in 1915.

and oldest homes in the city. It's bordered to the north by Quinpool Road, to the east and south by the harbor, and to the west by the beautiful North West Arm.

Downtown/Waterfront   This is undoubtedly Halifax's main draw. In this concentrated area of the city, you'll find museums, historic forts, all manner of seafaring vessels (military ships, ferries, and cruise ships), art galleries, hotels, theaters, cathedrals, public gardens, restaurants, casinos, breweries, and, at press time, 60 listed pubs, bars, and lounges. Halifax works hard and plays hard, and a lot of it is done downtown. Hotels, restaurants, and attractions in this part of the city are all reachable on foot. (See the suggested walking tours and map in chapter 7.) The more you walk, the better, because parking in downtown Halifax is atrocious. Several of the buildings and shops in the downtown are connected by covered walkways over the streets—very convenient when the weather is cold or wet. While none of the attractions are far away, some of the routes are uphill, and this can be challenging if you don't fancy or are unable to do more arduous trekking.

Halifax's waterfront is a popular tourist spot, with wooden buildings and stone structures dating to the 18th-century alongside more modern high-rise office buildings. The harbor is Halifax's most outstanding resource; it's the reason for the city's existence, and a fascinating place to visit. Harbor tours and boat trips are offered day and night, ranging from deep-sea fishing charters to the regular passenger ferry service between Halifax and Dartmouth. (See chapter 6 for more details on organized tours in Halifax.) Amid all this excitement, activity, and fun, though, it's disturbing to see the sewage, which is still allowed to drain into the harbor.

2 Getting Around

ON FOOT

If you can manage a fair amount of walking, this is the way to go. Halifax is best appreciated at street level, and parking is at such a premium—particularly in the attraction-rich downtown area—you'll save time, money, and a good deal of hassle by exploring the city on foot. Keep a close eye on children, especially at crosswalks.

The Halifax Explosion

This terrible explosion occurred on December 6, 1917, while war still raged in Europe. As a Belgian relief ship was heading out to sea from Halifax Harbour, a French ship, carrying a full cargo of explosives, was entering the harbor, awaiting a convoy to escort her back across the Atlantic to France. The two ships collided, and the French ship caught fire. The blast that followed is considered the biggest man-made explosion prior to the atomic bomb. More than 1,900 people died instantly, about 9,000 more were injured—many permanently—and 325 acres—almost all in the city's north end—were destroyed.

Three thousand houses had to be repaired in the first seven weeks after the explosion; by January 1918, temporary apartments were being constructed at the rate of one every hour. Rebuilding continued frantically, and a few months later, construction started on 328 houses in the area bordered by Young, Agricola, Duffus, and Gottingen streets. The houses were built from cement blocks, called hydrostones (so named perhaps because they were fire-resistant), and had gardens, modern plumbing, and electricity. This area, still known as the **Hydrostone District,** is considered one of the more attractive and desirable parts of Halifax in which to live.

A moving exhibit about the explosion, Halifax Wrecked, is at the **Maritime Museum of the Atlantic,** 1675 Lower Water St. (© 902/424-7490; http://museum.gov.ns.ca/mma). *Barometer Rising,* a powerful novel by the late Canadian author **Hugh MacLennan,** uses the explosion as its backdrop.

BY PUBLIC TRANSPORTATION

BY BUS   If you're tired of walking or wish to venture outside of the downtown core, **Halifax Metro Transit,** 200 Ilsley Ave., Dartmouth, NS B3B 1V1 (© **902/490-6600;** www.region.halifax.ns.ca/metrotransit) offers inexpensive transportation to all parts of the city and outlying areas. Bus routes you'd likely use include: **no. 7** (Robie Street to Gottingen Street via South Street and Downtown), **no. 9** (to Point Pleasant Park), and **no. 12** (to Downtown). Bus schedules vary, but most run from 7am to midnight, with extra runs at rush hour, fewer on holidays. One-way fares are C$1.65 (US$1.10) for adults, C$1.15 (US75¢) for seniors (65 and up) and for children 5 to 15, children 4 and under ride for free. Metro Transit also operates the ferry service between Halifax and Dartmouth. Ask for a bus transfer—no extra charge—to get you on to the ferry.

BY TAXI

You can try to hail a taxi on a downtown street, but it's easier to find one in front of hotels or in shopping districts. Some taxis serve only certain areas of the city, and for limited periods. For 24-hour, full-city service, call **Casino Taxi** (© **902/429/6666** or 902/425-6666). **Yellow Cab** (© **902/420-0000**) is also a 24-hour, full-city service. You can arrange payment by credit card when you phone in advance. Rides from one downtown attraction to another cost approximately C$4 (US$2.50). The fare from downtown to the Halifax International Airport is C$45 (US$30).

Halifax Firsts

World Firsts
Founding of the Cunard Steamship Line: 1840
Founding of Schwartz Spices: 1840
Use of pulp wood in making paper: 1844
Invention and testing of kerosene: 1846
Use of seawater for a computerized air-conditioning system in
   sky-scrapers: 1985

North American Firsts
First postal service: 1752 (to New York City)
First Board of Trade: 1789
The first city to use electric street lamps: 1890

Canadian Firsts
The first public school: 1749
The first Protestant church: 1750 (St. Paul's Anglican Church still stands)
The first English-language newspaper: 1752 (*The Halifax Gazette*)
The first Elective Assembly: 1758
The first university: 1789 (King's College, now affiliated with
   Dalhousie University)
The first black Sunday School: 1813
Winning of freedom of the press and freedom of speech: 1835
The first chocolate factory: 1844
The birthplace of Responsible Government: 1848
Founding of the Institute of Science: 1862
The first law school: 1884 (at Dalhousie University)
The first college of art: 1887 (founded by Anna Leonowens)
The first basketball game: 1892

BY CAR

Driving in Halifax isn't navigationally difficult, as there are four major arteries that will take you most anywhere once you become familiar with them. They are: Robie Street, Quinpool Road, Barrington Street, and Spring Garden Road. Parking is the hassle, however. If you're staying downtown, it's easier to walk or take buses and taxis. The money you'll save from avoiding parking meters and garages will more than cover your bus and taxis fares.

If you must drive a car, be alert to one-way streets, jaywalkers (Halifax drivers regularly stop for pedestrians, even if they're crossing the street where they shouldn't be), and street signs that are sometimes obscured by trees.

REGULATIONS   Every vehicle must have a vehicle permit (registration). If the car does not belong to you, carry a letter from the owner; or if rented, carry a copy of the vehicle rental contract. Wearing seat belts is mandatory throughout Nova Scotia, for drivers and passengers. Fines for not wearing a seat belt are close to C$100 (US$75) per person. Car insurance is also mandatory. Car rental agencies will provide insurance for an extra fee.

The Smart City

smart 1.*adj*. brisk, lively.
How can you tell Halifax is smart? Halifax is:
- Ranked as one of Canada's Five Smart Cities in which to do business by the *Globe and Mail*'s "Report on Business" magazine.
- The home of six degree-granting institutions: the Atlantic School of Theology, Dalhousie University, St. Mary's University, Mount Saint Vincent University, the University of King's College (affiliated with Dalhousie University), and The Nova Scotia College of Art and Design.
- Credited with having one of the best-educated workforces in Canada; 57% of workers have a post-secondary education.
- The most Internet-savvy city, with the highest per-capita Internet usage in all of Canada.
- Known nationally and internationally as a great place to do business due to its advanced telecommunications structure, the cluster of high-tech companies, and the diverse range of cultural and leisure activities available.
- Consistently rated in the top 10% of cities across North America in terms of quality of education, determined by student–teacher ratio, the proportion of the population attending post-secondary institutions, and the variety of programs offered.
- Full of students—with 5,700 graduate students, 20,000 undergraduate students, and 11,000 students attending three community colleges.
- A major North American medical center. The Izaak Walton Killam Children's Hospital is one of North America's top 10.
- The financial center of Eastern Canada.
- Canada's major naval base.
- Canada's second-largest science and research center after Ottawa.
- On the same latitude as Bordeaux, France.

In Halifax and throughout Nova Scotia, a right turn on a red light is permitted only after coming to a complete stop, unless posted otherwise. Even so, you must yield to oncoming traffic and pedestrians.

Tips **Do and See More for Less—Ride *fred!***

From June to September, daily from 11am to 6pm, hop aboard *fred* **(Free Rides Everywhere Downtown)** (② **902/423-6658;** www.downtownhalifax. ns.ca), a brightly colored bus that'll show you the Halifax sites for free. *fred* makes a 30-minute loop of the downtown, from Upper and Lower Water streets to Terminal Road, up South Street to South Park Street, down Spring Garden Road to Barrington Street, and back to Upper Water Street. You can get on and off as many times as you want. *fred* also stops at the **Scotia Square Mall** and **Barrington Place Shops,** as well as **Casino Nova Scotia** and **Pier 21.** Ask for schedules and a map at any of the city's visitor centers.

⌒ *Tips* Beating the Parking Problem

Park & Ride

Park your car and take the bus. Several areas are located throughout the city including:

- Halifax Shopping Centre Annex: This is the Mumford Terminal for all buses. There are 50 free parking spots here; you can leave your vehicle and take a bus to downtown or anywhere else in the city, as well as to Dartmouth or Bedford.
- Village at Bayer's Road: If you are driving in from out of town via the Bicentennial Highway (Route 102) this is a convenient location to leave your vehicle and catch a bus. There are 30 free parking spaces for this service.
- Halifax Shopping Centre: Another location where you can leave your car and hop the bus is near the Sobeys store on the middle deck. The mall has allotted 200 parking spaces for Park & Ride.

Paid Parking Downtown

Most downtown streets have metered parking (average cost is $1 per hour, either Canadian or American coin, Monday to Friday, 8am to 6pm) and most are full during the day, especially around noon when you want to stop for lunch. It's a little easier to find an evening parking spot during week days, but weekend evenings are busy.

There are several downtown parking garages and areas that you can try:

- **Scotia Square:** The entrance to the parking garage is on Market St. between Cogswell and Duke sts.
- **Prince George Hotel parking garage:** The entrance is on Market St. between George and Prince sts.
- **Purdy's Wharf:** With more than 1,000 outdoor parking spaces used by people who work in the city, as well as visitors.
- **Citadel Halifax Hotel:** Underground parking. The entrance is at 1960 Brunswick St.

SPEED LIMITS   All speed limits are posted in kilometers per hour. The speed limit on most highways is 100kmph (60 mph). On secondary roads, it's usually 80kmph (50 mph). The limit in cities, towns, and school zones when children are present is 50kmph (30 mph). Police impose substantial fines for speeding. Radar detectors are illegal in Nova Scotia and can be confiscated within city limits by the Halifax Regional Police and on highways by the RCMP (Royal Canadian Mounted Police).

RENTALS   During peak summer months (June through August), it's difficult to rent a car at the last minute, so book one before you leave home. Remember, too, that renting is difficult for visitors under age 25. Some companies will only rent on a cash basis, others only if you have a credit card, and many won't rent to you at all.

Most major car rental agencies have offices at the Halifax International Airport. Renting a mid-size car for 1 week during peak summer months (June through August) will run you C$300 (US$200) or more. Remember to check for special discounts, membership discounts, drop-off rates, free kilometers, and special promotional rates. Insurance is required on all cars in Nova Scotia, but this may be covered by some credit cards. Double-check for damage before accepting the vehicle—the company will certainly check it when you return it.

Companies with offices at the airport and in Halifax proper include **Avis** (© **800/879-2847;** www.avis.com), **Budget** (© **800/268-8900;** www.budget-maritimes.com), and **Hertz** (© **800/263-0600;** www.hertz.com). Companies with offices in Halifax include **Discount,** 1240 Hollis St. and 6160 Almon St. (© **800/263-2355** or © 902/468-7171; www.discountcars.ca), **Enterprise,** 3200 Kempt Rd., 107–1161 Hollis St. and 120 Susie Lake Cres. (© **800/325-8007;** www.enterprise.com), and **Thrifty,** 6419 Lady Hammond Rd. (main rental center) and 1589 Lower Water St. (© **800/847-4389;** www.thrifty.com).

FUEL   If you're visiting from outside Canada, don't get excited about the seemingly low price of gas, because it's priced by the liter—roughly ¼ of an American or Imperial gallon.

Tips Color-coded Parking Meters

Meter caps are color-coded according to the maximum time they allow you to park your vehicle.

Yellow: 5 hours, minimum $5
Green: 2 hours, minimum $2
Silver/Grey: 1 hour, minimum $1
Red: 30 minutes, minimum 50¢

If you're searching for a metered parking space on the street, keep in mind the length of time you plan to park. If you plan to stay a while, try to find a yellow or green cap so that you won't have to return as often to add money to the meter. Meters are in effect Monday to Friday from 8am to 6pm, excluding holidays.

BY OTHER MEANS

BICYCLES   Bikes are subject to the same laws as other vehicles on the highway, and cyclists must obey traffic signals and signs. Cycling is becoming more popular in the city; unfortunately there aren't any designated bicycle routes to use. Halifax has formed a task force and plans to hire a bicycle/pedestrian coordinator to work toward developing bike routes throughout the city. If you've brought your bicycle with you, remember that wearing a helmet is mandatory.

Bicycles can be rented from **Freewheeling Adventures Inc.** (© **902/857-3600;** www.freewheeling.ca). They're open June 15 to September 15 daily from 9am to 6pm, and September 16 to June 14 Monday through Friday from 9am to 6pm. The cost of a rental is C$25 (US$16.70) per day. Tandem bicycles cost C$55 (US$36.70) per day.

RICKSHAWS   Rickshaw services are available in the downtown area, with or without narrated tours, from May to September. Look for the black and red carts lined up anywhere from the waterfront to Spring Garden Road.

FAST FACTS: **Halifax**

Airport   The Halifax International Airport is 35km (21 miles) from downtown Halifax. For transportation to and from the airport see "Getting There" in chapter 2. To check arrival and departure times for all flights, visit www.hiaa.ca/todaysflights/index.htm. For telephone inquiries about flights or baggage, call the appropriate airline company; see listings in chapter 2.

Air Travel Complaints   The Canadian Transportation Agency's Air Travel Complaints Commissioner handles unresolved passenger complaints against air carriers. Information and complaint forms are available at www.cta.gc.ca. For more information, call ✆ **888/222-2592**.

American Express   For card member services, including traveler's checks and lost or stolen cards, call ✆ **800/869-3016**.

Area Codes   The telephone area code for Halifax is 902. This is also the area code for all of Nova Scotia and Prince Edward Island. It is not necessary to use the area code when calling locations within the city. To call long distance within Canada or the U.S., dial 1, plus the area code, plus the seven-digit local number.

ATM   Automated Teller Machines that are linked to the Cirrus or PLUS networks and can be found at bank branches, shopping malls, and most transportation depots. If you have an Interac card, and your personal identification number (PIN), you can also make cash withdrawals from your Visa or MasterCard account. There are charges for this service.

Automobile Clubs   The Canadian Automobile Association (CAA) provides member benefits to AAA cardholders while you are in Canada. When visiting, make sure you bring your membership card. For information about the CAA, call ✆ **800/268-3750**. For emergency road service, call ✆ **800/222-4357**.

Babysitting   Hotels can usually provide you with a list of names and phone numbers of reliable babysitters who can provide references.

Business Hours   Most banks are open weekdays, 9:30am to 5pm, with extended hours, including weekends, at some locations. Stores are usually open from Monday to Saturday, 9:30 or 10am to 6pm. Stores located in shopping malls are usually open on Thursday, Friday, and sometimes Saturday evenings until 9:30 or 10pm. Downtown shops have various hours that cater to people visiting the city. Nova Scotia by-laws do not allow shopping malls and larger stores to open on Sundays. This does not apply to smaller gift shops and boutiques. Office hours are usually Monday to Friday from 9am to 5pm.

Car Rentals   See "Getting Around" earlier in this chapter.

Climate   See "When to Go" in chapter 2.

Currency Exchange   To get the best rate, use your bank card at an ATM or exchange your money at a bank or currency exchange. Foreign exchange services are available at the **International Visitor's Centre**, 1595 Barrington St. (✆ **902/490-5946**), and at the **visitor information center at the Halifax International Airport** (✆ **902/490-1223**). All banks can exchange U.S. currency.

Directory Assistance   For numbers within the same area code, call ℂ **411**. There is a charge for this directory assistance if you're calling from a residential or private phone, but not if you're calling from a pay phone or a hospital. For other numbers, call ℂ **555-1212** prefixed by the area code of the number for which you are searching. There is a charge for this service.

Disability Services   Most of Halifax's museums, attractions, and public buildings are accessible to travelers with disabilities. See "Tips for Travelers with Disabilities" in chapter 2.

Doctors   For life-threatening emergencies, call ℂ **911**. For routine medical assistance, call the **Queen Elizabeth II Health Sciences Centre** general information number at ℂ **902/473-2700**. For minor problems, visit one of the many drugstores in the city and talk to a pharmacist. Many are open evenings and weekends.

Documents   See "Visitor Information & Entry Requirements" in chapter 2.

Driving Rules   See "Getting Around" earlier in this chapter.

Drugstores   Many Halifax pharmacies are open evenings and weekends. **Pharmasave** is located at the Queen Elizabeth II Health Sciences Centre, 1278 Tower Rd ℂ **902/473-7210**, Victoria General Hospital, 1796 Summer St. ℂ **902/473-7300**, and 2151 Gottingen St. ℂ **902/429-5218**. **Shoppers Drug Mart** is located at 5595 Fenwick St. ℂ **902/421-1683**. A **24-hour** location is at 5524 Spring Garden Rd. ℂ **902/429-2400**.

Electricity   Canada uses the same electrical current as the United States: 110–115 volts, AC.

Embassies/Consulates   All of the more than 100 embassies in Canada are located in Ottawa. See "Visitor Information and Entry Requirements" in chapter 2. Consulates are located in Vancouver, Toronto, and Montreal. Consulates located in Halifax include those of Austria, Belgium, Denmark, France, Germany, Italy, Lebanon, the Netherlands, Norway, and the United States. Check the Yellow Pages of the Halifax telephone directory or call ℂ **411** for assistance.

Emergencies   In life-threatening situations, call ℂ **911** for fire, police, or ambulance. For the **Poison Information Centre,** call ℂ **902/428-8161**.

Eyeglasses   For one-hour replacement service, contact **Hakim Optical,** at the Bayers Road Shopping Centre (ℂ **902/455-5082**), at 5511 Spring Garden Rd. (ℂ **902/422-9900**), or at 120 Susie Lake Cres. (ℂ **902/450-5701**). Or log on to www.hakimoptical.ca.

Holidays   See "When to Go" in chapter 2.

Hospitals   Halifax is serviced by a collection of hospitals under the umbrella of the **Queen Elizabeth II Health Sciences Centre**, 1278 Tower Rd. ℂ **902-473-2700**.

Internet Access   Stay in touch with those back home at the **Ceilidh Connection Internet Café,** 1672 Barrington St. (ℂ **902-422-9800**). Most public libraries also have Internet access. See "Libraries" below.

Kids Help Phone   Kids or teens in distress can call ℂ **800/668-6868** or ℂ **902/457-4779**.

Libraries   The main branch of the **Halifax Regional Library** is located at 5381 Spring Garden Rd. (℃ **902/490-5700;** www.halifax.library.ns.ca). Call or visit their website for other branch locations.

Liquor Laws   The legal drinking age in Nova Scotia is 19. Bars, licensed restaurants, and retail stores routinely ask for proof of age, so carry a photo identification card.

Lost Property   Block charges against your credit card accounts the minute you discover your wallet has been lost or stolen, and file a report at the nearest police station Your credit card company or insurer may require a police report number or record of the loss. Most credit card companies have an emergency toll-free number to call if your card is lost or stolen; they may be able to wire you a cash advance immediately or deliver an emergency credit card in a day or two. **Citicorp Visa's U.S. emergency number** is ℃ **800/336-8472.** American Express cardholders and traveler's check holders should call ℃ **800/221-7282.** MasterCard holders should call ℃ **800/307-7309.** For other credit cards, call the toll-free number directory at ℃ **800/555-1212.** If you need emergency cash over the weekend when all banks and American Express offices are closed, you can have money wired to you via **Western Union** (℃ **800/325-6000;** www.westernunion.com).

Identity theft or fraud are potential complications of losing your wallet, especially if you've lost your driver's license along with your cash and credit cards. Notify the major credit-reporting bureaus immediately; placing a fraud alert on your records may protect you against liability for criminal activity. Canadian citizens should contact **Equifax** (℃ **800/766-0008;** www. equifax.com). American citizens should contact **Experian** (℃ **888/397-3742;** www.experian.com) or **TransUnion** (℃ **800/680-7289;** www.transunion.com).

Mail   Mailing letters and postcards within Canada costs C48¢ (US30¢). The cost to send letters and postcards to the United States is C65¢ (US40¢). Mailing letters overseas costs C$1.25 (US80¢).

Maps   Free maps of the city and province are available from visitor centers or by ordering online at www.halifaxinfo.com or www.novascotia.com. Maps can also be purchased at bookstores and souvenir shops.

Newspapers/Magazines   Halifax's daily newspapers are the *Halifax Herald*, the *Mail Star*, and the *Daily News*. *The Coast* is a free weekly newspaper. *Where Halifax* is a free monthly guide to shopping, dining, and entertainment. *Saltscapes* is a bi-monthly magazine featuring the people, places, and nature of Atlantic Canada. The best place to shop for magazines and newspapers is at **Atlantic News,** corner of Queen and Morris Sts. (℃ **902/429-5468;** www.atlanticnews.ns.ca). They carry over 5,200 magazine titles and over 90 newspaper titles from local, national, and international publishers.

Police   For a life-threatening emergency, call ℃ **911.** For other matters, call ℃ **902/490-5020.**

Post Offices   The main outlet for **Canada Post** is at 1680 Bedford Row, (℃ **902/494-4734**). Postal services can also be found on a smaller scale at many pharmacies throughout Halifax.

Radio   The Canadian Broadcasting Corporation (CBC) broadcasts local, regional, and national programming on **90.1FM** and **102.7FM**. Easy listening and oldies are broadcast on **C100FM**, and **CHNS Oldies 960AM**. Country music is broadcast on **CFDR 780 KIXX Country** and **CHFX Hot Country 101.9**.

Restrooms   Public restrooms are available at visitor information centers, gas stations, major hotels, shopping malls, and restaurants.

Safety   Halifax is considered a safe city. Still, lock your car doors, don't walk alone after dark, and stay alert to your surroundings. The downtown can become rowdy (but not usually dangerous) at night and on weekends when the bar crowd spills onto the streets. See "Insurance, Health & Safety" in chapter 2.

Taxes   The Harmonized Sales Tax (HST) combines the provincial sales tax (8%) and the federal Goods and Services Tax (GST) (7%) into a flat rate of 15%, which is charged on all goods and services. Visitors to Canada may claim a rebate of the GST portion on non-consumable goods purchased in Canada to take out of the country. The rebate doesn't apply to meals, liquor, tobacco, transportation costs, and gasoline. To apply for a refund, present your original receipts at a participating duty-free shop for a cash refund of up to $500 when leaving Canada. Or mail a completed refund application to the address on the application. Allow six to eight weeks for a refund. For further information, call © **800/668-4748** or 902/432-5608.

Taxis   See "Getting Around" earlier in this chapter.

Telephone   A local call from a telephone booth costs C25¢ (Canadian and U.S. coins are accepted at face value, and pay telephones will accept U.S. coins). Local calls made from hotel rooms are often levied a surcharge, often as high as C$1 (US63¢). To make a long-distance call between Canada and the U.S., dial **1** followed by the **area code** followed by the **phone number**. For other **international calls**, dial **011** followed by the **country code, city code,** and **telephone number.** Some country and city codes are as follows: **Australia** 63, Melbourne 3, Sydney 2; **Ireland** 353, Dublin 1, **New Zealand** 64, Auckland 9, Wellington 4, **United Kingdom** 44, Belfast 232, Birmingham 21, Glasgow 41, London 71 or 81. For reversed-charge or **collect calls**, and for person-to-person calls, dial **0** followed by the **area code** and **phone number**; an operator will come on the line, and you should specify that you are calling collect, or person to person, or both. If your operator-assisted call is international, ask for the overseas operator. Calls to area codes **800, 888,** and **877** are toll-free. However, calls to numbers in area codes **700** and **900** (chat lines, bulletin boards, and so on) can be expensive, up to $1 or more per minute, plus an up-front minimum charge of several dollars. Phone cards, which are used in the same way as credit cards for long-distance calls, can be purchased throughout the city at pharmacies and shopping malls.

Temperature   Canada uses the Celsius system where the freezing point is 0°. To convert Celsius to Fahrenheit, multiply by ⅗ and then add 32. For example, 22°C is a pleasant summer morning (at 72°F).

Time Zone   Halifax is in the **Atlantic Standard Time Zone**, one hour ahead of Eastern Standard time (used in New England). Daylight Savings Time is in effect from the first Sunday in April to the last Sunday in October.

Tipping   Tips or service charges are not generally added to bills, except in the case of large parties. The usual practice is to tip 15% in restaurants and taxis and C$2 (US$1) per bag for porters at airports and hotels.

Weather   To obtain a local weather forecast in English call ℂ **902/426-9090;** in French, call ℂ **902/426-9095.** Check daily newspapers, or tune in to **The Weather Network,** on TV or online, at **www.theweathernetwork.ca**. Or ask a Haligonian—they've already checked it.

4

Accommodations

Halifax is the largest and busiest city in Atlantic Canada. It's the site of major conventions, national meetings, and international events, including G–7 meetings and Tall Ships extravaganzas. It has become a popular location for making movies (*K-19: The Widowmaker,* starring Harrison Ford, was filmed here, as was *Christmas Shoes,* starring Rob Lowe) and for filming TV series (*This Hour Has 22 Minutes, Made In Canada*). It is a major business center and government location. These are just a few of the reasons why it's sometimes hard to get a room, especially in the downtown area. But every cloud has a silver lining, and in Halifax, it's in the form of special deals offered to fill hotel rooms when the business travelers and movie stars head home.

Keep in mind that parking in downtown Halifax is a chore, so staying in a downtown hotel can save you time and money. Parking rates range from C$2.50 (US$1.50) per hour in public parking areas (hotels charge more) to C$20 (US$12) per day. Some places charge each time you leave and return; others have no one on duty overnight, so you can't leave—even if you want to! Besides, if you've come to Halifax for its history and museums, its restaurants, entertainment, and nightlife, most is within walking distance of any downtown hotel.

Halifax also offers many family-friendly options in the form of spacious, functional suites, or apartment-style accommodations. Many are located downtown; others, on the outskirts. Many hotels allow children to stay free-of-charge with parents, and offer complimentary meals for younger kids. This is noted in individual hotel reviews in this chapter. Still more hotels provide limited or full-kitchen facilities so that you can prepare your own meals at a lower cost. Even delicious restaurant food can be too much of a good thing if you have to stare it down three times a day.

Most hotels, motels, and B&Bs are wheelchair-accessible. Beyond elevators, most have one or more rooms with wider doors, and accessible bathrooms. There is a limited number of these rooms in the city, though, so try to book as early as possible, and explain exactly what you need.

RATES The rates listed in this chapter are "rack rates" for both the high and low season, double occupancy. *Note:* You can often better this by inquiring about weekend specials and package deals. Many hotels offer discounted rates for seniors, family packages, and membership discounts.

SMOKING Most hotels are either totally nonsmoking or have smoke-free rooms and/or floors. Be sure to ask for your preference when you book. Most bed-and-breakfast locations are nonsmoking, so double-check before you book.

PLAYGROUNDS AND POOLS Although many accommodations furnish pools and places for children to play, the facility is not responsible for providing supervision.

SAVING ON YOUR HOTEL ROOM

The **rack rate** is the maximum rate that a hotel charges for a room. It's the rate you'd get if you walked in off the street and asked for a room for the night. Hardly anybody pays these prices, however, and there are many ways around them.

- **Ask about special rates or other discounts**. Always ask whether a room less expensive than the first one quoted is available, or whether any special rates apply to you. You may qualify for corporate, student, military, senior, or other discounts. Mention membership in CAA, CARP, AAA, AARP, frequent-flier programs, or trade unions, which may entitle you to special deals as well. Find out the hotel policy on children—do kids stay free in the room or is there a special rate?
- **Dial direct.** When booking a room in a chain hotel, compare the rates offered by the hotel's local line with that of the toll-free number. A hotel makes nothing on a room that stays empty, so the local hotel reservation desk may be willing to offer a special rate unavailable elsewhere.
- **Remember the law of supply and demand**. Resort hotels are most crowded and therefore most expensive on weekends, so discounts are usually available for midweek stays. Business hotels in downtown locations are busiest during the week, so you can expect big discounts over the weekend. Avoid high-season trips if you're counting your pennies: planning your vacation just a week before or after official peak season can mean big savings.
- **Look into group or long-stay discounts**. If you come as part of a large group, you should be able to negotiate a bargain rate, since the hotel can then guarantee occupancy in a number of rooms. Likewise, if you're planning a long stay (at least 5 days), you might qualify for a discount. As a general rule, expect 1 night free after a 7-night stay.
- **Avoid excess charges and hidden costs**. When you book a room, ask whether the hotel charges for parking. And find out whether your hotel imposes a surcharge on local and long-distance calls. Many hotels charge a fee just for dialing out on the phone in your room. A pay phone, however inconvenient, will save you money, although many calling cards charge a fee or take away minutes from your card when you use it on a pay phone. And don't be tempted by the room's minibar offerings: Most hotels make you pay through the nose for water, soda, and snacks. Finally, ask about local taxes and service charges, which can increase the cost of a room by 25% or more.
- **Book an efficiency**. A room with a kitchenette allows you to shop for groceries and cook your own meals. This is a big money-saver, especially for families on long stays.

LANDING THE BEST ROOM

Somebody has to get the best room in the house. It might as well be you. Always ask about a corner room. They are often larger and quieter, with more windows and light, and they often cost the same as standard rooms. When you make your reservation, ask if the hotel is renovating; if it is, request a room away from the construction. Ask about nonsmoking rooms, rooms with views, rooms with twin, queen-, or king-size beds. If you're a light sleeper, request a quiet room away from vending machines, elevators, restaurants, bars, and discos. Ask for one of the rooms that has been most recently renovated or redecorated.

If you aren't happy with your room when you arrive, say so. If another room is available, most lodgings will be willing to accommodate you. Join the hotel's frequent visitor club; you may qualify for upgrades.

CAMPING

You'd rather sleep out under the stars? Pitch your tent at **Woodhaven Park**, 1757 Hammonds Plains Rd., Hammonds Plains, NS B4B 1P5 (© **902/835-2271**; carolebuchanan@webtv.net). Less than a 30-minute drive from downtown Halifax, Woodhaven Park has 235 sites (including electrical and modem hookups), as well as a pool and playground for the kids. To get to Woodhaven Park from downtown Halifax, take Highway 102 to exit 3 and drive 6.5km (4 miles) west on route 213.

Halifax West KOA, 3070 Highway 1, Upper Sackville (© **877/865-2228** or 902/865-4342; colonial.camp@ns.sympatico.ca), has 83 sites. Amenities include electrical and modem hookups, a Laundromat, an on-site grocery store, plus a pool and playground. To get to Halifax West KOA from downtown, take Highway 102 to exit 4B, turn west on Highway 101 and take exit 3 to route 1, turn right and drive 2km (1.2 miles).

Shubie Park Campground, Box 36058, 5675 Spring Garden Rd., Halifax, NS B3J 3S9 (© **902/435-8382** or 902/490-4096 off season; www.shubie campground.com), has 100 sites. It's an open campground, with electrical hookups, supervised lake swimming, a canteen, volleyball court, horseshoes, and walking trails. Services were upgraded in 2002. To get to the campground from downtown Halifax, cross the A. Murray MacKay Bridge to Dartmouth and follow the signs for Highway 7. Traveling towards Dartmouth on Highway 7 turn right onto Highway 107 west. Follow the 107 approximately 5km (3 miles) to Exit 14. Turn left at the top of the ramp to the intersection of Waverley Road/Braemar Drive/Highway 318. Turn left and travel approximately 2.2km (1.5 miles) more to Jaybee Drive. Turn right on Jaybee and go straight through the 4-way stop, to the campground.

1 Downtown

A harbor-side room is the most popular in town, and two of Halifax's premier hotels, the **Casino Nova Scotia Hotel** and the **Westin Nova Scotian Halifax**, have an unobstructed view of the ships and sailboats that ply the waters of **Halifax Harbour**. Stroll the 3.8-km (2.3-mile) boardwalk that runs along the waterfront. Take the time to enjoy the numerous restaurants, museums, and nightspots clustered by the water.

In addition to the must-see Maritime Museum of the Atlantic (see "The Top Attractions" in chapter 6), you'll find Pier 21, a National Historic Site giving testament to Canada's immigration experience (also see "The Top Attractions" in chapter 6), Murphy's on the Water (see "Organized Tours" in chapter 6), where you can shop for fine crafts and souvenirs or book tickets on a harbor cruise, a dozen or so restaurants ranging from coffee and doughnuts to world cuisine, and **Casino Nova Scotia** (see chapter 9), where you might win (or lose) your fortune. On clear nights, you'll be charmed by the reflection of twinkling lights on the water, or mesmerized by the strings of car lights as they cross the bridge between Halifax and Dartmouth.

Just a few blocks up from the waterfront is a bevy of hotels, all within walking distance of downtown shopping, dining, and entertainment. Streets are

Halifax Accommodations

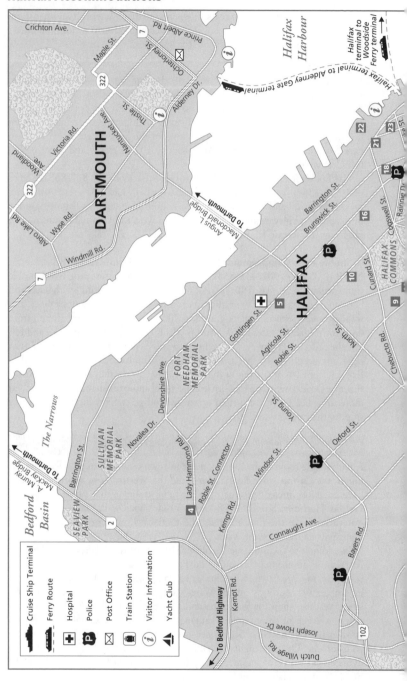

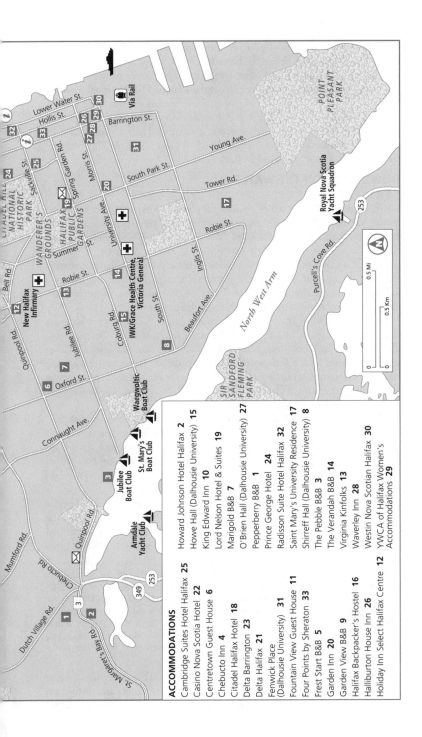

Lower Water St.
Hollis St.
Barrington St.
Young Ave.
South Park St.
Tower Rd.
Robie St.
Inglis St.
Via Rail
POINT PLEASANT PARK
Royal Nova Scotia Yacht Squadron
Purcell's Cove Rd.
253

Morris St.
Spring Garden Rd.
Sackville St.
University Ave.
Summer St.
Robie St.
Coburg Rd.
South St.
Beaufort Ave.
Bell Rd.
Quinpool Rd.
Jubilee Rd.
Oxford St.
Connaught Ave.
Mumford Rd.
Chebucto Rd.
Dutch Village Rd.
St. Margaret's Bay Rd.
Quinpool Rd.

CITADEL HILL NATIONAL HISTORIC PARK
WANDERER'S GROUNDS
HALIFAX PUBLIC GARDENS
New Halifax Infirmary
IWK/Grace Health Centre, Victoria General
North West Arm
SIR SANDFORD FLEMING PARK

Waegwoltic Boat Club
St. Mary's Boat Club
Jubilee Boat Club
Armdale Yacht Club

349
253
3

N
0.5 Mi
0.5 Km

ACCOMMODATIONS

Cambridge Suites Hotel Halifax **25**
Casino Nova Scotia Hotel **22**
Centretown Guest House **6**
Chebucto Inn **4**
Citadel Halifax Hotel **18**
Delta Barrington **23**
Delta Halifax **21**
Fenwick Place (Dalhousie University) **31**
Fountain View Guest House **11**
Four Points by Sheraton **33**
Frest Start B&B **5**
Garden Inn **20**
Garden View B&B **9**
Halifax Backpacker's Hostel **16**
Haliburton House Inn **26**
Holiday Inn Select Halifax Centre **12**

Howard Johnson Hotel Halifax **2**
Howe Hall (Dalhousie University) **15**
King Edward Inn **10**
Lord Nelson Hotel & Suites **19**
Marigold B&B **7**
O'Brien Hall (Dalhousie University) **27**
Pepperberry B&B **1**
Prince George Hotel **24**
Radisson Suite Hotel Halifax **32**
Saint Mary's University Residence **17**
Shirreff Hall (Dalhousie University) **8**
The Pebble B&B **3**
The Verandah B&B **14**
Virginia Kinfolks **13**
Waverley Inn **28**
Westin Nova Scotian Halifax **30**
YWCA of Halifax Women's Accommodations **29**

busy, and parking is lousy, so leave your car in your hotel's parking area and put on your walking shoes. This is the business district, so, on weekdays, alongside the museums, restaurants, and other attractions, expect to see people rushing to and from meetings. Escape to the grass at the **Citadel Hill National Historic Site** (see "The Top Attractions" in chapter 6), or meander through the **Halifax Public Gardens** (also see "The Top Attractions" in chapter 6). If the weather doesn't cooperate, remember that much of downtown Halifax is connected by the **Downtown Link,** a series of covered pedways and tunnels linking hotels to convention centers to shopping areas.

DOWNTOWN ON THE WATER
VERY EXPENSIVE
Casino Nova Scotia Hotel ⭐ _(Overrated)_   If you're looking for a place right next to the harbor with nightlife, entertainment, and a view, this is your hotel. Located on the waterfront, this hotel, with its copper roof and sandstone exterior is a view in itself. Formerly known as the Halifax Sheraton, it recently underwent a C$15-million (US$9-million) renovation that included updating the guest rooms, and adding a new restaurant/lounge, new meeting rooms, a self-serve business center, and a spa. There are 300 attractive, if not elegant, traditional guest rooms furnished with contemporary pieces.

Suites are available, including the Specialty Junior Suites, with a king-size canopy bed, living area, and an oversize Jacuzzi. Even so, most are located within the interior of the hotel—only one has a harbor view—and the original, rather small bathrooms look a little worn. The one-bedroom suites have a king-size bed, two bathrooms, and a separate living area with enough room for a dining room table that seats six. The Elite Suites have all this, plus they're larger. They also sport a wet bar, pantry, and a harbor view.

The hotel is connected to Casino Nova Scotia by the Downtown Link, and offers rooms on its Player's Club VIP Floor to people who purchase a Stay and Play package. This floor includes more lavish rooms and a private Crown Club lounge with complimentary buffet, continental breakfast, evening hors d'oeuvres, and cocktail services. The Downtown Link also connects the hotel to downtown boutiques, shops, and restaurants.

It's expensive to stay here, and because it's expensive, we expected a superior experience. We were disappointed. The minibar ran all night—loudly—and the canopy bed, while comfortable enough, was nothing but a piece of unfinished plywood on the inside. Despite a multi-million-dollar facelift, the overall quality just isn't here.

1919 Upper Water St., Halifax, NS B3J 3J5. ℭ **866/425-4329** or 902/421-1700. Fax 902/428-7850. www.casinonovascotiahotel.com. 352 units. April 15–Nov 15 C$300 (US$200) double; C$425 (US$283) 1-bedroom suite; C$1100 (US$733) executive suite. Nov 16–April 14 C$99 (US$66) double; C$425 (US$283) 1-bedroom suite; C$1100 (US$733) executive suite. Weekend, Stay and Play, and other packages available. Extra person C$20 (US$13.30). Children 18 and under stay free in parents' room. AE, DC, DISC, MC, V. Parking C$10 (US$6). Metro Transit nos. 7, 9, 2. Pets accepted. **Amenities:** 2 restaurants (Canadian, pub), lounge; indoor heated pool; exercise room; spa; Jacuzzi; sauna; concierge; business center; limited room service. _In room:_ A/C, TV w/pay movies, minibar, hair dryer, iron.

The Westin Nova Scotian Halifax ⭐⭐⭐ _(Kids)_   This place has elegance and polish. As soon as you step inside, you feel a sense of history and distinction in this grand hotel that over the years has hosted fancy balls, historic events, and royalty. Built in 1929 by the Canadian National Railway, the Nova Scotian has long been a landmark in downtown Halifax. The considerable renovations completed in 2002 have preserved most of the gentility of the rooms, while adding modern amenities.

Half of the guest rooms look onto the harbor and George's Island, while the others view Cornwallis Park with its lawn, playground, and Heritage Garden (a memorial to the immigrants who entered Canada via Pier 21, located nearby. Standard in every room are two telephones—one with a data/fax port, a safe, and windows that open to let you smell that salt air. The bathrooms are not overly large, but they are new and spotless. Suites are available with one and two bedrooms, all with at least two bathrooms. The hotel has the largest convention space in the city, but is also suitable for families.

The staff is gracious and helpful to everyone—from the famous to the family dog (the concierge keeps treats in his desk for four-legged guests). Children are greeted on arrival with special age-appropriate gifts; for younger children, there's a telephone bedtime Story Line, accessible from room phones. Complimentary high chairs and cribs are available. There are pet-designated guest rooms, and staff will walk dogs and feed pets, with advance notice.

1181 Hollis St., Halifax, NS B3H 2P6. ℂ Westin, **800/228-3000** or 902/421-1000. Fax 902/422-9465. www.westin.com. 297 units. April 1–Nov 30 C$255 (US$170) double; C$295 (US$197) 1-bedroom suite; C$550 (US$367) executive suite. Dec 1–March 31 $C135 (US$90) double; C$295 (US$197) 1-bedroom suite; C$550 (US$367) executive suite. Weekend and other packages available. Extra person C$20 (US$13). AE, DC, DISC, MC, V. Valet parking C$14 (US$8.50); self-parking C$9 (US$5.50). Metro Transit nos. 7, 9, 2. Pets accepted with some restrictions. **Amenities:** Restaurant (Canadian), coffee shop, lounge; indoor pool; outdoor tennis court; health club & spa; sauna; children's programs; concierge; free shuttle to downtown; business center; limited room service; massage; babysitting; laundry service; same-day dry cleaning. *In room:* A/C, TV w/pay movies, dataport, fridge, coffeemaker, hair dryer, iron, safe.

DOWNTOWN ABOVE THE WATER
VERY EXPENSIVE
Prince George Hotel ⊀   This is a modern hotel in the heart of downtown, connected via enclosed Pedways and underground tunnels to shopping and business. The Prince George caters to visitors attending events at the Metro Centre and World Trade & Convention Centre, both next door, but you'll find the service agreeable even if you're not staying here on business. A complete renovation in 2000 has kept the marble looking fresh and the mahogany polished. Along with regular guest rooms, there are Business Rooms, with a work desk, dual-line speakerphone with dataport, fax machine, and free local calls. Executive Suites feature a separate bedroom, and the Crown Suite has a dining room, living room, and Jacuzzi. Bathrooms are small but serviceable. Children receive an Activity Pak when visiting, and have their own special menu. Breakfast on the terrace is a delight on a sunny day. Spa services are available at **Bliss,** 1477 Lower Water St. (ℂ **902/420-8555**), and **Harbour House Day Spa,** 1326 Barrington St. (ℂ **902/ 446-4772**), each several blocks away, but hotel guests receive a discount.

1725 Market St., Halifax, NS B3J 3N9. ℂ **800/565-1567** or 902/425-1986. Fax 902/429-6408. www.prince georgehotel.com. 207 units. May 1–Oct 31 C$149 (US$99) double; C$450 (US$300) 1-bedroom suite; C$650 (US$433) executive suite. Nov 1–April 30 C$119 (US$79) double; C$225 (US$150) 1-bedroom suite; C$450 (US$300) executive suite. Extra person C$20 (US$13). Children 17 and under stay free in parents' room. AE, DC, DISC, MC, V. Parking C$12.95 (US$8). Metro Transit nos. 7, 9, 18. **Amenities:** Restaurant (Californian), bar; large indoor pool; exercise room; Jacuzzi; sauna; concierge; business center; limited room service; in-room massage; babysitting; laundry service; same-day dry cleaning; safe deposit boxes at front desk. *In room:* A/C, TV w/pay movies, coffeemaker, hair dryer, iron.

EXPENSIVE

Cambridge Suites Hotel Halifax *★* *(Kids* *(Value*   Located next to Citadel Hill and only a few minutes' walk from the waterfront and other points of interest, this is a great place for a prolonged stay or for families who need space. The regular Studio Suites are larger than the typical hotel room; Junior Suites are slightly larger again, with the bedroom area screened off from the sitting area; and one-bedroom suites are almost twice as large, with the bedroom on a slightly raised level. All include kitchenette and pullout sofas, great views of either Citadel Hill or the harbor, and access to rooftop barbecues. The bathrooms are spacious and clean. The Gold Club Floor is suited to business travelers. Along with a kitchenette, its one-bedroom suites are equipped with dual phone lines, dataport, and fax machine. A complimentary continental breakfast is available to all visitors, along with a free grocery shopping service—guests provide a list of items to hotel staff, who purchase and deliver them to their suite. The cost of the items is charged to your hotel bill. Children will enjoy the welcome basket containing cookies and microwave popcorn, refilled daily.

1583 Brunswick St., Halifax, NS B3J 3P5. © **888/417-8483** or 902/420-0555. Fax 902/420-9379. www. cambridgesuitehotel.com. 200 units. May 1–Sept 30 C$159 (US$106) double; C$179 (US$119) 1-bedroom suite; C$209 (US$139) executive suite. Oct 1–April 30 C$129 (US$86) double; C$149 (US$99) 1-bedroom suite; C$179 (US$119) executive suite. Packages available. Children 17 and under stay free in parents' room. AE, DC, DISC, MC, V. Parking C$11.50 (US$7). Metro Transit nos. 1, 3, 10. **Amenities:** Restaurant (Canadian), lounge; Jacuzzi; sauna; concierge; secretarial services; limited room service; babysitting; coin-op washers and dryers; laundry service; same-day dry cleaning; safe deposit boxes at front desk. *In room:* A/C, TV w/pay movies, coffeemaker, hair dryer, iron.

Citadel Halifax Hotel   This hotel was renovated from carpets to ceiling in 2001, giving it a fresh, contemporary look. Business rooms provide more space and amenities than regular guest rooms. There are four suites. The rooms have a choice of harbor views or city views, and with the renovations the bathrooms are modern and immaculate. Its location across from the Halifax Citadel and proximity to the Metro Centre and World Trade and Convention Centre make it popular and convenient for vacationers and business travelers. A 10-minute walk takes you to most of downtown's highlights.

1960 Brunswick St., Halifax, NS B3J 2G7. © **800/565-7162** or 902/422-1391. Fax 902/429-6672. www. citadelhalifax.com. 267 units, 4 suites. C$169 (US$113) double; C$199 (US$133) business room; C$250 (US$167) junior suite; C$450 (US$300) executive suite. Packages available. Extra person C$15 (US$10). Children 18 and under stay free in parents' room. AE, DC, DISC, MC, V. Parking C$12.95 (US$8). Metro Transit nos. 2, 4, 6. Pets accepted. **Amenities:** Restaurant (Canadian), lounge; small indoor pool, wading pool; exercise room; Jacuzzi; sauna; limited room service; laundry service. *In room:* A/C, TV w/pay movies, dataport in business rooms, coffeemaker, hair dryer, iron.

Delta Barrington *★★*   This hotel caters to vacationers and business travelers, and when it comes to a convenient downtown location, it has the best in the city. It's a 3-minute indoor walk to shops, it's in the core of the business district, surrounded by historic buildings and entertainment venues, and it's only three short blocks away from the waterfront. Like the Casino Nova Scotia Hotel, the Barrington is connected by the Downtown Link (a combination of tunnels and above-ground covered walkways) to six business towers, the Scotia Square shopping complex, Casino Nova Scotia, the World Trade and Convention Centre— if you're attending a conference or tradeshow—and the Halifax Metro Centre, for hockey games and entertainment.

The hotel completed a C$4.5-million (US$3-million) renovation in 2000, which included a refurbishing of regular guest rooms along with the introduction of a Signature Club Floor. Guest rooms on this floor are decorated with pine sleigh beds covered in goose-down duvets, and guests have access to a lounge with complimentary continental breakfast, evening reception, and honor bar. Deluxe rooms are larger, with an adjoining sitting room. Service at the Barrington has always been good, and the staff is friendly. Be sure to let them know if you are celebrating a special occasion; they'll usually go out of their way.

1875 Barrington St., Halifax, NS B3J 3L6. © **877/814-7706** or 902/429-7410. Fax 902/420-6524. www. deltahotels.com. 200 units. C$139–$220 (US$92–$147). AE, DC, DISC, MC, V. Valet parking C$18.95 (US$11.40). Metro Transit nos. 2, 4, 6. Small pets accepted. **Amenities:** Restaurant (Maritime), lounge; indoor heated pool; exercise room; Jacuzzi; sauna; concierge; business center; limited room service; massage; laundry service; same-day dry cleaning. *In room:* A/C, TV w/pay movies, minibar, hair dryer, iron.

Delta Halifax ⟨✦⟩   Popular and well-equipped for business travelers, the high-rise Delta Halifax boasts a boardroom and two rooftop ballrooms that offer a panoramic view of the harbor and city. Built in 1972, and formerly known as the Chateau Halifax, this hotel is also connected via indoor Pedway to downtown shopping, business, and entertainment centers, and is only four blocks up from the waterfront. The structure consists of a six-level parking garage serving the hotel and shopping mall, with the hotel located above. The guest rooms include Regular, Signature Service, and Resort Wing rooms, plus Deluxe and 1-bedroom suites. The Delta Halifax caters to business people; its Signature Service rooms make up 60% of all guest rooms in the hotel. These provide a desk with extra working space, dual phone lines, cordless phone, dataport, printer, and fax service, and office stationery supplies. The Resort Wing rooms have direct access to the indoor pool as well as access to private outdoor balconies. Bathrooms are small but very clean.

1990 Barrington St., Halifax, NS B3J 1P2. © **800/268-1133** or 902/425-6700. Fax 902/425-6214. www. deltahotels.com. 296 units. C$129–$209 (US$92–$150). AE, DC, DISC, MC, V. Valet parking C$18.95 (US$11.40). Metro Transit nos. 2, 4, 6. Pets accepted. **Amenities:** Restaurant (Continental), lounge; small indoor pool; exercise room; Jacuzzi; 2 saunas; concierge; limited room service; babysitting; laundry service; same-day dry cleaning; safe-deposit boxes at front desk. *In room:* A/C, TV w/pay movies, minibar, coffeemaker, hair dryer, iron.

The Four Points by Sheraton Halifax ⟨✦⟩   Built in 2001, this hotel is the newest in the city and is connected to the Maritime Centre, a complex of retail shops and offices, where Spring Garden Road meets Barrington Street. Be sure to check out the second largest three-dimensional mural in the world—a life-size streetscape of historic Halifax—located in an open-air courtyard attached to the hotel. It's especially impressive under lights after dark. The hotel itself is a nondescript building, with a lobby that's all business. The hotel was designed, not surprisingly, with business travelers in mind; the Deluxe Rooms include complimentary high-speed Internet, dataport access, large desk, and a dual-line speakerphone. The C-Level Floor is a private secure-access floor with views of the city and harbor. The C-Level Lounge, which you can often have all to yourself, has a relaxing shiatsu massage chair, fireplace, computer station, and flat-screen TV with more than 200 digital channels. Suites have a living room, separate bedroom, and a Jacuzzi in the bathroom. The decor in all rooms is contemporary, but plain, and the bathrooms are rather small. Room service is very quick and breakfast is plentiful. A variety of fashionable shops and restaurants is just a 5-minute walk up Spring Garden Road.

1496 Hollis St., Halifax, NS B3J 3Z1. ℂ **866/444-9494** or 902/423-4444. Fax 902/423-2327. www.fortis properties.com/hotels/fourpoints. 177 units. C$199 (US$133) double; C$249 (US$166) 1-bedroom suite; C$299 (US$199) executive suite. Extra person C$15 (US$10). AE, DC, DISC, MC, V. Parking C$14 (US$8.50). Metro Transit nos. 7, 9, 2. **Amenities:** Restaurant (Continental), bar; outdoor heated pool; exercise room; Jacuzzi; concierge; business center; limited room service; babysitting; laundry service; same-day dry cleaning; safe deposit boxes at front desk. *In room:* A/C, TV w/pay movies, coffeemaker, hair dryer, iron.

Halliburton House Inn ✦

An upscale historic hotel located on a quiet side street convenient to downtown attractions, this is a great place for romantic getaways or any special occasion. The inn is made up of three separate, adjacent town houses, built in 1809 and converted to an inn during the mid-1990s. The buildings remain separate from each other on the inside, but are connected on the exterior by a series of decks and balconies. Spend some time in the delightful gardens enjoying coffee and the newspaper in the mornings, or cocktails and seafood hors d'oeuvres before dinner. The gardens are lit at night, adding to the air of romance. The cozy restaurant (see chapter 5) is considered one of the best in the city for its regional cuisine, including locally farmed game and fresh seafood.

Each guest room is uniquely decorated, with antique furnishings and down-filled duvets. Some have working fireplaces; others have views of the gardens. All have four-piece bathrooms (tub and shower, sink and toilet), the result of a renovation completed in 2001. The Grand Suite is impressive, with its four-poster bed and large bathroom with Jacuzzi, while the Studio Apartment suite has a full kitchen and loft. The main floor includes a library and an Internet kiosk where visitors can check their e-mail or plan their trip. The inn also has conference facilities for smaller groups, and the boardroom doubles as a private dining room for special occasions. The inn offers discounted spa services in cooperation with **Harbor House Day Spa,** 1326 Barrington St. (ℂ **902/446-4772**), across the street.

5184 Morris St., Halifax, NS B3J 1B3. ℂ **902/420-0658.** Fax 902/423-2324. www.halliburton.ns.ca. 29 units. May 1–Oct 31 C$140 (US$93) double; C$225 (US$150) 1-bedroom suite; C$350 (US$233) executive suite. Nov 1–April 30 C$110 (US$73) double; C$150 (US$100) 1-bedroom suite; C$250 (US$167) executive suite. Packages available. Extra person C$20 (US$13). AE, DC, MC, V. Free parking. Metro Transit nos. 7, 9, 10. **Amenities:** Restaurant (Canadian); limited room service; same-day dry cleaning. *In room:* A/C, TV, coffeemaker, hair dryer, iron upon request.

Lord Nelson Hotel & Suites ✦✦

Another hotel with a history, the Lord Nelson is among the best in Halifax. Built in 1928, it was one of the most distinguished hotels of its time. The Lord Nelson's location is one of its best features, located on the corner of South Park Street and Spring Garden Road, close to shopping and dining, next to the beautiful Halifax Public Gardens, and within walking distance of Citadel Hill, downtown, and the waterfront. Although it went through a downturn in the late 1990s, it has since been purchased and renovated from top to bottom, with the last phase of work completed in 2001. The guest rooms have been redone in a contemporary Art Deco style. Some have kitchenettes. But the rest of the hotel retains its traditional grand ambience, especially in the lobby, where the ceiling is decorated with intricately carved wooden panels depicting the provincial shields of Canada. This is the same design as found in the parliament buildings in Ottawa. Suites are available, and include a variety of sizes from simply extra space to separate bedrooms and a kitchen. Ask for a room with a view of the park; it's well worth the extra charge. But if you're looking for a deal, a few of the interior suites can be rented for a price comparable to a room rate. The hotel also provides Flagship Business Rooms, which include in-room fax and dual-line telephone.

1515 South Park St., Halifax, NS B3J 2L2. © **800/565-2020** or 902/423-6331. Fax 902/491-6148. www.lord nelsonhotel.com. 243 units. July 1–Oct 31 C$139 (US$93) double; C$349 (US$233) 1-bedroom suite. Nov 1– April 30 C$99 (US$66) double; C$189 (US$126) 1-bedroom suite. Packages available. Extra person C$15 (US$10). Children 18 and under stay free in parents' room. AE, DC, DISC, MC, V. Parking C$8 (US$5). Metro Transit nos. 1, 10, 14. **Amenities:** Restaurant (English Pub), bar; sauna; concierge; limited room service; babysitting; coin-op washers and dryers; same-day dry cleaning; safe deposit boxes at front desk. *In room:* A/C, kitchenettes in 60 units.

Radisson Suite Hotel Halifax ★★ If comfort and satisfaction is your aim, you've come to the right place. This particular Radisson has won the company's President's Award five years running, for quality of product and guest services. All suites are spacious and have a separate living room. Medium-size bathrooms are clean and shiny. If you want to do a little business on your trip or just want to surf the Net, high-speed Internet access is available in each suite, plus there's a telephone in your bathroom. Located just one block up from the waterfront, roughly 75 of the 104 units have a harbor view. The building was remodeled from an old office building—from the outside it hardly looks like a hotel—and renovations were completed in 2002. Although it doesn't have its own restaurant, **East Side Mario's** is located in the lower lobby. Meals can be charged to your hotel bill. The Club Room Lounge is open to guests every evening for drinks and complimentary hors d'oeuvres, served at the bar or around the fireplace. The staff is very helpful and courteous.

1649 Hollis St., Halifax, NS B3J 1V8. © **800/333-3333** or 902/429-7233. Fax 902/429-9700. www.radisson halifax.com. 104 units. C$255 (US$170) suite. Packages available. Extra person C$20 (US$13). Children 18 and under stay free in parents' room. AE, DC, DISC, MC, V. Valet parking C$14 (US$8.50). Metro Transit nos. 7, 9, 2. **Amenities:** Restaurant (Italian/American); lounge; small indoor pool; exercise room; Jacuzzi; sauna; concierge; limited room service; coin-op washers and dryers; same-day dry cleaning; safe deposit boxes at front desk. *In room:* A/C, TV w/pay movies, dataport, minibar, coffeemaker, hair dryer, iron.

Waverley Inn ★ *Finds* This is a fun and fascinating place to stay. When you book your room, your name will join those of Oscar Wilde (who stayed in room 122) and P. T. Barnum in the reservation ledger, and you can even walk the same halls as those famous visitors. This is because, while necessary improvements have been made, the inn has retained much of its original late-19th-century character.

The Waverley has been an inn since it was purchased in 1876, 10 years after it was built as a private residence for a wealthy Halifax merchant. The elegant, three-story house is Victorian in every way, with walnut trim and red upholstered furniture in the sitting room, antique beds with Gothic-style headboards, and a myriad of staircases (but no elevators). Some guest rooms have propane fireplaces, all have private, mostly spacious bathrooms, and nine guest rooms have private Jacuzzis. There's even a room with a carved Chinese wedding bed. The new Waverley Suite is located in an annex, and has two bedrooms, a full kitchen, living/dining room, and laundry—ideal for couples or for families who want to stay a while. Located on the main floor, the breakfast/friendship room is stocked with coffee and a variety of teas, juice, fruit, croissants, bagels, and muffins for breakfast, while cookies and cake will tempt you for afternoon tea or a bedtime snack. This inn is simply a treasure, and it's a 15-minute walk from shops, restaurants, and top attractions.

1266 Barrington St., Halifax, NS B3J 1Y5. © **800/565-9346** or 902/423-9346. Fax 902/425-0167. www. waverleyinn.com. 34 units, 1 suite. May 15–Oct 31 C$139 (US$93) double; C$159 (US$106) deluxe; C$249 (US$166) executive suite. Nov 1–May 14 C$99 (US$66) double; C$139 (US$93) deluxe; C$199 (US$133) executive suite. Packages available. Extra person C$15 (US$10). DC, MC, V. Free parking. Metro Transit nos. 2, 4, 6. **Amenities:** Babysitting; laundry service; safe deposit boxes at front desk. *In room:* A/C, TV, dataport in 10 units, iron upon request.

MODERATE

Fresh Start B&B   This is a modest Victorian home, furnished with an eclectic assortment of antiques and contemporary pieces, and decorated in period style. Two of the guest rooms have kitchens and private bathrooms; the other six rooms share bathrooms. All are spacious. One guest room has a small balcony—appealing on a sunny morning or warm evening—complete with flower boxes. Bathrooms are small, but very clean. It's a 20-minute walk to Citadel Hill and the waterfront, but close to the Angus L. Macdonald Bridge if you decide to experience a bridge walk. Breakfasts are delicious and healthy, served in a friendly, relaxed atmosphere. There's a cat on the premises (he doesn't mind visitors).

2720 Gottingen St., Halifax, NS B3K 3C7. © **888/453-6616** or 902/453-6616. Fax 902/453-6617. www. canoe.bbcanada.com/2262.html. 8 units, 2 w/bathroom. May 16–Nov 14 C$80 (US$53) w/shared bath; C$90 (US$60) w/private bath. Nov 15–May 15 C$70 (US$47) w/shared bath; C$80 (US$53) w/private bath. Rates include full breakfast. AE, DC, MC, V. Limited free parking. Metro Transit nos. 3, 7, 12. Pets accepted. **Amenities:** Lounge. *In room:* Kitchen in 2 units, hair dryer on request, no phone.

The Verandah B&B   This B&B is a charming Victorian home, on a quiet street in a residential area. It's located only two blocks from the Halifax Public Gardens, and Spring Garden Road, with lots of shopping and dining. A 15-minute walk will take you downtown or to the waterfront. Decorated simply but tastefully, each guest room has a small private bathroom, and the apartment is suitable for a family with one or two children. There is a piano in the living room; guests are welcome to play. You can't help but admire the beautiful antique fireplace mantel, just another reason you feel pampered staying here. Host Joan Robillard and her little dog, Cody, are the best part of the package, though. Joan will make you feel right at home and part of the family.

1394 Edward St., Halifax, NS B3H 3H6. © **902/494-9500**. www.theverandahbb.com. 2 units, 1 apartment. May 1–Oct 31 C$95 (US$63) double; C$125 (US$83) studio apartment. Nov 1–April 30 C$75 (US$50) double; weekly rates by arrangement for studio apartment. Rates include continental breakfast. MC, V. Extra person C$15 (US$10). Children 10 and under stay free in parents' room. Free parking. Metro Transit nos. 1, 3, 10. **Amenities:** Lounge. *In room:* TV.

INEXPENSIVE

Halifax Backpacker's Hostel   This hostel is located in a less affluent part of the downtown core, but it's only a 10-minute walk to Citadel Hill or the waterfront. The owners have hosteled in over 20 countries around the world, and offer friendly and helpful service for visitors who prefer this type of accommodation. There are both private and shared rooms, with basic decor, and linen is provided. There are also laundry facilities. Other amenities include a kitchen, lounge with TV and VCR, and a movie library. Bicycles can be rented for C$15 (US$10) per day, and Internet use is available for C$5 (US$3) an hour.

2193 Gottingen St., Halifax, NS B3K 3B5. © **902/431-3170**. www.halifaxbackpackers.com. 24 units. C$19 (US$12.60) dormitory; C$25 (US$16.60) single; C$35 (US$23.35) double; C$65 (US$43.35) family. V. Metro Transit nos. 3, 7, 12. **Amenities:** Lounge, coffee shop; bike rental; coin-op washers and dryers. *In-room:* No phone.

O'Brien Hall (Dalhousie University) *(Kids)*   Located on the corner of Morris and Barrington streets, close to the train station and downtown, this university residence is a great spot if all you need is a roof over your head. They provide basic dorm rooms, single and double, shared bathrooms, as well as lounges and kitchenettes on each floor. Guests have access to the Dalplex Athletic Facility, one of Dalhousie University's main sports facilities, which includes a Fun Zone play area that's great for kids, Cybex weight-training equipment, ¼-km (.17-mile) indoor running track, international-size swimming pool, two hardwood basketball courts, indoor climbing wall, squash and racquetball courts, fitness areas, a golf driving cage, and a 74-sq.-m (800-sq.-ft.) putting green.

5217 Morris St., Halifax, NS B3J 1B7. For reservations contact: Conference Services & Summer Housing, Room 407, Student Union Building, 6136 University Ave., Halifax, NS B3H 4J2. © **902/494-8840.** Fax 902/494-1219. www.dal.ca/confserv. 85 units. C$37 (US$25) one single bed; C$58 (US$39) two single beds. Rates include continental breakfast. MC, V. Parking C$4 (US$2.70). Metro Transit nos. 7, 9, 10. Closed Aug 26–May 9. **Amenities:** Lounge; access to nearby health club; coin-op washers and dryers. *In room:* No phone.

YWCA of Halifax Women's Accommodations   This is a great place for women traveling on a budget. It's within walking distance of the VIA Rail station, restaurants, downtown nightclubs, theaters, museums, and the historic waterfront. There are single and twin rooms with shared kitchen and bathroom, plus laundry facilities on-site, a smoking lounge for guests, and a TV lounge. Mini-fridges are available for rent for C$11 (US$7.35) per month. The rooms are basic and clean, and the kitchen is well stocked with equipment. An added bonus is the opportunity to meet other travelers.

1239 Barrington St., Halifax, NS B3J 1Y3. © **902/423-6162.** Fax 902/423-7761. www.ywcahalifax.com. 26 units. C$45 (US$30) per night; C$270 (US$180) per week. MC. Metro Transit nos. 2,4, 6. **Amenities:** Lounge; large indoor pool; sauna; exercise room. *In room:* No phone.

2 North of Quinpool Road

Much of this area is quiet and residential, save for a few shopping malls here and there. And since it's one of the city's main arteries, all of the accommodations are easy to locate. There are some lovely bed-and-breakfasts and a couple of economical motor inns. Room rates are slightly less than downtown, because it's further removed—you'll need to use the Metro Transit or your car to get around.

EXPENSIVE

Pepperberry B&B ⟨⊀⟩   This lovely house was built in 1915, and first belonged to a ship's captain. Present owners Jim and Elizabeth Trites have restored it with loving care and hard work. If you relish older homes—antique radiators, claw-foot bathtubs, period furniture, and the ambience that goes with it, this B&B delivers. Jim and Elizabeth have a knack for making you feel right at home. Each of the four guest rooms has a private bathroom, one with Jacuzzi. While three of the rooms are spacious, The Coast room is smaller. There's a large library with a good supply of books and magazines, and a small den that opens onto a private patio and back garden. Outside, there's plenty of room to relax on the spacious grounds, or on the patio. Breakfasts are scrumptious. The Pepperberry is located close to the Armdale Rotary, which provides convenient access to both Quinpool Road, a main artery to downtown Halifax, and Highway 102.

2688 Joseph Howe Dr., Halifax, NS B3L 4E4. © **877/246-3244** or 902/479-1700. Fax 902/477-9701. www.pepperberryinn.com. 4 units. June 23–Oct 31 C$135 (US$90) double; C$195 (US$130) w/Jacuzzi and fireplace. Nov 1–June 22 C$115 (US$77) double; C$140 (US$93) w/Jacuzzi and fireplace. Rates include full breakfast. AE, MC, V. Free parking. Metro Transit nos. 3, 17. **Amenities:** Jacuzzi. *In room:* No phone.

MODERATE

Centretown Guest House (★) (*Finds*) This sea captain's house was built in 1916, and restored and updated by the present owners in the early 1990s. It's tastefully decorated and cozy, and caters primarily to gay and lesbian travelers from North America and Europe. Hosts Serge Gionet and Stephen Parsons are happy to give you an orientation to Halifax, and to make sure your stay is enjoyable. The living room is a gathering place for eclectic conversation with other guests. Two of the four comfortable guest rooms have private bathrooms, the other two share a bathroom. The rooms are spacious. The glassed-in deck, with Jacuzzi and seating area, overlooks a small city garden.

2016 Oxford St., Halifax, NS B3L 2T2. © **902/422-2380**. Fax 902/425-0605. www.centretown.com. 4 units. C$99–$109 (US$62–$68). AE, MC, V. Limited free parking. Metro Transit nos. 14, 20. **Amenities:** Jacuzzi; coin-op washers and dryers.

Chebucto Inn   A two-story wooden complex, this would be better described as a motel or motor hotel, set in a quiet area near the north end of Robie Street. The restaurant's food is not creative, but it is generous and tasty. The rooms are basic and clean, the decor rudimentary, but it's city accommodation at an affordable price.

6151 Lady Hammond Rd., Halifax, NS B3K 2R9. © **800/268-4330** or 902/453-4330. Fax 902/454-7043. http://users.eastlink.ca/~chebuctoinn/about_us.htm. 32 units. May 1–Oct 31 C$95 (US$63) 1 double bed; C$130 (US$87) 2 double beds. Nov 1–April 30 C$60 (US$40) 1 double bed; C$65 (US$43) 2 double beds. Extra person C$10 (US$7). Children 12 and under stay free in parents' room. AE, DC, MC, V. Free parking. **Amenities:** Restaurant (Canadian), bar; coin-op washers and dryers. *In room:* A/C, TV.

Garden View B&B   This Victorian home is located on a quiet, peaceful street near the Halifax Public Gardens. The elegant leaded glass entryway suggests an equally elegant interior decorated with antiques and original art. One of three guest rooms has a private bathroom; the other bathroom is shared. Guests can chat in the lovely living room with fireplace and piano, or relax and unwind with a good soak in an antique bathtub. But the best part is the gourmet breakfast— five different dishes to choose from, including a raisin-apple bread pudding, and the delicious house specialty, crepes with yummy fruit sauce. It's a breezy 15-minute walk to downtown.

6052 Williams St., Halifax, NS B3K 1E9. © **888/737-0778** or 902/423-2943. Fax 902/423-4355. www.inter design.ca/gardenview. 3 units. June 16–Oct 20 C$95 (US$63) double w/shared bath; C$115 (US$77) suite w/private bath. Oct 21–June 15 C$60 (US$40) double w/shared bath; C$65 (US$43) suite w/private bath. Rates include full breakfast. Extra person C$20 (US$13). Children 4 and under stay free in parents' room. MC, V. Metro Transit nos. 7, 17, 80. **Amenities:** Jacuzzi.

King Edward Inn   This Edwardian-style inn was built in 1903 and has an interesting history, surviving two explosions (one of which was, of course, the Halifax Explosion of 1917) and a variety of fires. It was renovated in the late 1980s; guest rooms and bathrooms were modernized. The furniture is a combination of modern and traditional, with four-poster beds in most rooms. There are two rooftop patios, one with a Jacuzzi, and a great view of Citadel Hill. The continental breakfast is simple but adequate. Staff and other guests are open and friendly; a pleasant contrast to larger hotels in the city. It's a 15-minute walk to Citadel Hill and the downtown.

5780–88 West St., Halifax, NS B3K 1H8. On the corner of West and Agricola sts. © **800/565-5464** or 902/484-3466. Fax 902/423-8910. www.kingedward.com/index.htm. 40 units. April 20–Oct 30 C$100 (US$67) double; C$115 (US$77) deluxe; C$170 (US$114) suite. Nov 1–April 19 C$80 (US$55) double; C$95 (US$64) deluxe; C$130 (US$87) suite. Children 16 and under stay free in parents' room. AE, DC, MC, V. Free parking. Metro Transit nos. 7, 17, 80. **Amenities:** Jacuzzi. *In room:* A/C in 12 units, TV.

INEXPENSIVE

Fountain View Guest House *(Finds)*   This attractive blue-and-white row house is located opposite the Halifax Commons (where the fountain is located) and is a 5-minute walk to Citadel Hill. Guest rooms, though not spacious, are clean and comfortable. Guests share two four-piece bathrooms, one three-piece bathroom and two powder rooms. On pleasant days, the backyard garden is a good spot to relax or enjoy a picnic. Note that credit cards are not accepted, but you can use cash, traveler's checks, or Interac. A light breakfast can be brought to your room for an extra charge. If you have a hankering to marry while in Halifax, host Helen Vickery can contact an officiant, arrange the wedding, and even provide witnesses.

2138 Robie St., Halifax, NS B3K 4M5. ℭ 800/565-4877 or 902/422-4169. Fax 775/418-4991. http://browser.to/fountainviewguesthouse. C$24 (US$16) single; C$30 (US$20) double; C$35 (US$24) triple. No credit cards. Free parking. Metro Transit nos. 7, 17, 80. *In room:* TV, no phone.

3 South of Quinpool Road

This area includes trendy **Spring Garden Road,** as well as some beautiful homes—old and new. If you enjoy walking, you can make it to downtown within 20 minutes, or stroll through the 186 acres of **Point Pleasant Park.** Head to **Tower Road** to admire some especially stately homes.

EXPENSIVE

Garden Inn   Built in 1875, this Heritage Victorian inn has been newly renovated for guests' convenience, but still retains the charm of high ceilings and antique furniture. It is named for the Halifax Public Gardens, less than a 10-minute walk away. This is a lovely spot for a romantic getaway, or simply to pamper yourself. A 20-minute walk will take you to downtown shopping, restaurants, and attractions.

1263 South Park St., Halifax, NS B3J 2K8. ℭ 877/414-8577 or 902/492-8577. Fax 902/492-1462. www.gardeninn.ns.ca. 23 units. May 15–Oct 31 C$109 (US$73) double w/shared bath; C$149 (US$99) suite w/private bath. Nov 1–May 14 C$79 (US$53) double w/shared bath; C$149 (US$99) suite w/private bath. Rates include continental breakfast. Packages available. Extra person C$20 (US$14). Children 4 and under stay free in parents' room. MC, V. Free parking. Metro Transit nos. 1, 10, 14. **Amenities:** Coin-op washers and dryers. *In room:* TV, dataport.

Holiday Inn Select Halifax Centre *(★) (Kids)*   This is a high-rise, full-service hotel in the center of Halifax overlooking the Halifax Commons. The hotel is a popular spot for both business conferences and vacationers, and as an extra benefit there are among the hotel staff people who speak Chinese, Dutch, English, French, German, Italian, and Spanish. Although newly renovated in 2001/2002, the ambience is still strictly basic hotel fare. The exception is the view of the Halifax Commons. Many of the hotel rooms, and the **Willow Restaurant,** overlook this green area, which is home to summer tournaments, and a large fountain lit at night. For business visitors, guest rooms include Internet connections, and the Executive floor features private elevator-key access. For vacationers, there's a convenient free shuttle service to the waterfront and shopping districts from June to September, and the Halifax Citadel, the Public Gardens, and the Nova Scotia Museum of Natural History are within a 15-minute stroll. The **Willow Restaurant** features a popular Saturday and Sunday brunch year-round.

1980 Robie St., Halifax, NS B3H 3G5. © **800-HOLIDAY (800/465-4329)** or 902/423-1161. Fax 902/423-9069. www.holiday-inn.com/halifax-centre. 232 units. May 1–Oct 14 C$185 (US$123) double; C$210 (US$140) deluxe. Oct 15–April 30 C$170 (US$113) double; C$195 (US$130) deluxe. Packages available. Extra person C$15 (US$10). Children 18 and under stay free in parents' room. AE, DC, DISC, MC, V. Heated underground parking. Metro Transit nos. 7, 17, 80. Small pets accepted. **Amenities:** Restaurant (Canadian), lounge; indoor pool; wading pool; Jacuzzi; sauna; concierge; free shuttle to waterfront and shopping (May–Oct); business center; coin-op washers and dryers. *In room:* A/C, TV w/pay movies, dataport, coffeemaker, hair dryer, iron.

The Pebble B&B ✸ *Finds*   This is a delightful bed-and-breakfast located on the beautiful North West Arm. The house is charming, and you are pampered with Irish hospitality by host Elizabeth O'Carroll and her West Highland terrier, Dugal. Breakfasts are divine; imagine fresh waffles with local berries and fruit, smothered in a hot orange syrup. Each of the two spacious suites is outfitted with quality linens, and one has a feather bed with goose-down duvet. Both suites have luxurious, large, squeaky-clean bathrooms, with a pedestal tub and high-quality towels and toiletries. There's also a lovely living room with a fireplace, equally suited to chatting or reading.

1839 Armview Terrace, Halifax, NS B3H 4H3. © **902/423-3369.** www.thepebble.ca. 2 units. June 1–Oct 31 C$175–$195 (US$117–$130). Nov 1–May 31 C$100–$124 (US$67–$83). Rates include full breakfast. V. Free parking. Metro Transit nos. 6, 32. Pets accepted with advance notice. *In room:* No phone.

MODERATE

Virginia Kinfolks ✸   This is another lovely bed-and-breakfast, with antiques, canopy beds with crocheted lace coverings, fireplaces, and Jacuzzi. There's also a library, well stocked with books and magazines. Each of the four units has a quiet balcony for reading and relaxing. Plus, you're only one block away from the Halifax Public Gardens and Citadel Hill. Your hosts are Lucy and Dick Russell.

1722 Robie St., Halifax, NS B3H 3E8. © **800/668-7829** or 902/423-6687. Fax 902/423-6687. www.members.aol.com/vakinfolkz. 4 units. May 1–Nov 30 C$99 (US$66) double; C$139 (US$93) deluxe. Dec 1–April 30 C$69 (US$46) all rooms. Rates include full breakfast. C$159 (US$106) honeymoon package. AE, MC, V. Free parking. Metro Transit nos. 7, 17, 80. Pets accepted. Children under 4 not accepted. *In room:* A/C, TV, hair dryer, no phone.

INEXPENSIVE

Dalhousie University Residences   The university has three residences—Howe Hall, at 6230 Coburg Road, Shirreff Hall, at 6385 South Street, and Fenwick Place, a 33-story, 252-unit apartment complex, at 5599 Fenwick Street. If you only need a room, choose Shirreff Hall, built in 1923, with elegant architecture, a Victorian-style lounge, and a library. Some rooms on the fourth floor have a beautiful view of the North West Arm. For families or longer stays, Fenwick Place has fully furnished two- and three-bedroom apartments with full kitchen. All three residences are within a 20-minute walk of downtown.

Conference Services & Summer Housing, Room 407 Student Union Building, 6136 University Ave., Halifax, NS B3H 4J2. © **902/494-8840.** Fax 902/494-1219. www.dal.ca/confserv. C$60 (US$36) residence room; C$57 (US$35) 2-bedroom apartment; C$81 (US$49) 3-bedroom apartment. Residence room rate includes continental breakfast. Closed Aug 26–May 9. Metro Transit nos. 1, 7, 9. **Amenities:** Lounge; coin-op washers and dryers. *In room:* No phone.

Marigold B&B   This unassuming B&B is located in an old family home owned and operated by Joan Doherty. The house is surrounded by gardens, and one of the two rooms has a balcony with a garden view. The rooms share a single bath. Along with peace and quiet on the pleasant street, you'll find unique hand-made dolls, canvas floor mats, and table mats made in Joan's in-house studio. A 20-minute walk will take you to downtown shopping and attractions.

6318 Norwood St., Halifax, NS B3H 2L1. ℂ **902/423-4798**. 2 units. C$60 (US$36). Rates include full breakfast. V. Free parking. Metro Transit nos. 1, 18, 58 *In room:* No phone.

Saint Mary's University Residence Though located a little farther from downtown Halifax, this university residence offers good accommodation at a rock-bottom price. Basic rooms have two single beds and shared bathrooms; two-bedroom apartments have four single beds, plus a living/dining room, kitchen, and bathroom. There are also Travel Suites, private single rooms with bathroom, telephone, and TV, plus a shared kitchenette. There's a coffee shop and cafeteria in the building, and 24-hour security.

5865 Gorsebrook Ave., Halifax, NS B3H 3C3. ℂ **888/347-5555** or 902/420-5049. Fax 902/496-8118. www.stmarys.ca/conferences/. 500 units. C$28–$43 (US$17–$26) double; C$55–$69 (US$33–$42) suite and apartment. MC, V. Free parking. Metro Transit nos. 7, 9, 17. Closed Aug 16–May 14. **Amenities:** Cafeteria, lounge; access to university health club; coin-op washers and dryers. *In room:* No phone.

4 West of the North West Arm

This area is on the outskirts of Halifax. Instead of office towers and concrete, however, you can look forward to forests and lakes. A drive along route 253 promises lovely glimpses of the North West Arm and several yacht clubs. It's a 15- to 30-minute drive downtown by automobile, and Metro Transit services are available.

MODERATE
Howard Johnson Hotel Halifax While this nine-floor, high-rise hotel with attached motel doesn't look very impressive from the street, the location over-looking Chocolate Lake and the indoor amenities salvage it somewhat. The hotel caters to both business travelers and vacationers. There's a variety of room sizes; some with kitchenettes. There are also family-appropriate suites. A continental breakfast is complimentary; however, at press time the dining room was only open from 4pm to 6pm for the evening meal. The hotel is a 15-minute drive from downtown, and the rates reflect this. The Metro Transit bus service stops at the door for downtown transportation, if you'd rather not deal with downtown parking.

20 St. Margaret's Bay Rd., Halifax, NS B3N 1J4. ℂ **800/561-7666** or 902/477-5611. Fax 902/479-2150. www.hojo-canada.com. 135 units. C$104 (US$70). Rates include continental breakfast. Packages available. Extra person C$10 (US$7). Children 18 and under stay free in parents' room. AE, DC, MC, V. Free parking. Metro Transit no. 6. Pets accepted. **Amenities:** Restaurant (Canadian), lounge; indoor pool; safe deposit boxes at front desk. *In room:* A/C, TV, dataport, 12 units w/kitchenette, coffeemaker, hair dryer, iron.

5

Dining

You'd be right to expect that Halifax restaurants do a good job with seafood. And they do, on the whole. But they also do a good job of steak to accompany that seafood, as well as Italian, Greek, Chinese, and vegetarian.

For a quick, inexpensive bite at lunch, grab a generous pizza slice at **Pizza Corner** (a collection of outlets at the corner of Blowers and Grafton streets, including **Sicilian Pizza Donairs Subs**, 5245 Blowers St. (© **902/423-5555**), and **King of Donairs**, 1560 Grafton St. (© **902/422-0000**). Donairs are a combination of shaved meat and spices made into a loaf and placed on a spit to season. The meat is served in pita bread spread with special donair sauce, and served hot. There's also **Bud the Spud**, Halifax's well-known chip wagon that you'll find parked next to the **Spring Garden Road Memorial Public Library** (5381 Spring Garden Rd.). Revel in a large dish of old-fashioned french-fried potatoes, complete with vinegar, ketchup, gravy, or all three.

Enjoy an extended break at one of the city's many cafes or bistros, and, during the warmer months, delight in a snack at one of the outdoor patios that spring up in honor of summer. For those who prefer the ocean breezes and lots of company, **Salty's on the Waterfront,** 1868 Upper Water St. (© **902/423-6818**), has outdoor seating for 200 on a harbor-front patio. If your taste tends to the more intimate, the sidewalk patio at **Opa! Greek Taverna,** 1565 Argyle St. (© **902/492-7999**), seats 20. But if the

rooftop is where you want to be, **Your Father's Moustache,** 5686 Spring Garden Rd. (© **902/423-6766**), has almost 200 rooftop seats overlooking the street.

Evening dining can be as casual or formal as you like, served open-air on the waterfront, or in an elegant, candlelit historic building. Sit down to a meal accompanied by classical music or by foot-stomping Celtic fiddle tunes.

NOTES ON TAX AND TIPPING The **Harmonized Sales Tax** (HST) on meals in Nova Scotia is 15%, and just about the only good thing about that is that it's easy to figure out the standard 15% tip: it's the same amount as the tax. The choice to tip or not, and in whatever amount, is up to you. However, if you're a group of 10 or more, a 15% gratuity is often included in the bill.

Wine is sold by the bottle, half-liter (approximately one pint), or glass, usually for twice what you'd pay in a liquor store. House wines are generally imported, although Nova Scotia produces gold- and silver-medal-winning wines in its own wineries. In better venues (we highlight restaurants with stellar service throughout this chapter) your server should be able to recommend a good local wine.

NOTES ON THE REVIEWS This chapter groups restaurants by district and then lists them alphabetically under the following main-course price ranges: **Expensive,** C$20 (US$13) and up; **Moderate,** C$10 to C$20

(US$6–US$13); and **Inexpensive,** under C$10 (US$6). Many restaurants' offerings veer into higher and lower categories, so keep in mind that these price ranges are general guidelines. Also, remember that many restaurants change their menus on a moment's notice. Menus at the higher priced spots usually offer one or more less expensive dishes, or specials. Another cost-effective option is to visit a particular restaurant for lunch instead of dinner. You'll probably be able to enjoy a lot of the same menu items as you would in the evening, without breaking the bank.

1 Restaurants by Cuisine

BAKERY
Heartwood Bakery & Café (Quinpool Road, Inexpensive, *p. 91*)

BISTRO
Maple ★★★ (Downtown above the Water, Expensive, *p. 83*)
Sweet Basil Bistro ★★★ (Downtown above the Water, Moderate, *p. 87*)

CAFE
Café Chianti ★★ (Downtown above the Water, Moderate, *p. 84*)
Cheapside Café (Downtown above the Water, Inexpensive, *p. 88*)
Dio Mio Gelato Desserts Café (Spring Garden Road, Inexpensive, *p. 93*)
Economy Shoe Shop Café and Bar ★★ (Downtown above the Water, Inexpensive, *p. 89*)
Steve-O-Reno's ★★ (Spring Garden Road, Inexpensive, *p. 93*)

CANADIAN
44 North Restaurant (Downtown above the Water, Moderate, *p. 83*)
Apple Barrel 24-Hr Restaurant (Downtown above the Water, Inexpensive, *p. 88*)
Maple ★★★ (Downtown above the water, Expensive *p. 83*)
Your Father's Moustache Pub & Eatery (Spring Garden Road, Inexpensive, *p. 93*)

CHINESE/DIM SUM
Cheelin (Downtown above the Water, Moderate, *p. 84*)

Great Wall (Downtown above the Water, Inexpensive, *p. 89*)
King Wah (Quinpool Road, Inexpensive, *p. 91*)

CONTINENTAL
Alfredo Weinstein & Ho (Downtown above the Water, Inexpensive, *p. 88*)
La Cave ★ (Downtown above the Water, Moderate, *p. 84*)
O'Carroll's Restaurant & Irish Pub ★ (Downtown above the Water, Expensive, *p. 83*)

DESSERTS
Dio Mio Gelato Desserts Café (Spring Garden Road, Inexpensive, *p. 93*)
La Cave ★ (Downtown above the Water, Moderate, *p. 84*)

DINER
Bluenose II Diner (Downtown above the Water, Inexpensive, *p. 88*)

ECLECTIC
Bish World Cuisine ★★★ (Downtown on the Water, Expensive, *p. 77*)

FUSION
Georgio's Restaurant & Bar ★★ (Downtown above the Water, Expensive, *p. 82*)

GAME
Halliburton House Inn ★★★ (Downtown above the Water, Expensive, *p. 82*)

King Wah Restaurant (Quinpool Road, Inexpensive, *p. 91*)

THAI

Chicken Tandoor (Quinpool Road, Moderate, *p. 90*)

VEGETARIAN

Heartwood Bakery & Café (Quinpool Road, Inexpensive, *p. 91*)

Satisfaction Feast (Downtown above the Water, Inexpensive, *p. 89*)

2 Downtown on the Water

Every old salt knows that some of the best restaurants in any maritime port are found on the waterfront, and Halifax is no exception. Of course, you'll pay a little extra for the privilege of watching the harbor comings and goings while you dine.

EXPENSIVE

Bacchus ★★★ NOUVEAU CUISINE   Blending traditional tastes with exotic flair is how Bacchus describes its menu, and I have to agree. The seafood salad combines warm lobster, shrimp, scallops, and calamari with wild mesclun greens, asparagus, avocado, and papaya for a different and refreshing flavor. If your taste runs toward fowl, there's pheasant breast stuffed with chanterelles, herbs, caramelized shallots, and fig compote. The stuffing keeps the pheasant moist and gives it an earthy essence. The desserts are perfectly proportioned— not too large to enjoy once you've finished your main course, and as tantalizing to the eye as they are to the taste buds. This is likely because they're made fresh on-site daily. Each menu item, including dessert, is paired with a recommended wine.Wine connoisseurs can make their own choices, or you can ask for suggestions from the knowledgeable and helpful staff. The overall atmosphere, warmed by two fireplaces, is classy and refined, exemplified by fine china and linens. Though the room is an intimate size—about six tables and a few stylish booths—you won't feel crowded. Located in Casino Nova Scotia, this is a great place for celebrations, especially if what you're toasting is a windfall at the slot machines.

In Casino Nova Scotia. 1983 Upper Water St. ✆ **902/428-7846.** Reservations required. Main dinner courses C$20–$38 (US$14–$26). AE, DC, MC, V. Daily 6pm–midnight. Metro Transit nos. 2, 4, 6.

Bish World Cuisine ★★★ ECLECTIC   Opened in 2001, this is one of the newest restaurants in the city. Bish is short for Bishop's Landing, a newly constructed residential complex on the Halifax waterfront. Although designed and decorated with a casual feel—including an outdoor patio—this restaurant still exudes high-class elegance, with its circular bar and waterfront view. The menu is diverse and varies daily. If you enjoy seafood, try the fresh Digby scallops with wasabi butter, or the Chilean sea bass with Cuban mojo (a citrus-and-spice vinaigrette that is Cuba's national table sauce). For those who prefer something a little more earthbound, the beef tenderloin is a good choice. The staff is quietly attentive and helpful. This is the third restaurant opened by executive chef and restaurateur Maurizio Bertossi—the force behind two Italian delights, da Maurizio (see the following review) and the popular Il Mercato bistro (p. 92). Bertossi's European ingenuity ensures a loyal following of local connoisseurs.

1475 Lower Water St. ✆ **902/425-7993.** Reservations required. Main dinner courses C$21–$29 (US$14–$20). AE, DC, MC, V. Mon–Sat 5:30–10pm. Metro Transit nos. 7, 9, 18.

Halifax Dining

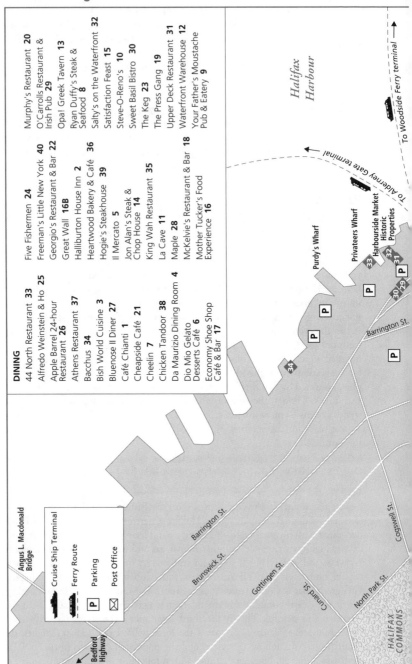

DINING

44 North Restaurant **33**
Alfredo Weinstein & Ho **25**
Apple Barrel 24-hour
Restaurant **26**
Athens Restaurant **37**
Bacchus **34**
Bish World Cuisine **3**
Bluenose II Diner **27**
Café Chianti **1**
Cheapside Café **21**
Cheelin **7**
Chicken Tandoor **38**
Da Maurizio Dining Room **4**
Dio Mio Gelato
Desserts Café **6**
Economy Shoe Shop
Café & Bar **17**

Five Fishermen **24**
Freeman's Little New York **40**
Georgio's Restaurant & Bar **22**
Great Wall **16B**
Haliburton House Inn **2**
Heartwood Bakery & Café **36**
Hogie's Steakhouse **39**
Il Mercato **5**
Jon Alan's Steak &
Chop House **14**
King Wah Restaurant **35**
La Cave **11**
Maple **28**
McKelvie's Restaurant & Bar **18**
Mother Tucker's Food
Experience **16**

Murphy's Restaurant **20**
O'Carrolls Restaurant &
Irish Pub **29**
Opal Greek Tavern **13**
Ryan Duffy's Steak &
Seafood **8**
Salty's on the Waterfront **32**
Satisfaction Feast **15**
Steve-O-Reno's **10**
Sweet Basil Bistro **30**
The Keg **23**
The Press Gang **19**
Upper Deck Restaurant **31**
Waterfront Warehouse **12**
Your Father's Moustache
Pub & Eatery **9**

*Halifax
Harbour*

To Woodside Ferry terminal →

To Alderney Gate terminal ←

Purdy's Wharf

Privateers Wharf

Harbourside Market
Historic
Properties

Barrington St.

Angus L. Macdonald
Bridge

Cruise Ship Terminal
Ferry Route
P Parking
⊠ Post Office

Bedford
Highway

Barrington St.

Brunswick St.

Gottingen St.

Cunard St.

Cogswell St.

North Park St.

HALIFAX
COMMONS

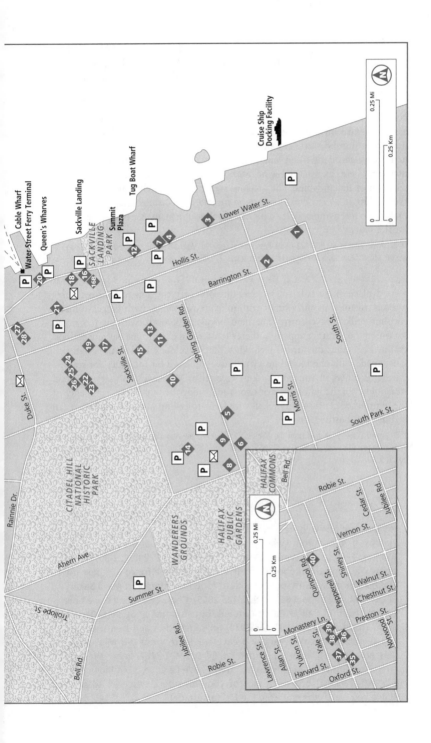

Cable Wharf

Water Street Ferry Terminal

Queen's Wharves

Sackville Landing

Summit Plaza

Tug Boat Wharf

SACKVILLE LANDING PARK

Cruise Ship Docking Facility

Lower Water St.

Hollis St.

Barrington St.

Spring Garden Rd.

Sackville St.

South St.

South Park St.

Morris St.

Duke St.

CITADEL HILL NATIONAL HISTORIC PARK

WANDERERS GROUNDS

HALIFAX PUBLIC GARDENS

Rainnie Dr.

Ahern Ave.

Summer St.

Trollope St.

Bell Rd.

Jubilee Rd.

Robie St.

0.25 Mi

0.25 Km

HALIFAX COMMONS

Bell Rd.

Robie St.

Vernon St.

Cedar St.

Jubilee Rd.

Quinpool Rd.

Pepperell St.

Shirley St.

Walnut St.

Chestnut St.

Monastery Ln.

Lawrence St.

Allan St.

Yukon St.

Yale St.

Harvard St.

Preston St.

Norwood St.

Oxford St.

0.25 Mi

0.25 Km

79

da Maurizio Dining Room ★★★ *Finds* NORTHERN ITALIAN   This is the best upscale, fine-dining Italian restaurant in Nova Scotia. The appetizers are extremely inventive, though some are quite rich, made with both cream and butter. Turning to main courses, of special note is the grilled polenta with mushrooms, and a rich squash ravioli with duck maigret. The servings might be considered on the small side, except for the pasta, though this does let you have a multi-course meal of three or four dishes—in true Italian fashion—not to mention a sinful dessert. The tiramisu is sublime. The decor and atmosphere is luxurious—the dark colors and Italian bric-a-brac make it comfortable and inviting. There's an extensive wine list, both imported and domestic, with a great selection of Italian wines. The gracious staff provides intelligent suggestions at the bidding. This is a great place to go for special occasions because the service makes you feel pampered. It's a bit of a climb to the main entrance. Be prepared for the stairs.

1496 Lower Water St. © 902/423-0859. Reservations required. Main dinner courses C$30–$45 (US$20-$30). AE, DC, MC, V. Mon–Sat 5:30–10pm. Metro Transit nos. 7, 9, 20.

McKelvie's Restaurant & Bar ★★ SEAFOOD   For seafood lovers, this is a good place to start. If you're adventuresome, try the appetizer of red curry mussels, steamed in curry broth with julienne vegetables, fresh ginger, tomato, coconut milk, and cilantro. The crab bisque is smooth, without too much seasoning. For heartier appetites, there's lobster and champagne pasta or seafood gratin, a generous mixture of seafood, scallops, haddock, and shrimp, in a rich sauce made with cheese and heavy cream—perhaps a bit too saucy for seafood purists. If others in your group don't favor fish, McKelvie's also serves a good steak and even the odd burger or two. You'll enjoy the more casual ambience of the refurbished century-old firehall with floor-to-ceiling windows, though it can be busy and bustling.

1680 Lower Water St. Across from the Maritime Museum of the Atlantic. © 902/421-6161. Reservations required. Main courses C$21–$30 (US$14–$20). AE, MC, V. Daily 11:30am–10:30pm. Metro Transit nos. 7, 9, 20.

 Anyone for a Picnic?

It's a shame not to have a picnic—with all the parks and green areas in Halifax. If you're on the waterfront, pick up take-out at the **Harbourside Market,** 1869 Upper Water St. Historic Properties (© 902/422-3077) and enjoy watching the tugboats on the water. Plan an alfresco lunch on the **Halifax Commons** with some nutritious food from the **Heartwood Bakery & Café,** 6250 Quinpool Rd. (© 902/425-2808). Choose to spend some time at the beautiful **Halifax Public Gardens,** but stop first at **Steve-O-Reno's,** 1536 Brunswick St. (© 902/429-3034) for sandwiches and treats. Or visit the revitalized **Victoria Park** and eat your lunch from **Dio Mio Gelato Desserts Café,** 5670 Spring Garden Rd. (© 902/492-3467) under the gaze of Robbie Burns's statue. For a real treat, have **La Cave,** 5244 Blowers St. (© 902/429-3551) box up a slice of your favorite cheesecake to savor while you watch the city from the **Halifax Citadel.**

MODERATE

Murphy's Restaurant SEAFOOD   Rustic, casual, and expansive, this a great place to hang out with a group, or to bring your whole extended family for a boisterous dinner. Murphy's makes you feel as though you're not just eating by the water, but right on top of it! Located on Cable Wharf, between the ferry terminal and the Maritime Museum of the Atlantic, the restaurant's screened-in patio floats on the water, with an unparalleled view of Halifax Harbour. While the specialty is fresh seafood—Atlantic salmon comes to mind, poached or pan-fried, dressed with a Dijon green-onion sauce—there's steak, chicken, pasta, and burgers on the menu, as well. If you're undecided, or just want a snack, there's a variety of seafood appetizers, plus bruschetta and barbecued chicken wings. It can get a little cool at night out on the patio, even in the summer, so bring a sweater or jacket. The kitchen closes at 11pm, but the bar stays open until 2am.

1751 Lower Water St. At Cable Wharf. ✆ **902/420-1015**. Main courses C$7–$22 (US$5–$15). AE, DC, DISC, MC, V. Daily 11am–11pm. Closed Nov 1–April 30. Metro Transit nos. 7, 9, 2.

Salty's on the Waterfront *(Kids)* SEAFOOD   Like Murphy's (see the previous review), Salty's is another "on the water" waterfront restaurant, located on the Historic Properties Pier. The dining area is upstairs, and the view of the harbor is accordingly better because of the height. During the day, you can watch ships ply in and out of the harbor, and at night, take in the lovely Dartmouth city lights. For a moderately priced restaurant, Salty's does a good job of presenting food, with attention to appetizing color combinations on the plate and artistic garnishes made from celery and such. Don't miss the seafood chowder, full of lobster, scallops, and haddock, not to mention flavor. The rack of lamb is tender, and the crab cakes, served with Caesar salad, are delicious. There's even a special children's menu that includes hot dogs, hamburgers, and fish and chips. The experience here is all fun; unfortunately, our waitress didn't seem to like her job very much, and that detracted from the meal.

1869 Upper Water St. At the end of Historic Properties Pier. ✆ **902/423-6818**. Reservations required. Main courses C$11–$30 (US$7–$30). AE, MC, V. Daily 11:30am–10pm. Hours may vary from Oct–May, call to confirm. Metro Transit nos. 7, 9, 2.

Waterfront Warehouse *(Kids)* SEAFOOD   *Warehouse* is the operative word here; the place is large and open, with a casual nautical theme. The house specialty is cedar-planked salmon, seasoned with brown sugar and soya—not the best I've had, but not bad. There's also baked halibut with crab, or, for something lighter, a traditional Maritime lobster roll: pieces of boiled fresh lobster mixed with mayonnaise and diced celery, stuffed into a toasted roll. Hilary's Fish Shack is a special spot for kids. It's a child-size replica of a fishing shanty, where children can watch videos while mom and dad relax over coffee, or something stronger. The staff is friendly and accommodating, but the atmosphere of the main room is somewhat cold and impersonal—just like a warehouse, funnily enough. The wingback chairs in the pub are a cozier option. There's a patio in the summer. Overall, a good place to take the whole family for a night out.

1549 Lower Water St. ✆ **902/425-7610**. Main dinner courses C$14–$16 (US$9–$11). DC, MC, V. Daily 11:30am–11pm. Closed Nov 1–April 30. Metro Transit nos. 7, 9, 2.

Value   The Harbourside Market

So you spent longer than you'd anticipated gawking at Maud Lewis's tiny house in the Art Gallery of Nova Scotia, and now you've only got half an hour for lunch. Not really enough time to sit down and order somewhere, but more than enough time to nip in to the **Harbourside Market**, 1869 Upper Water St. (*℃* **902/422-3077**), grab a take-out sandwich, pizza slice, or salad, and be on your way. It's like a food court in function, but with more style. The large seating area is open-air during summer; glassed-in during winter. It's a popular lunch spot during the week with office workers, so you may have to wait a few minutes to get your food. But finding a seat shouldn't be a problem—there's room for 100. Depending on what kind of food you're in the mood for, choose from **Captain John's Fish Company, The Brisket Boardwalk Deli,** the **Wildfire Grill,** and the **Loaf Leaf N Ladle Bakery,** among others. Top it off with a specialty brew from **John Shippey's Brewing Company.** It's a great place to pick up some sandwiches for a picnic, or take-out to enjoy in your hotel room.

The market is open Sunday through Thursday from 7am to 9pm, and Friday and Saturday from 8am to 10pm. Take Metro Transit no. 2, 7, or 9.

3 Downtown above the Water

Though not right on the water, there are nevertheless wonderful restaurants in Halifax's downtown core. They tend to cater to corporate lunches and special dinners, so you get an idea of the general caliber of fare in this part of the city. Here's where you'll find the widest variety of cuisine, from seafood and steak to nouveau cuisine, from Chinese food to Greek, from sushi to wild game. Parking availability is always a concern, so walk or take a cab.

EXPENSIVE

Georgio's Restaurant & Bar *★★* FUSION   Located in the Prince George Hotel, Georgio's has a quiet, relaxed elegance with comfortable upholstered chairs, dark wood, and rich red accents. The service is attentive, professional, and friendly, but doesn't infringe on your personal space. The menu includes a reliable NY striploin—juicy, pink, and tender, just as ordered, with accompanying vidalia onions and poached potatoes, crisp and golden. For something a little different, try the lamb cooked with a blueberry mustard in a sweet onion broth, served with basil-asiago mashed potatoes. The whole experience is relaxing and enjoyable; this is a good spot for conversation and lingering over dinner. If you visit during the summer, take advantage of the **Terrace Patio** for midday dining.

In the Prince George Hotel. 1725 Market St. *℃* **902/425-1986.** Reservations required. Main courses C$30–$45 (US$20–$30). AE, DC, DISC, MC, V. Daily 11am–11pm. Metro Transit nos. 7, 9, 18.

Halliburton House Inn *★★★ (Finds* GAME   This is definitely a unique dining experience, and not for the faint of palate. Housed in an award-winning century-old inn, Halliburton House has a menu that features local and imported game and Atlantic seafood. A regular on the menu is grilled medallions of caribou with house-filled caribou raviolis and a blackberry zinfandel sauce. One of the tamer dishes is a roasted breast of free-range chicken, served with a ginger-tiger shrimp mousseline and sweet scallion cream. Although the dining area is made up of four adjoining small rooms, the feel is intimate and relaxing instead of crowded. Indulge in a before- or after-dinner drink in the library, or in the back garden courtyard in the summer. The service is excellent, and the staff is professional and friendly, but the Windsor-style wood chairs can become uncomfortable if you want to linger. This food experience is one of the city's better-kept secrets. Despite this, the menu *is* limited overall.

5184 Morris St. © **902/420-0658**. Reservations required. Main dinner courses C$30–$45 (US$20–$30). AE, MC, V. Daily 5:30pm–9pm. Metro Transit nos. 7, 9, 18.

Maple ★★★ BISTRO/CANADIAN   Although it was rated one of the best restaurants in the city shortly after opening in 2001, the popular Maple is nevertheless suffering from the loss of its original owner/chef Michael Smith, star of TV's *Inn Chef*, who has moved on. The menu, while still very good, doesn't have the same creative edge that it did originally. The restaurant continues to use local products and ingredients, which include fresh Atlantic seafood, Canadian beef and chicken, Annapolis Valley fruits and vegetables, and a variety of freshly grown herbs. The restaurant occupies three levels—with the open kitchen on the mezzanine level. It's both impressive and entertaining. Impressive because the whole place is quite stylish, and entertaining because, from certain vantage points—especially from the second and third levels—you get a bird's-eye view of the action in the kitchen. But it's not all flash. Ask for a quiet table for two tucked away in a corner, if that's what you have planned. There's also a private room that accommodates up to 45. One of the most popular menu items is the surprise seven-course **Chef's Table.** Order it only if you've brought your biggest appetite, and be prepared for adventure—every Chef's Table is unique. If you're not quite that famished, try the halibut polenta in a sautéed spinach, tomato, and lemon caper sauce, or the beef tenderloin roasted with horseradish and Dijon, accompanied by caramelized onions, brown butter potato crisp, and port veal jus. You won't be disappointed.

1813 Granville St. © **902/425-9100**. Reservations required. Main courses C$30–$45 (US$20–$30). AE, DC, MC, V. Mon–Fri 11:30am–2:30pm and 5:30–10pm; Sat 11:30am–10pm. Metro Transit nos. 7, 9, 18.

O'Carroll's Restaurant & Irish Pub ★ PUB/SEAFOOD   This is an inviting restaurant, whether you choose the fine dining side or the raucous Irish pub. It's another good spot for seafood, as well. If you prefer a simple dish, try the halibut grilled with caramelized onion in a remoulade sauce, or the Atlantic salmon charbroiled or poached with herbed butter. If you've had your fill of the bounty of the sea, there's also a decent steak on offer, as well as roast duck, and a daily pasta creation. Over on the pub side, try the fish and chips, made the traditional way with fresh haddock in a beer batter, or the steak-and-kidney pie in puff pastry with a side of fresh vegetables—a tasty, filling meal for a reasonable price. The live musical entertainment by the Evans and Doherty duo will bring out the Irish in you.

1860 Upper Water St. © **902/423-4405**. Reservations required. Main courses C$30–$45. (US$20–$30). AE, MC, V. Daily 11am–11pm. Metro Transit nos. 7, 9, 18.

MODERATE
44 North Restaurant SEAFOOD/CANADIAN   This restaurant is located in the Casino Nova Scotia Hotel (see the section "Downtown" in chapter 4), not to be confused with the actual casino (see chapter 9), which is a little

farther north on Upper Water Street. Inspired by the nautical coordinates of Halifax, the elegant **44 North Restaurant** and sister business, the **63 West Lounge,** both have floor-to-ceiling windows revealing a wonderful view of the harbor, particularly enchanting after dark. The open-kitchen style lets you watch the culinary team at work. If you're here for the seafood, choose the Seafood Feast buffet, served on Fridays and Saturdays from May to October. This way, you can pick and choose your favorites from a variety of offerings, including mussels, oysters, crab, scallops, and lobster. The wine list is decent, and so is the Sunday Brunch.

In the Casino Nova Scotia Hotel. 1919 Upper Water St. ✆ **902/428-7852.** Reservations recommended on weekends. Main courses C$13–$30 (US$9–$20). AE, DC, DISC, MC, V. Daily 11:30am–10:30pm. Metro Transit nos. 7, 9, 2.

Café Chianti ★★ Finds CAFÉ/NORTHERN ITALIAN/EASTERN EURO-PEAN   Eat here. The menu is extensive, with seafood, chicken, duck, beef, and lamb, along with pastas and vegetarian dishes. You can appease your appetite with the generous-sized appetizers alone, which include everything from stewed octopus (gently pan-fried with garlic, chilies, paprika, and white wine) to homemade Hungarian sausage with Dijon sauce and rye toast. The Borscht—authentic, homemade Russian beet soup—is hearty and delicious. For simple beauty, not to mention wonderful taste, try the Linguine Pescatore, with scallops, mussels, shrimp, green onions, red peppers, and mushrooms, heaped on a bed of pasta. There's also a Chicken alla Valdostana, stuffed with spinach, mushrooms, asiago cheese, and capicollo ham. The atmosphere is intimate even though the space is open-concept. It probably has something to do with the low ceilings. If you're tall, watch out for the hanging bottles. There's a patio in the summer, and a separate dining room for private parties. Ask for a tour of the extensive, state-of-the-art wine cellar. Don't miss this little jewel of a restaurant.

5165 South St. ✆ **902/423-7471.** Reservations recommended on weekends. Main courses C$15–$30 (US$10–$20). AE, DC, MC, V. Mon–Fri Noon–2pm and 5–10pm; Sat–Sun 5–10pm. Metro Transit nos. 7, 9, 18.

La Cave ★ Moments CONTINENTAL/DESSERT   If you have even an ounce of passion in your soul, you'll love this little gem of an eatery. Private "caves" (booths, really) are located off the main dining area, whose centerpiece is a beautiful stone fireplace. The whole place is candlelit. Although it's been around for almost 20 years, the present owner has improved the menu and service. The menu now offers steak, chicken, and seafood, including the Seafood Vol-au-Vent, a combination of shrimp, scallops, and salmon, with a creamy chive sauce in a freshly baked puff pastry shell. A favorite is the Brie plate: dip your French bread, vegetables, or fruit into this baked and toasted treat. It's topped with almonds. Good as the main courses are, they're a bit of a formality, since the real reason for coming to La Cave is the dessert. Cheesecake, to be precise. The pastry chef prepares more than two-dozen decadent cakes daily; everything from Banana Lemon and Black Forest to Strawberry Shortcake and Peanut Butter Chocolate Chip. Rarely does one of these cakes live to see another day, and the staff is continually wiping finger smudges off the glass display case. La Cave ships these yummy cakes across North America—orders have come in from fans as far away as Calgary and San Francisco. Even if you don't have room for dessert, order a slice to take with you. The restaurant's extended hours make it a great spot for an after-theater sugar fix.

5244 Blowers St. ✆ **902/429-3551.** Reservations recommended on weekends. Main dinner courses C$15–$30 (US$10–$20). AE, MC, V. Sun–Wed 5pm–2am; Thur–Sat 5pm–4:30am. Metro Transit nos. 7, 9, 18.

Cheelin SZECHUAN   This restaurant is located just across the street from the waterfront, so you can still catch a glimpse of the harbor as you peruse the menu. This is authentic Szechuan—so authentic, in fact, that you'll be hard pressed to find a single North American–style Chinese dish. (This is a good thing, since those sorts of dishes go heavy on the sauces to the point where you're not sure what you're eating at all.) Well, Cheelin's not like that. Its menu offerings are light and rife with unusual flavor combinations. One such example is the haddock, served with a forceful, but somehow not overpowering, chili-flavored sauce. Combine the pleasing menu with friendly, efficient service, and you've found a relaxing spot to indulge your Szechuan cravings. The Friday lunch buffet is a little pricey (C$25 (US$17)), but delicious. Eat on the terrace in summer. Take-out and delivery are also available.

1496 Lower Water St. (✆) 902/422-2252. Reservations recommended on weekends. Main courses C$15–$30 (US$10–$20). AE, DC, MC, V. Daily 11:30am–2:30pm and 5:30–10:30pm. Metro Transit nos. 7, 9, 18.

Finds **For Sushi Fans**

Suddenly sushi seems to be everywhere in Halifax. How's a fan to choose? **Doraku**, 1579 Dresden Row (✆ **902/425-8888**), has given its name to a tasty dish—the mouth-watering Doraku roll is stuffed with shrimp tempura, avocado, cucumber, grilled eel, and spicy sauce. **Hamachi House**, 5190 Morris St. (✆ **902/425-7111**), has the only floating sushi bar in the city, and it's not even on the waterfront. The **Sushi House**, 6196 Quinpool Rd. (✆ **902/425-2333**), offers the best and spiciest tuna roll. **Momoya**, 1671 Barrington St. (✆ **902/492-0788**), has especially good service, and **Maki Maki**, 5974 Spring Garden Rd. (✆ **902/422-3818**), offers a tasty smoked salmon salad. **I Love Sushi**, 5232 Blowers St. (✆ **902/429-6168**), has the most varied menu. Last, but definitely not least, is **Dharma Sushi**, 1576 Argyle St. (✆ **902/425-7785**), with delicious food and generous servings at a reasonable price.

Five Fishermen ★★ SEAFOOD   A Halifax fixture for 25 years, this restaurant has repeatedly earned its reputation for great seafood and Maritime hospitality. The mussel bar, with its choice of four sauces, is second to none, as is the salad bar. Choose this restaurant for traditional Nova Scotia lobster, boiled to perfection and served with fresh vegetables (although the true Maritimer fills up on the lobster and saves the vegetables for another meal). Order the deep-fried plate of Digby scallops, haddock filets, clams, and shrimp, for a taste of how Maritimers used to prepare fish—there was no poaching or gentle sautéeing—it was all deep-fried! Don't get the wrong impression, though: Five Fishermen isn't lost in a time warp. The linguine with shrimp prepared in a garlic, tomato, Pernod, fennel, and cream sauce proves that it isn't. Not as well heralded, but just as good, are the non-fish dishes, such as the rosemary and pommery roasted game hen with garlic mashed potatoes and roasted vegetables. With all this to tempt you, it's hard to save room for dessert, but do try. There's a selection of ice creams and sorbets, which go down easily after a big meal. The maple *crème brûlée* is especially good. Enjoy your meal in a comfortable setting of brass, timber, and stained glass, along with a campy collection of nautical items.

1740 Argyle St. (✆) 902/422-4421. Reservations required. Main dinner courses C$15–$30 (US$10–$20). AE, MC, V. Daily 5–10pm. Metro Transit nos. 7, 9, 18.

The Keg STEAK/SEAFOOD   This is a popular spot for doing business over dinner as well as simply enjoying a meal. The Keg serves good steak at a reasonable price, in a relaxing atmosphere. Dark wood and dim lighting give it a cozy feel. High dividers between tables and booths ensure intimacy, despite the large, multilevel layout. The steak is cooked to your specifications, and there's quite a good variety to choose from, including sirloin, striploin, tenderloin, and prime rib. The sourdough bread is baked on the premises and is a tasty, hearty accompaniment to red meat. Seafood makes an appearance on the menu, but stick with the steak—and skip the garlic mashed potatoes. The staff is attentive and courteous.

1712 Market St. ℂ **902/425-8247**. Reservations recommended on weekends. Main courses C$15–$30 (US$10–$20). AE, MC, V. Daily 4:30–10pm. Metro Transit nos. 7, 9, 18.

 Patio Lanterns

It seems as though every restaurant and bar in Halifax has a patio that migrates into the city around the end of May and then to parts unknown come the end of September. In fact, there are more than 60 locations that offer this summer treat. It really gives the city an air of celebration and fun with the colorful umbrellas and pots of flowers hanging or placed about. Some of the best patios are rooftop patio's, offering a bird's-eye view of the city. Others are located beside the harbor where you can watch the blue water turn to inky black when the sun goes down, and see the lights twinkle from the opposite shore. Here's a selection of our favorites:

On the Waterfront:
- **Bish World Cuisine**, 1475 Lower Water St. (ℂ **902/425-7993**)
- **Harbourside Market**, 1869 Upper Water St. (ℂ **902/423-3077**)
- **Salty's on the Water**, 1869 Upper Water St. (ℂ **902/423-6818**)
- **The Waterfront Warehouse**, 1549 Lower Water St. (ℂ **902/425-7610**)

Streetside:
- **Café Chianti**, 5165 South St. (ℂ **902/423-7471**)
- **Economy Shoe Shop**, 1663 Argyle St. (ℂ **902/423-7463**)
- **Opa! Greek Taverna**, 1565 Argyle St. (ℂ **902/492-7999**)
- **Split Crow**, 1855 Granville St. (ℂ **902/422-4366**)

Rooftop:
- **The Argyle**, 1575 Argyle St. (ℂ **902/492-8844**)
- **Your Father's Moustache**, 5686 Spring Garden Rd. (ℂ **902/423-6766**)

Mother Tucker's Food Experience STEAK/SEAFOOD   This restaurant on the west side of Lower Water Street has become an institution in downtown Halifax. Legions of hungry diners converge daily, so be prepared for a lineup. And while you can order prime rib, steak, seafood, and lobster a la carte, why bother? Everybody comes for the buffet and salad bar. With over 100 items to choose from, you can sample 10 dishes for the price of one. The food is reliable, if not outstanding, and the service is friendly. If you're not an adventuresome eater, you'll find lots of comfort food you recognize. The lunch buffet is a real steal, at C$6 (US$4).

1668 Lower Water St. ✆ **902/422-4436**. Reservations recommended on weekends. Main courses C$12–$25 (US$8–$17). DC, MC, V. Daily 11:30am–10pm. Metro Transit nos. 7, 9, 18.

Opa! Greek Taverna ⭐ *Finds* GREEK/MEDITERRANEAN   This is an enjoyable spot for lunch or dinner. The restaurant is set in a bright atrium, and the walls are done in warm colors. The fake plants and trees take a little away from the otherwise pleasing atmosphere. The menu is generous, however—so generous, that it will take a while to decide what to order. The food is Mediterranean, and includes such appetizers as grape leaves stuffed with rice, raisins, and herbs, and charbroiled octopodi (tender marinated octopus, mixed with onions and bell peppers). For the main course, opt for traditional Greek dishes such as souvlaki (lamb, chicken, pork), or marinated and charbroiled swordfish, scallops, or shrimp, brushed with special "Opa sauce," and served with vegetables. The braised lamb with Orzo in tomato sauce, topped with kefalograviera cheese (a Greek cheese), is another tasty main. The wine list includes vintages from around the world, and the staff gladly deconstructs the at times overwhelming menu in a friendly, helpful manner. Opa! is popular with the corporate crowd at lunch, and with everyone in the evenings. In the summer, tables spill out onto the sidewalk patio. It's great if you don't mind the bustle and crowds, but opt for somewhere else if you have a more quiet evening in mind.

1565 Argyle St. ✆ **902/492-7999**. Reservations recommended on weekends. Main courses C$15–$25 (US$10–$17). AE, MC, V. Daily 11am–11pm. Metro Transit nos. 7, 9, 18.

The Press Gang ⭐⭐ SEAFOOD   This trendy, upscale restaurant opened in 1999. It's located in Carleton House, one of the many historic downtown buildings, reportedly built using stones from Fortress Louisburg (built by the French in the 1700s and located in Cape Breton). Seafood is the specialty, and it shows. I recommend the grilled salmon with caviar and cream sauce. Some people are put off by the fact that there are no prices listed on the menu; still, no one needs to be "pressed into service" to dine here, as it's usually busy and you'll need reservations. A good spot for a romantic dinner and long, lingering conversations.

5218 Prince St. ✆ **902/423-8816**. Reservations required. Main dinner courses C$15–$35 (US$10–$24). AE, MC, V. Daily 6–11pm. Metro Transit nos. 7, 9, 18.

Sweet Basil Bistro ⭐⭐⭐ *Value* BISTRO/SEAFOOD   Restaurant-goers (both local and visiting) chose this establishment as the 2001 Restaurant of the Year. These people know what they're talking about, for Sweet Basil has great food at great prices, in an informal, relaxed atmosphere. Be sure to make a reservation; the place is busy every night of the week. It's hard to pick just one item from the menu, so you might consider creating a meal from the appetizers. The crab cakes are delicious, especially when paired with the sun-dried tomato chutney. There's excellent seafood chowder, smoked scallops, and spicy coconut shrimp. The pasta is homemade and creatively served; the herb and hazelnut-crusted chicken is flavorful and comes with a fruit salsa. The menu also offers shark. Unlike some restaurants, Sweet Basil doesn't fade after the main course. The desserts are divine, especially the apple flan pie. While the menu is imaginative, the wine list lacks variety.

1866 Upper Water St. ✆ **902/425-2133**. Reservations required. Main courses C$15–$30 (US$10–$20). AE, MC, V. Summer daily 11:30am–11pm; winter daily 11:30am–10pm. Metro Transit nos. 7, 9, 2.

Upper Deck Restaurant ★★ STEAK/SEAFOOD   This classy restaurant is popular with Haligonians for special occasions because of its romantic atmosphere and attentive service. The menu boasts a decent variety, including roast duck, game, lamb, steak, and seafood. I enjoyed the roast pork tenderloin with rum-Pasilla chili glaze. The appetizer selection could be better, with several seafood dishes and only two salads. Fortunately, both of them, a Caesar salad and an Arugula salad with pears, roasted hazelnuts and blue cheese, are quite successful. The wine list is adequate, and you can order by the glass.

1869 Upper Water St. (Level 3 in Privateer's Warehouse). ℂ 902/422-1289. Reservations required. Main courses C$15–$30 (US$10–$20). DC, MC, V. Daily 5–10pm. Metro Transit nos. 7, 9, 2.

INEXPENSIVE

Alfredo Weinstein & Ho (Kids) CONTINENTAL   A good restaurant for those who can't make up their minds, or a large group with varied tastes, because the menu includes Italian, Deli, and Chinese. The atmosphere is relaxed and friendly. The signature dish is the Oriental Steak Pizza, and it's quite a feast, with sliced steak, onions, mozzarella, cheddar and Ho's oriental sauce. Another good choice is the traditional Reuben sandwich: corned beef, sauerkraut, mustard, and Swiss cheese on rye bread. For vegetarians, or those who just don't feel like meat, there's a tasty vegetable cashew stir-fry, cooked with roasted garlic and topped with cashews. It arrives at the table tender-crisp. There's a varied children's menu that also offers basics such as hamburgers and french fries. All items are under C$5 (US$3.50). Remember that "relaxed" sometimes means busy and noisy, but the good-natured staff handles it efficiently, if not too speedily.

1739 Grafton St. ℂ 902/454-9344. Reservations recommended on weekends. Main courses C$7–$15 (US$5–$10). DC, MC, V. Sun–Thur 11am–11pm; Fri–Sat 11am–4am. Metro Transit nos. 7, 9, 2.

Apple Barrel 24Hr Restaurant (Kids) (Value) CANADIAN   The Apple Barrel is certainly not the best restaurant in Halifax, but it has the virtue of being open 24 hours a day, and the bonus of being located downtown. This makes it a convenient stop with almost everybody at some point, if you're in a rush or out late. These extended hours should give you a hint about the bulk of the Apple Barrel's clientele, however: be prepared for university students wolfing down plates of nachos. Still, it's a good place for a quick family meal. A family of four can eat for under C$30 (US$20). The apple crisp is good—even better if you enjoy dessert at 4am.

1726 Grafton St. ℂ 902/425-0500. Main courses C$7–$15 (US$5–$10). MC, V. Daily 24 hours. Metro Transit nos. 7, 9, 2.

Bluenose II Diner (Value) DINER   This is a classic downtown diner: reliable and unobtrusive service and ultra-affordable fare. There's lots of comfort food on offer, including fish and chips, fried clams, and hot beef sandwiches with gravy. The milkshakes are good. The coffee is average. Come here for a traditional greasy spoon breakfast of eggs, bacon, sausage, and toast. The portions are generous, and you'll get to meet an eccentric local or two.

1824 Hollis St. ℂ 902/425-5092. Main courses C$7–$15 (US$5–$10). MC, V. Mon–Fri 6:30am–10pm; Sat–Sun 8am–10pm. Metro Transit nos. 7, 9, 2.

Cheapside Café (Value) (Kids) CAFE   The Cheapside Café is only open for lunch, but you get more than just food if you opt to eat here. Located in the Art Gallery of Nova Scotia (see "The Top Attractions" in chapter 6), there's colorful art on the walls, colorful plates on the tables, and colorful food in front of you. It's all delicious—especially the desserts. The Café Torte ranks especially high. The menu includes sandwiches, fish cakes, and quiche. The food presentation is very artistic, which is appropriate, considering the location. There's comfort food for kids, too, like peanut butter and jelly and egg salad sandwiches. Space is unfortunately limited, so it's often cramped.

In the Art Gallery of Nova Scotia. 1723 Hollis St. ✆ 902/425-6806. Main courses C$7–$15 (US$5–$10). AE, MC, V. Tue–Fri 10am–5pm; Sat–Mon Noon–5pm. Metro Transit nos. 7, 9, 2.

Economy Shoe Shop Café & Bar ★★ ⟨Finds⟩ CAFE   This is the trendiest restaurant in Halifax. Get ready for a coterie of actors and writers, some celebrated, some not, along with university students and business types. The owner's background in set and production design is evident: The restaurant comprises a series of uniquely decorated rooms, from the crowded bar to the dusky cantina overhung with a giant faux tree and grape vines, to the large, bright atrium, whose centerpiece is a raised balcony and from which authors give readings. Here and there are quiet nooks with one or two tables. Monday nights are jazz nights, while Tuesday nights have a literary theme, as local and visiting writers read from their work. After all this build-up, the food is, refreshingly, not a disappointment. The Shoe Shop has some of the city's best mussels, served with Thai green curry and coconut milk. Or if you're just in awe of your surroundings and in the mood for something a little tamer on your plate, go for the delicious nachos—topped with tomatoes, onions, green peppers, jalapenos, sour cream, and the Shoe Shop's homemade salsa. Main courses are varied and include fish, chicken, and beef. Desserts and breads are baked fresh daily.

1663 Argyle St. ✆ 902/423-8781. Main courses C$9–$20 (US$6–$15) AE, MC, V. Daily 11am–2am. Metro Transit nos. 7, 9, 2.

⟨Fun Fact⟩ **Ever Heard of a Donair?**

The donair has a Mediterranean heritage. The first restaurant that served donairs opened in Halifax in the early 1970s, and it spread to the rest of Canada from here. The recipe varies, but a traditional Halifax donair is a concoction of ground beef, spices, onions, and garlic, made into a loaf. The loaf is placed vertically on a skewer, where it cooks in an open barbecue-style oven. The traditional donair is served hot with a spicy sauce in pita bread. A couple of enterprising individuals have even come up with donair subs and pizza donairs. Whether you're trying it for the first time or you're already hooked, the best place in Halifax to enjoy a donair is **Bash Toulany's Fine Foods**, 5553 Duffus St. (✆ 902/455-5120).

Great Wall CANTONESE/SZECHUAN   This is Halifax's landmark Chinese restaurant, with a wide selection of individual dishes and combination plates. There are separate menus: one in English, one in Chinese. As you might expect, the former features more standard selections; you can order more authentic fare off the Chinese menu, such as tripe and chicken feet. If you like spicy food, try the salt & pepper squid. The ginger-fried beef is also good. Great Wall was voted the best place for dim sum in the city in 2002, and the place is packed every

Sunday, when dim sum is featured. The restaurant can accommodate large groups. It'll also deliver free to major hotels in the downtown area.

1649 Bedford Row. (C) **902/422-6153**. Main courses C$7–$15 (US$5–$10). AE, MC, V. Daily 11:30am–10pm. Metro Transit nos. 6, 7, 9.

Satisfaction Feast VEGETARIAN   The food here is so nutritious, delicious, and filling, it makes you forget why you order meat. Soups and casseroles are flavorful, and the desserts are too tempting. Try the "Neat" Loaf or the lasagna. Open for 20 years, Satisfaction Feast has made it into *Where To Eat In Canada* for 14 of them. It draws both confirmed vegetarians and others who are simply looking for a healthy meal. The prices are reasonable, and the service, serene. There's a sidewalk patio in summer.

1581 Grafton St. (C) **902/422-3540**. Main courses C$11–$20 (US$7–$13). AE, MC, V. Daily 8am–10pm. Metro Transit nos. 7, 9, 2.

4 Quinpool Road

Quinpool Road is in a predominantly residential part of town. However, it has a diverse selection of ethnic eateries, including Chinese, Greek, Japanese, and Indian. Many are family-friendly, with children's menus, and all are moderate to inexpensive. All the restaurants reviewed in this section are wheelchair-accessible.

MODERATE

Chicken Tandoor NORTH INDIAN/THAI   From the outside it's mundane, but the first thing you notice when you step inside Chicken Tandoor is the ceiling hung with Indian cotton and the walls dappled in sunset yellow. The lights are turned low, and you begin to relax almost immediately. The food is prepared with care in this intimate little restaurant. You may have to wait a bit, but it's worth it, especially if you like dishes hot enough to make your eyes water, like the cilantro-infused pad Thai or the butter chicken. The peanut curry chicken is also excellent. For something a little different to cool the fire in your mouth, try the sangria with mango. Though the restaurant bills itself as both Indian and Thai, the menu is predominantly Indian.

6285 Quinpool Rd. (C) **902/423-7725**. Reservations recommended. Main courses C$15–$30 (US$10–$20). AE, MC, V. Tue–Sat 4–10pm; Sun 4–9pm. Metro Transit nos. 6, 32, 14.

Freeman's Little New York ITALIAN   Freeman's is the uptown equivalent of the Apple Barrel 24Hr Restaurant (reviewed earlier in the chapter), a good spot for a reasonably priced lunch or for a late bite. The restaurant itself is small, but the booths can seat four comfortably. Pizza is a specialty. Service can be slow, and consequently your hot meal might arrive cold. There's a patio in summer. Takeout is available.

6092 Quinpool Rd. (C) **902/429-0241**. Main courses C$15–$30 (US$10–$20). AE, MC, V. Daily 11am–5pm. Metro Transit nos. 6, 32, 14.

Hogies Steakhouse *(Kids)* STEAK   A Halifax tradition, Hogies has been in business for over 40 years. Its most recent facelift took place in summer 2002, and while there were no radical changes to the decor, a few fresh paint coats certainly revitalized it. The restaurant is famous for warm, crusty bread served with steak, ribs, and seafood. One of the most popular dishes is the Hogies Surf & Turf: grilled sirloin with oven-baked scallops or hot garlic shrimp. It's a good spot for families, with big booths and sturdy furniture. There's also plenty of free parking on both sides of the restaurant, which is a treat in itself—especially in Halifax.

6273 Quinpool Rd. © **902/422-4414**. Main courses C$15–$30 (US$10–$20). AE, MC, V. Daily 11am–10:30pm. Metro Transit nos. 6, 32, 14.

INEXPENSIVE

Athens Restaurant *(Value* GREEK   This is an unpretentious, family-owned restaurant, with a colorful atmosphere reminiscent of an old-fashioned eatery. The menu is large—a seemingly limitless list of Greek, Canadian, and Italian dishes. On offer is everything from the dependable (albeit mundane) hot turkey sandwich, to *kleftiko*—spiced lamb wrapped in foil with an herbed lemon sauce and feta cheese, served with Greek salad and roasted potatoes. The signature dish is souvlaki—pork, lamb, chicken, beef, or shrimp—and served with the predictable Greek salad, rice, pita bread, and tsatziki sauce. Portions are generous and prices really affordable, which explains the crowded, noisy atmosphere.

6303 Quinpool Rd. © **902/422-1595**. Main courses C$7–$15 (US$5–$10). AE, MC, V. Daily 9am–11pm. Metro Transit nos. 6, 32, 14.

Heartwood Bakery & Café *(Finds* BAKERY/VEGETARIAN   A great choice for vegetarians, and anyone else, for that matter. It specializes in foods for people with dietary restrictions, such as allergies to wheat and gluten. The cafe has an interesting menu that changes daily, but the buffet always includes soup, cold salads, hot dishes, brown rice, and steamed greens. The weight of your plate determines the price of your meal. Besides the buffet, the most popular entree is the vegetarian lasagna, but the savory bean pie is also good. Aside from traditional cakes and pies, there's a complete line of wheat-, dairy-, egg-, and gluten-free desserts, which still manage to taste like a treat. The staff is knowledgeable, especially so when it comes to recommending dishes for those with dietary limitations.

6250 Quinpool Rd. © **902/425-2808**. Main courses C$7–$15 (US$5–$10). AE, MC, V. Daily 10am–8pm. Metro Transit nos. 6, 32, 14.

Kids **Family-Friendly Restaurants**

I know your children are perfect little angels and you can take them anywhere, but for the rest of the families who are looking for a spot that will provide (a) food their children will eat, (b) something to keep their children amused while they are waiting for the food to be served, and (c) enough background noise that their children won't be easily identified as the ones causing a ruckus, we offer the following suggestions.

The **Waterfront Warehouse,** 1549 Lower Water St. (© **902/425-7610**), provides a children's menu, lots of decorative distractions, and a child-size fisherman's shanty where they can watch videos. **Alfredo Weinstein & Ho,** 1739 Grafton St. (© **902/421-1977**), has an inexpensive children's menu in a bustling environment. If you want to infuse them with a little culture while you eat, the **Cheapside Café,** 1723 Hollis St. (© **902/425-4494**) in the Art Gallery of Nova Scotia, caters to children's tastes. **Hogies Steakhouse,** 6273 Quinpool Rd. (© **902/422-4414**), has big booths and a children's menu.

King Wah Restaurant *(Value)* SZECHUAN/CANTONESE Don't come here for the ambience, because this place resembles a truck stop. Come for the food. Better yet, get it delivered. It's worth it. A Cantonese feast for two is less than C\$25 (US\$17), including tax and tip. If you want a smaller meal, try the hot-and-sour soup or General Gao's spicy chicken. Service can be slow.

6430 Quinpool Rd. *©* **902/423-2587**. Reservations required on weekends. Main courses C\$7–\$15 (US\$5–\$10). AE, MC, V. Mon–Wed 4pm–11pm; Thur–Sat Noon–Midnight. Metro Transit nos. 6, 32, 14.

5 Spring Garden Road

This is the trendiest street in Halifax, and the restaurants here reflect this. Cafes and pub-style eateries serve quick lunch; most of them extend their hours to welcome the dinner crowd. There's also fine dining at the two best steakhouses in the city: **Jon Alan's Steak & Chop House** and **Ryan Duffy's Steak & Seafood.** (Haligonians are often caught up in heated debate over which is the best.)

EXPENSIVE

Jon Alan's Steak & Chop House *(★★)* STEAK/SEAFOOD Haligonians are fortunate to have two excellent steak houses within a stone's throw of each other on Spring Garden Road. Jon Alan's Steak & Chop House serves certified U.S. Angus beef—lots of it—cooked to your specifications. The menu also includes fresh seafood, herb-crusted rack of lamb, pork chops with green apple chutney, and Chicken Cordon Bleu, but most everyone comes for the steak. The service is excellent; attentive rather than bothersome, and the atmosphere is relaxed. Once you've finished your meal, stroll next door and visit Atlantic Canada's largest walk-in humidor. It is also part of the Jon Alan complex, and there are over 600 varieties of cigars available, including Cuban ones (see chapter 8).

5523 Spring Garden Rd. *©* **902/422-5267**. Reservations required. Main courses C\$30–\$45 (US\$20–\$30). AE, MC, V. Mon–Thur 11am–10pm; Fri 11am–11pm; Sat 5–11pm; Sun 5–10pm. Metro Transit nos. 1, 10, 14.

Ryan Duffy's Steak & Seafood *(★)* STEAK/SEAFOOD Duffy's is located on the second floor of Spring Garden Place, on the corner of Spring Garden Road and Dresden Row. The specialty is corn-fed U.S. beef, cut and weighed at your table (an experience in itself), then cooked to your specifications. There's also a variety of seafood, lamb, lemon, and chicken (try the chicken marinated in garlic and roasted with traditional vegetables). The roast duck is excellent, and so is the Caesar salad. Some diners feel that the quality of service has lagged recently, although I've always thought Jon Alan's was better—both in terms of service and food. **Duffy's Bar & Grill** is attached to the restaurant. It's an elegant pub, although that sounds a bit like a contradiction in terms. But the rich red plaid and dark wood really work, aided by substantial, overstuffed wingback chairs and soft lighting. The menu is more relaxed and slightly less expensive than the steakhouse.

In Spring Garden Place. 5640 Spring Garden Rd. *©* **902/421-1116**. Reservations recommended on weekends. Main courses C\$30–\$45 (US\$20–\$30). AE, MC, V. Daily 11:30am–1am. Metro Transit nos. 1, 10, 14.

MODERATE

Il Mercato *(★★)* NORTHERN ITALIAN Part of the da Maurizio and Bish family (see pages 77 and 92, respectively), little Il Mercato is just as trendy and popular as her big sisters. Many consider it the best Italian restaurant in the city. The European-style setting has warm, sunny walls, terra-cotta floor tiles, and a fountain that's relaxing to watch—not to mention good cover for intimate conversations. The menu offers lots of tempting dishes; it's difficult to choose. The penne sautéed with Italian sausage, garlic, onions, fresh tomato, and chilies is excellent, not to mention filling. The antipasti should not be missed, and it would be a shame to not save room for one of the wonderful desserts. With all this going for it, the paper tablecloths and napkins seem really out of place. Remember to arrive early because it's always busy, and, for some reason, reservations aren't accepted.

5475 Spring Garden Rd. ✆ **902/422-2866**. Reservations not accepted. Main courses C$15–$30 (US$10–$20). AE, MC, V. Mon–Sat 11am–11pm. Metro Transit nos. 1, 10, 14.

INEXPENSIVE

Dio Mio Gelato Desserts Café CAFE/ICE CREAM/DESSERT   People come from all over the city to enjoy the Italian ice cream made on site. It's creamy and light, and low in fat—what more could you ask of an ice cream? They also serve a type of gelato that's called soy magic, worth a try even for those who abhor soy, especially the mint–carob chip flavor. Though Dio Mio is known for homemade gelati and sorbetti, it also serves soups, salads, and sandwiches that make a delicious, inexpensive lunch.

5670 Spring Garden Rd. ✆ **902/492-3467**. Most meals under C$10 (US$7). No credit cards. Mon–Fri 8am–10pm; Sat–Sun Noon–10pm. Metro Transit nos. 1, 10, 14.

Steve-O-Reno's ★★ (Value CAFE   Located just off of Spring Garden Road, this is a great spot for lunch or a quick refreshment. Authentic Italian panini sandwiches, homemade vegetarian soups, Greek and Caesar salads, plus desserts and pastries are available in a relaxing setting. On warm summer days, enjoy a mocha or chai freeze, or a fruit smoothie on the patio. The prices are a pleasant treat and the staff is welcoming.

1536 Brunswick St. Beside the Halifax Folklore Centre, just off Spring Garden Rd. ✆ **902/429-3034**. Most meals under C$10 (US$7) . No credit cards. Mon–Fri 7:30am–6pm; Sat 8am–6pm. Metro Transit nos. 1, 10, 14.

Your Father's Moustache Pub & Eatery CANADIAN   This is a popular spot for the university crowd, partially because the food is fast and inexpensive, but also because there's a variety of entertainment. The menu includes fish and chips, lobster, steaks, and pasta, and a wide variety of classic pub specialties. Try the clubhouse sandwich made with grilled chicken, Cajun mayonnaise, and sweet Spanish onions, served on grilled French bread. For a shared snack, go for the wings with the restaurant's own hot sauce. In summer, head up to the rooftop patio that overlooks Spring Garden Road. This place doesn't lack for on-site entertainment, with computerized trivia games, the Friday night Open Mike for up-and-coming talent, and Saturday afternoon blues music sessions. The Cape Breton ceilidh is a treat, if you happen to be there on a night when one's scheduled. What's a ceilidh? Think of foot-tapping fiddle music and Celtic songs with a bit of step-dancing thrown in. Call to find out when the next ceilidh is scheduled.

5686 Spring Garden Rd. ✆ **902/423-6766**. Main courses C$7–$15 (US$5–$10). AE, MC, V. Daily 11am–midnight. Metro Transit nos. 1, 10, 14.

Moments The Chickenburger

This landmark burger joint about a 20-minute drive north of Halifax will send you on a nostalgia kick back to the 1950s. Also known as "The Chick," the place does all the usual diner foods exceptionally well, including fish & chips and the ever-popular burger and fries. But it's known for its namesake: the chickenburger, made with chunks of roasted chicken in a gravy-style sauce. Just delicious. Order from the counter, which is open to the parking lot, or go inside and sing along with the jukebox. Choose Pat Boone's "Love Letters in the Sand" or "I'm Walking," by Ricky Nelson, and let your mind slip back into bobby socks and Brylcreem. Hollywood even brought Jason Priestley, star of *Beverly Hills 90210,* to The Chick in 1996, for the filming of *Love and Death on Long Island*. Take the Bedford Highway (Route 2) north to **1531 Bedford Highway**, on the right. Just look for the rooster enshrined in neon lights.

6

Exploring Halifax

Founded in 1749, Halifax is one of the oldest cities in North America, with a strong European heritage that has left its impact on the city's buildings and culture. But that doesn't mean Halifax is lacking in modern ideas. With six universities—the highest concentration in Canada—and a leading edge in Information Technology, Halifax has found a happy mix of old and new. If you like this mix, and want to dig a bit deeper, you'll find a lot on offer, whether exploring the historic architecture of **Province House,** or the **Maritime Museum of the Atlantic,** strolling through **Point Pleasant Park,** or taking in an exhibit at the **Art Gallery of Nova Scotia.**

When the weather cooperates, be sure to spend a few hours at the **water-front,** with its working piers, visiting ships, and shops. If you visit during the warmer months (May through September) don't miss the **Halifax Public Gardens** with its Victorian splendor. Remember that Halifax hosts a variety of festivals and regional events, from the **International Tattoo,** every July, to the **International Boat Show,** each February. See the Halifax Calendar of Events in chapter 2 for a complete list of annual festivals and events.

If you are traveling with children, be sure to check the "Especially for Kids" section later in this chapter.

Halifax is a friendly city. Residents enjoy having a good time and meeting new people. You will feel welcome.

SUGGESTED ITINERARIES

If You Have 1 Day

If the weather allows, visit the **Halifax Citadel National Historic Site** in the morning, and discover the city's roots. Because so much of Halifax is military or maritime, take some time to stroll along the **waterfront boardwalk** to get a feel, and smell, of the harbor. While there, visit the **Maritime Museum of the Atlantic,** and take in exhibits about the 1917 Halifax Explosion, view artifacts from the *Titanic,* and learn about the hundreds of shipwrecks along Nova Scotia's shores. For lunch, go to the **Cheapside Café,** located in the **Art Gallery of Nova Scotia.** Delight in the paintings on the walls and the artfully presented food on your plate. That afternoon, head to the ornate and lovely **Halifax Public Gardens.** Feed the ducks (and pigeons) amid flowers, shrubs, and trees laid out in the Victorian style. Continue to the **Museum of Natural History,** and discover a different facet of Nova Scotia's history through interactive wildlife exhibits. End the afternoon with a tour of **Alexander Keith's Nova Scotia Brewery**. If you feel like a splurge for dinner, indulge in a meal at **Bish World Cuisine** (make a reservation), or enjoy a hearty pub meal and live music at **The Old Triangle Irish Alehouse** (see chapter 9). If you're visiting in colder weather, skip the stroll in the Public Gardens and visit the **Anna Leonowens Gallery at the Nova Scotia College of Art and Design**. There's some fantastic contemporary art on display by students, faculty, and visiting artists.

If You Have 2 Days

On the first day, follow the itinerary above. Begin day 2 with a visit to the **Pier 21 National Historic Site.** Sometimes called Canada's Ellis Island, this was the front door to Canada for more than a million immigrants from the 1920s to the 1970s. Next, take a cab to the **Hydrostone district,** in the north end of the city. The houses and other buildings in this charming area were built just a few short months after the Halifax Explosion of 1917, which leveled all the residences in the area. The **Hydrostone Market** has a lovely variety of European-style shops, with antiques, crafts, flowers, and food. In fact, **Epicurious Morsels,** 5529 Young St. (© **902/455-0955**), with its international menu of gourmet specialties, would be a great place to have lunch. Spend the afternoon exploring the trendy shops on **Spring Garden Road** or the historic buildings and boutiques of the **Historic Properties.** Try some authentic Greek cuisine for dinner at **Opa! Greek Taverna** (see chapter 5), or opt for the classy ambience and Italian fare at **da Maurizio** (see chapter 5).

If You Have 3 Days

If you visit Halifax in June, July, or August, on day 3 stop in at **Nova Scotian Crystal,** 5080 George St. (© **902/492-0416**), Canada's only crystal-making establishment. During the summer, the glassworks doors are open to let visitors watch the craftsmen at work, while a guide explains the process. Artisans craft both mouth-blown and hand-cut crystal on the premises. Afterwards, grab a quick lunch at the **Harbourside Market** (© **902/ 422-3077**) at the **Historic Properties.** In the afternoon, put on your walking shoes and take a cab to **Point Pleasant Park.** Acres of natural parkland beckon you. Groomed paths take you along the shores of the Halifax Harbour, through forests, and past the ruins of several fortresses, including the **Prince of Wales Tower National Historic Site.** (Before you leave the Harbourside Market for the park, buy a bag of peanuts to feed the squirrels, or some sunflower seeds for the chickadees—many will eat right from your hand if you are patient and still.) After a few hours of exploring and hiking, you might welcome some passive entertainment for the evening. Take in a performance by **Symphony Nova Scotia,** or a play by the **Neptune Theatre.**

If You Have 4 Days or More

With the luxury of more time, why not include a day trip in your itinerary? What about a trip to across the harbor to **Dartmouth,** or, if it's warm, a drive to one of the beaches along the **Eastern Shore**? It's also a good chance to get some exercise— try **kayaking the North West Arm** or **hiking** in hilly Hemlock Park. Check out the "Organized Tours" section, later in this chapter, for something that catches your interest. Or turn to chapter 10, "Side Trips from Halifax," if you want to venture further afield.

1 The Top Attractions

History is front and center when it comes to the most popular attractions in Halifax—those that are really worth your time. But other equally absorbing cultural and outdoor highlights are a close second. These destinations are also easy to get to. From hotels downtown, some are within walking distance. If you're taking a Metro Transit bus, this section tells you where to get off. If you're traveling with children, try to visit these top attractions on summer weekdays. To avoid crowds, mornings are the best time.

Alexander Keith's Nova Scotia Brewery ⭐ The legendary Alexander Keith and his India Pale Ale are popular with Haligonians and visitors alike. Located in the ironstone and granite Brewery Market, amid potters' studios, offices, and shops, the restored brewery tells the story of Keith's life and his famous ale. A number of costumed guides, speaking in the manner befitting persons in the 1800s, lead a tour where you learn about the secrets of brewing beer, complete with a split-second glance at Keith's original recipe for India Pale Ale. Sample everything from the dry hops in the brewery office, to the finished brew at the Stag's Head tavern. The tavern staff entertains with a song or two while you enjoy the free samples. You can purchase such questionable necessities as coasters, T-shirts, playing cards, etc., in the adjoining store. And yes, this includes Keith's India Pale Ale—to take home, of course! Tours run every half-hour. Plan to spend an hour to an hour-and-a-half.

1496 Lower Water St., ℂ **902/455-1474**. www.beer.com/brands/ca/keiths. Admission C$8 (US$5.35) adults, C$6 (US$4) seniors, students & children all ages. May–Oct Mon–Sat 10am–9pm; Sun 10am–5pm. Nov–April Mon–Thurs pre-booked tours only; Fri 5–8pm; Sat noon–8pm. Metro Transit nos. 7, 9, 20.

Art Gallery of Nova Scotia ⭐ *Kids* Inside these impressive sandstone heritage buildings are surprisingly modern gallery facilities with a wide collection of artwork. Recent exhibitions have included **The Group of Seven** and **The Impressionists,** including Monet. Upcoming exhibitions in 2003 include **Canvas of War,** the Canadian War Museum's definitive exhibition of Canada's war art, and **Alex Colville: Metaphors of Eternal Return,** featuring recent works. In 2004, the gallery will host **Acadie/Acadia,** a collection of works by francophone artists from Canada, the United States, and France, in celebration of the Congrès Mondiale Acadien, being held in Nova Scotia. Along with temporary exhibitions such as these, there are over 8,000 works in the gallery's permanent collection. These include historic and contemporary Nova Scotian art, Canadian and international art, and an acclaimed collection of folk art. One of the highlights is the **house of Nova Scotian folk artist Maud Lewis,** with its delightful painted flowers on every conceivable surface: doors, steps, and inside walls. There is also an artist-in-residence studio, an art sales and rental gallery, a gift shop, and the **Cheapside Café,** serving lunch and snacks (see chapter 5). You might want to attend the public lectures, or take your children to one of the art classes provided by the gallery. If you really enjoy galleries, plan to spend at least 2 hours here.

1723 Hollis St. ℂ **902/424-7542**. www.agns.gov.ns.ca. Admission C$5 (US$3.35) adults, C$4 (US$2.70) seniors, C$2 (US$1.35) students, free for children 12 and under. Tue–Fri 10am–6pm; Sat, Sun & holiday Mondays noon–5pm. Metro Transit nos. 2, 7, 9.

Halifax Citadel National Historic Site ⭐⭐ *Kids* Situated high on a hill overlooking the harbor and downtown Halifax, the Citadel is one of the world's finest remaining examples of a 19th-century star-shaped fortification. It's also the ideal spot to take panoramic photographs of the city and harbor. The present

Halifax Attractions

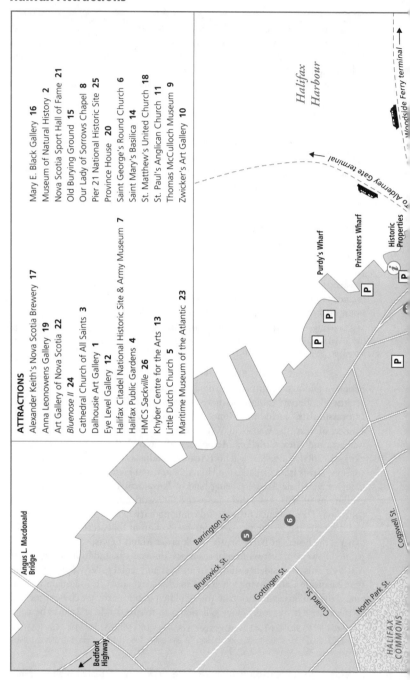

ATTRACTIONS

Alexander Keith's Nova Scotia Brewery **17**
Anna Leonowens Gallery **19**
Art Gallery of Nova Scotia **22**
Bluenose II **24**
Cathedral Church of All Saints **3**
Dalhousie Art Gallery **1**
Eye Level Gallery **12**
Halifax Citadel National Historic Site & Army Museum **7**
Halifax Public Gardens **4**
HMCS *Sackville* **26**
Khyber Centre for the Arts **13**
Little Dutch Church **5**
Maritime Museum of the Atlantic **23**

Mary E. Black Gallery **16**
Museum of Natural History **2**
Nova Scotia Sport Hall of Fame **21**
Old Burying Ground **15**
Our Lady of Sorrows Chapel **8**
Pier 21 National Historic Site **25**
Province House **20**
Saint George's Round Church **6**
Saint Mary's Basilica **14**
St. Matthew's United Church **18**
St. Paul's Anglican Church **11**
Thomas McCulloch Museum **9**
Zwicker's Art Gallery **10**

Halifax Harbour

→ Woodside Ferry terminal

To Alderney Gate terminal ←

Historic Properties

Privateers Wharf

Purdy's Wharf

Angus L. Macdonald Bridge

Bedford Highway

Barrington St.

Brunswick St.

Gottingen St.

Cunard St.

North Park St.

Cogswell St.

HALIFAX COMMONS

Cable Wharf

Water Street Ferry Terminal

Queen's Wharves

Sackville Landing

Summit Plaza

Tug Boat Wharf

Cruise Ship Docking Facility

SACKVILLE LANDING PARK

Lower Water St.

Hollis St.

Barrington St.

Barrington St.

Sackville St.

Spring Garden Rd.

Morris St.

South St.

South Park St.

Duke St.

Rainnie Dr.

Ahern Ave.

CITADEL HILL NATIONAL HISTORIC PARK

WANDERERS GROUNDS

HALIFAX PUBLIC GARDENS

University Ave.

Emergency Site

Trollope St.

Bell Rd.

Summer St.

Jubilee Rd.

Robie St.

Emergency Site

0.25 Mi
0.25 Km

	Cruise Ship Terminal
	Ferry Route
	Hospital
P	Parking
	Post Office
	Train Station
i	Visitor Information

Citadel, completed in 1856, is the fourth in a series of forts that have stood on the hill since 1749. It sports a defensive ditch, ramparts, musketry gallery, powder magazine, and signal masts. Although never attacked, the fort was garrisoned by the British Army until 1906, and by Canadian forces during the World Wars. Today, Parks Canada operates the Citadel, which is one of the most visited and important historic sites in the country.

When you visit, you will be drawn into the mid-Victorian period by summer students who portray members of the 78th Highland Regiment and the Royal Artillery on parade or going about their work. You'll also meet the soldiers' wives and typical tradespeople, all dressed in period costume and pursuing period activities. Inside the fort, it's easy to believe that the world of the 21st century does not yet exist. There are guided tours available, and a 50-minute audiovisual presentation, *The Tides of History*, depicting the four different periods of the fort's history, beginning with the Mi'kmaq, through the British era, the two World Wars, and ending in the present. Children will enjoy playing in a "real fort"—with cannons and underground storage rooms to explore, ramparts to climb, and soldiers to watch. To see everything you'll need almost 3 hours. *Note:* From November 1 to May 6, you can tour the grounds free of charge, but none of the buildings are open to the public, and there are no costumed guides.

Sackville St. Near Dresden Row. © **902/426-5080.** www.parcscanada.gc.ca/parks/Ns_nhs_e.htm. Admission C$8 (US$5.35) adults, C$6 (US$4) seniors, C$4 (US$2.70) children 6–16, free for children 5 and under, C$20 (US$13.35) families. May 7–Oct 31 daily 9am–5pm; Nov 1– May 6 daily 9am-5pm grounds only, admission free. Metro Transit nos. 6, 4, 2.

⌐Fun Fact How Many Shipwrecks?

Nova Scotia has more shipwrecks per kilometer of coastline than almost anywhere else in North America. Wrecks range from aboriginal vessels to modern craft, and involve virtually every type and size of boat. There are an estimated 10,000 to 25,000 wrecks, in some places so thick that ships are piled on top of each other.

Halifax Public Gardens ★★ ⌐Kids ⌐Moments   A quick jaunt through the Gardens will take no more than half an hour, but if you're a gardener—or even a wannabe gardener—and if you visit between May and November, you'll likely spend a full hour at least. The Halifax Public Gardens were recognized as a National Historic Site in 1984 because they are a valuable resource in the study of heritage plants and landscape design. A formal Victorian public garden that has survived intact and relatively unspoiled in the heart of a modern city is rare indeed in the 21st century. The idea for these gardens first germinated when the Nova Scotia Horticultural Society expanded a private garden, planted in 1753, almost 100 years later (in 1836). A civic garden was added in 1867. The city took charge of the gardens in 1874, and the present design was adopted the following year. The 7-hectare (17-acre) park is surrounded by a wrought-iron fence and contains a **water garden, rose garden, mixed perennial and annual borders, and rare shrubs and trees.** The stunningly beautiful rhododendron shrubs in bloom will impress gardeners visiting in June. July and August showcase dahlias and begonias. And people are often startled by the display of cacti in such a northern garden. Although they appear to grow year-round, the cacti are moved into a greenhouse during the winter. Several of the trees carry plaques stating the species and the name of those who donated them. Non-living additions to the garden include **ornate fountains, ponds,** winding gravel walkways, and wooden benches. The large **Jubilee Fountain,** located in the northeast section of the Gardens, was erected in 1897 to honor Queen Victoria's Diamond Jubilee. It is classical in style with a heavy Corinthian column base, surrounded by four water babies riding on sea monsters. The large basin holds the nymph Egeria, who, according to mythology, was turned to stone when she tried to hide in the forest after her husband's death. Sassy ducks and persistent pigeons will insist on making your acquaintance. They expect every human, large or small, to feed them. There's a **Victorian bandstand,** with a bright red roof and intricate gingerbread architecture. Free concerts are held from late June to early September on Sunday afternoons at 2pm, and last about an hour. It's a great place to relax or enjoy a picnic lunch.

Corner of Spring Garden Rd. and South Park St. Admission free. May–Oct dawn–dusk. Closed Nov–April. Metro Transit nos. 1, 10, 14.

Maritime Museum of the Atlantic ★★ *Kids* Make sure you take time to visit this museum, because there are so many fascinating exhibits that reveal the history and character of Halifax. From Sable Island shipwrecks to the *Titanic* disaster, from the Halifax Explosion to the Canadian Navy, the museum houses more than 24,000 artifacts representing the period from 1850 to the present. One of the most haunting pieces in the exhibit, *Titanic,* **the Unsinkable Ship and Halifax,** is an original deck chair recovered from the liner after it sank. Another must-see is the **Halifax Wrecked** exhibit, about the 1917 Halifax Explosion: It has a moving audio recording of citizens of Halifax telling their amazing stories of survival. Moored on the wharf behind the museum is the **CSS Acadia,** a retired hydrographic survey vessel, and the museum's largest artifact. The newest exhibit, **Shipwreck,** explores the staggering number of shipwrecks that have taken place along Nova Scotia's shores. On display are more than 100 artifacts, as well as a life-size diorama of an underwater archaeologist at work. Adults and children can participate in several activities and projects. The museum staff build replicas of small boats in the museum's collection as part of an ongoing program to demonstrate and preserve traditional boat-building skills. Visitors are welcome to observe. You can also learn how to make such things as rope mats used on ships, or a model lighthouse. Allow 2 hours to visit all the exhibits.

1675 Lower Water St. ✆ **902/424-7490.** http://museum.gov.ns.ca/mma. Admission C$6 (US$4) adults, C$5 (US$3.35) seniors, C$2 (US$1.35) children 6–17, free for children 5 and under, C$15 (US$10) families. May–June Mon, Wed–Sat 9:30am–5:30pm; Tue 9:30am–8pm; Sun 1–5:30pm. June–Sept Mon, Wed–Sat 9:30am–5:30pm; Tue 9:30am–8pm; Sun 10:30am–5:30pm. Oct Mon, Wed–Sat 9:30am–5:30pm; Tue 9:30am–8pm; Sun 1–5:30pm. Nov 2–April 30 Wed–Sat 9:30am–5pm; Tue 9:30am–8pm; Sun 1–5pm. Closed Mon. Call for holiday operating hours. Metro Transit nos. 7, 9, 20.

Museum of Natural History ★★ *Kids* This is a fun and interactive museum with displays of plants, animals, and rocks of Nova Scotia—a great place to go anytime, but a perfect place to spend a couple of hours on a rainy day. You might see local wild mice, snakes and turtles, frogs and salamanders, fish, bats, spiders, bugs, poison ivy, carnivorous plants, or fossils. The newest exhibit, **Trace Fossil Mysteries,** takes a look at the habits of ancient lizards, crabs, and the Earth's first dinosaurs that lived in Eastern Canada 550 million years ago. An interactive exhibit, this is one in which adults and children alike can follow a trail of clues, play a game of chance, peer into past lives, and learn how to identify trace fossils. There are also stationary displays of native animals, which have been mounted and placed in natural-looking environments, a life-size replica of a whale, and dinosaur bones. Plus, you'll find interactive displays—match bird calls to birds, play in the Bone Zone (dinosaur bones, that is), or visit Gus, the Gopher Tortoise and the museum's official mascot—that are fun and educational. Naturalists are on duty to explain and assist. Ask about the one-session programs for children and/or adults in the afternoons, evenings, and during school holidays. These can be anything from a nature hike to identify snakes, to a peek into the collection vaults of the museum, to a presentation on local geology. Plan on spending 1 to 2 hours.

1747 Summer St. ✆ **902/424-7353**. www.nature.museum.gov.ns.ca. Admission C$4 (US$2.70) adults, C$3.50 (US$2.35) seniors, C$2 (US$1.35) children 6–17, free for children 5 and under, C$8 (US$5.35) families (one adult plus their children), C$12 (US$8) families (two adults plus their children). June 1–Oct 15 Thurs–Sat 9:30am–5:30pm; Sun 1–5:30pm; Mon–Tues 9:30am–5:30pm; Wed 9:30am–8pm. Oct 16–May 31 Tues, Thurs–Sat 9:30am–5pm; Sun 1–5pm; Wed 9:30am–8pm; closed Mon except special holidays. Free Wed 5–8pm. Metro Transit nos. 3, 14, 21.

 Titanic Sites in Halifax

All of these locations are in some way connected with the sinking of the *Titanic,* in 1912.

- **Camp Hill Cemetery,** Robie St. Titanic survivor Hilday Lacon (nee Slayter) was buried here in 1965.
- **Coaling Jetty No. 4,** just north of the Halifax side of the Angus L. Macdonald Bridge. The site is now part of the Naval Dockyard and is not open to the public. The bodies of the Titanic victims were landed at this wharf and then taken by horse-drawn hearses to the temporary morgue on Agricola Street.
- **Fairview Lawn Cemetery,** Chisholm Ave. off Connaught Ave. Halifax is home to the largest number of Titanic graves in the world. This cemetery contains 121 graves that bear witness to the range of cultures and social classes on board the *Titanic.* All the victims thought to be Protestant were buried in this nondenominational cemetery.
- **Maritime Museum of the Atlantic,** 1675 Lower Water St. A permanent exhibit honors those who lost their lives and explores the close ties between Halifax and the *Titanic.* The exhibit features a number of authentic documents and photographs. There are also numerous wooden artifacts recovered at the scene of the disaster, including richly carved pieces of *Titanic'*s grand staircase, and one of the only known intact Titanic deck chairs.
- **Mount Olivet,** 7076 Mumford Rd. There are 19 victims of the *Titanic* interred in this Catholic cemetery, including J. F. P. Clarke, the bass player in the ship's band.
- **Site of Snow's Funeral Home,** 1740 Argyle St. The original building of Snow's Funeral Home is still standing, and is now the site of My Apartment restaurant and bar. John Snow & Sons were the chief embalmers of the *Titanic* victims' bodies. They directed the large team of undertakers from Nova Scotia, New Brunswick, and Prince Edward Island.

Making Their Way to Canada

Pier 21, 1055 Marginal Rd. (𝒞 **902/425-7770**; www.pier21.ns.ca), is Canada's Ellis Island—the first stop for many people who entered Canada between 1928 and 1971. More than 100,000 refugees and Displaced Persons eventually arrived on Canada's doorstep at Pier 21. Some of the most desperate even sailed across the Atlantic Ocean in small fishing vessels. Following are some interesting facts about Pier 21 and immigration to Canada:

- The Red Cross operated a nursery from Pier 21, so families with small children could bathe and rest before boarding the train for the next stage of their journey.
- The YWCA offered counseling and organized social gatherings so the newcomers could meet others and practice their English.
- The Sisters of Service helped non–English-speaking immigrants make up food lists or send telegrams to loved ones.
- 3,000 British youngsters were evacuated to Canada during the first few years of World War II to keep them safe in case the Nazis overran England. They became known as "guest children."
- When the war was over, approximately 48,000 war brides and their 22,000 children eventually did make the journey to far-off Canada to begin their new lives.
- During World War II, ocean liners were transformed into troop ships. In all, 484,000 troops departed from Pier 21 between the war years 1939 and 1945.

Pier 21 National Historic Site ★★ *Kids* *Moments*   More than a million immigrants, troops, war brides, evacuee children, and displaced persons entered or left Canada through this immigration shed between 1928 and 1971. Pier 21 was reopened in 1999 to honor the contribution of immigrants in building Canada, and to acknowledge the sacrifices of Canadian troops during World War II. As you explore the building you can hear the taped voices of many of the immigrants and soldiers—it's almost as though the walls are whispering—sharing their memories and stories. The displays are designed to allow visitors to trace the path an immigrant would follow upon arriving in Canada: the hard wooden benches of the seating area (called the listening benches, as you can hear simulated conversations between families and authorities), the seemingly unending wait, and finally the questioning by the officials in charge. The recorded voices and images portray the mixture of joy, hope, and fear experienced by the immigrants. There are video testimony stations showing immigrants and their family members telling their stories, as well as a station where visitors can videotape their own. A special display lists all the ships that brought immigrants to Canada, and a database to find out more information about the ships. There is a reproduction of a train such as immigrants would board to travel from Halifax to other parts of Canada. Visitors can walk along a replica of a World War II ship's deck, and imagine soldiers and sailors doing the same. A 24-minute video presentation, ***Oceans of Hope,*** uses stage props, video, sound effects, and real actors to present the Pier 21 story. Many visitors find it a very emotional encounter, as they relive their own experience or those of their parents or grand-parents. Upstairs is the **Resource Centre,** with a photo library, books, videos, a database of ship arrival schedules, firsthand arrival accounts, and 10 years' worth of Canadian immigration records.

1055 Marginal Rd. At the south end of Barrington St. © 902/425-7770. www.pier21.ns.ca. Admission C$6.75 (US$4.50) adults, C$5.75 (US$3.85) seniors, C$4.75 (US$3.15) students, C$3.75 (US$2.50) children 6–16, free for children 5 and under, C$15.75 (US$10.50) families. May 13–Nov 17 daily 9:30am–5pm. Nov 18–May 12 Wed–Fri 10am–5pm; Sat–Sun noon–5pm; closed Mon–Tue. Metro Transit nos. 7, 9, 17.

2 Museums & Galleries

Along with the museums reviewed in the first section, including the **Maritime Museum of the Atlantic,** the **Museum of Natural History,** and **Pier 21,** Halifax is home to museums focusing on other areas of interest as well. From the Canadian military to Victorian clothing, from sports to birds, the city invites you to explore. Visual art has been important in Halifax since the British gentry brought their European art collections with them when they moved to this New World. Though the level of art appreciation may ebb and flow with economic tides, the city has numerous galleries specializing in historical and contemporary art.

Anna Leonowens Gallery   The gallery is an exciting spot for people who enjoy contemporary art. This display area of the Nova Scotia College of Art and Design features exhibits that change weekly. When the gallery opened in 1968, the college felt that the name should in some way reflect the tradition of the school, and at the same time embody a progressive spirit. Anna Leonowens had taught in various parts of the world (the movie *The King and I* was based on her teaching in Siam) and was instrumental in founding the college. The history of her life is a testament to a probing, creative spirit directed toward service. It was this attribute that made the Anna Leonowens Gallery an appropriate name. The gallery complex is made up of three exhibition spaces, all at street level. **Gallery 1** is primarily reserved for faculty, alumni, visitors to the college, and guest exhibitions. **Galleries 2 and 3** are reserved for the work of students, usually those in their final semester, and represent the various program areas within the college. About 130 exhibitions take place here each year.

1891 Granville St. © 902/494-8823. www.nscad.ns.ca/~gallery. Admission free. Tue–Thur 11am–7pm; Fri 11am–5pm; Mon 5:30–7pm. Closed Aug 19–Sept 8, Dec 16–Jan 6, and holidays. Metro Transit nos. 7, 9, 18.

Army Museum ⊛   This museum is located in the Cavalier Building of the Citadel complex, and houses an extensive collection of historic uniforms, decorations, edged weapons, and small arms associated with Nova Scotia. Exhibits include the Croak Victoria Cross, the largest collection of Nova Scotia Highland Brigade insignia in Canada, light artillery, and artifacts from the Fenian Raids, the 1885 Rebellion, and the Boer War. There are also special memorial displays on the **First Special Service Force** (a unique combat unit in Italy made up of a bi-national group of elite Canadian and American fighters during World War II), and the **Battle for Hong Kong.** (Almost 2,000 Canadian soldiers were sent to Hong Kong in 1941, only to find themselves facing overwhelming odds in a fight they couldn't win. Some 550 were killed in battle.) There is an exhibition on the **Defense of Halifax Harbour,** a tribute to Atlantic Canadians in World

War II. The museum also provides information, evaluation, and restoration services for military artifacts.

Cavalier Building, Halifax Citadel National Historic Site, Sackville St. at Dresden Row. © **902/422-5979.** museum.gov.ns.ca/musdir/armymuseum.htm. Admission free. June 15–Labour Day daily 9am–6pm; Labour Day–Oct 15 daily 9am–5pm; Oct 16–May 14 by appointment; May 15–June 15 daily 9am–5pm. Metro Transit nos. 6, 4, 2.

Dalhousie Art Gallery   This gallery was established in 1954, and houses a permanent collection of more than 1,000 works of art by Canadian and international artists. There are also rotating exhibitions of historic and contemporary art, including **About Memory and Archive,** selections from the permanent collection of the Musée d'art contemporain de Montréal, and an exhibition of contemporary abstract painting titled **Hungry Eyes.** There is an annual December display of student, staff, and faculty and alumni art in the genres of painting, graphic art, photography, mixed media, video, sculpture, and crafts. The gallery also presents a film series with screenings from September to May, every Wednesday at 12:30pm and 8pm. The selection is eclectic, and ranges from biographies of artists, to films that complement current exhibits at the gallery, to contemporary international films. Visitors are welcome to use the gallery's reading room, stocked with art periodicals and catalogues.

6101 University Ave. In Dalhousie University. © **902/494-2403.** http://is.dal.ca/~gallery. Admission free. Tue, Thurs–Sun 11am–5pm; Wed 7pm–8pm. Closed Mon. Metro Transit nos. 7, 9, 10.

Finds **Archives & Records**

If you enjoy history and research, you might want to spend a few hours in some of Halifax's extensive archives. The **Dalhousie University Archives**, in the Killam Memorial Library, 6225 University Ave. (© **902/ 494-6490;** www.library.dal.ca/archives/archives.htm), has rich resources on Dalhousie University, business, labor, Nova Scotia shipping, music, theater, and collections of private manuscripts and photographs. Admission is free. The archives are open Monday to Friday from 9am to noon, and from 1pm to 5pm.

The **Maritime Command Museum Library and Archives**, 2725 Gottingen St. (© **902/427-0550** ext. 8250), contains a treasure chest of intelligence on the history of the Canadian naval forces, especially if there's a Halifax connection. Admission is free. It's open Monday to Friday from 10am to 3:30pm.

If you have an interest in genealogy, you'll enjoy spending some time at the **Nova Scotia Archives & Records Management**, 6016 University Ave. (© **902/424-6060;** www.gov.ns.ca/nsarm). The holdings include papers of families and individuals, and records of churches, businesses, organizations, communities, and government departments. There's also a 50,000-title library, newspapers, genealogical sources, photographs, maps, and architectural plans. The staff is very knowledgeable and helpful. Admission is free. The archives are open Monday to Friday from 8:30am to 4:30pm, and Saturday from 9am to 5pm.

Eye Level Gallery   The gallery moved to a new, larger, street-level location two years ago, making room for a major expansion of exhibition space and public visibility. It's a nonprofit, artist-run center focusing on the work of emerging and established contemporary Canadian artists. And it's often controversial. Halifax police removed a recent video exhibit, **Byte,** by Toronto-based artist Lyla Rye. The video was playing in the gallery's window, and police began receiving complaints that the video was pornographic. Other recent exhibitions include **Drift,** by Isabelle Hayeur, of Montreal, and **Drinking Stories,** by Halifax artist Craig Francis Power. Check the website for upcoming exhibitions.

1587 Barrington St. ℂ 902/425-6412. www.eyelevelgallery.ca. Admission free. Tue–Sat Noon–5pm. Closed Sun–Mon. Metro Transit nos. 3, 7, 9.

Khyber Centre for the Arts   This is a nonprofit, artist-run center located in a historic, three-story building in downtown Halifax. Built in 1888 to house the Church of England Institute, it's a highly decorative Victorian composition in the ornate Gothic style. The third-floor Turret Room is a multidisciplinary space made available for theater, dance, and other performance initiatives. The gallery actively supports local, regional, and national artistic communities, and presents contemporary art exhibitions in a wide variety of disciplines, including visual arts, theater, and music. Recent exhibitions have included **Coast to Coast,** with works by Jo Cook, Paul Zylstra, and Drew Classen, three Canadian artists. **We Build Excitement** was an exhibit by six recent graduates of the Nova Scotia College of Art and Design (NCAD). Call or check the website to see what's showing.

1588 Barrington St. ℂ **902/422-9668.** www.khyberarts.ns.ca. Admission free. Tue–Wed Noon–5pm; Thur noon–10pm; Fri–Sat Noon–5pm. Closed Sun–Mon. Metro Transit nos. 3, 7, 9.

Mary E. Black Gallery   Also known as the Nova Scotia Center for Arts and Design, this is a government-sponsored center with ongoing exhibitions by Nova Scotia craftspeople and designers. Folk Art has become a popular and valuable collectible, and Atlantic Canada has a rich history of artists producing unique pieces in wood, clay, and paint. The gallery features one-of-a-kind craft displays, including folk art. Upcoming exhibits include the Lieutenant Governor's Design Awards in Architecture 2003 (June 13 to July 26, 2003), Svava T. Juliusson: Blanket Sacrifice (October 3 to November 15, 2003), and Colour and Light: An International Exhibition of Contemporary Stained Glass (November 28 to January 10, 2004).

1683 Barrington St. ℂ **902/424-4062.** www.craft-design.gov.ns.ca. Admission by donation. Mon–Fri 9am–4pm; Sat 10am–4pm. Metro Transit nos. 3, 7, 9.

Nova Scotia Sport Hall of Fame ★ (Kids)   If you or anyone traveling with you enjoys sports, be sure to allow a couple of hours to spend here. Not only will you be amazed at the quality of the displays on sport heritage in Nova Scotia, but also you'll have fun shooting hoops on a regulation-height net or shooting against an NHL goalie in the Action Corner. Visitors can use interactive computers to play trivia games and research information on more than 300 members of the Hall of Fame. The displays include awards, uniforms, photographs, equipment, and other significant artifacts spanning over 120 years. Discover Nova Scotia's connection to the evolution of hockey, and the very first basketball game ever played (in 1891). The museum also houses a research room, a sport film library, and a collection of books, programs, and files on the history of numerous sports and sporting individuals. The best time to visit is weekdays during school hours. If you're traveling with children during summer vacation, try first thing in the morning.

1645 Granville St. © **902/421-1266**. www.novascotiasporthalloffame.com. Admission free. Year-round Mon–Sat 10am–4:30pm; July–Aug also open Sun 10am–4:30pm. Metro Transit nos. 7, 9, 18.

Thomas McCulloch Museum Located in the Biology Department of Dalhousie University, this museum houses an exhibit of mounted birds of Nova Scotia, prepared by Thomas McCulloch, first principal of Dalhousie College over 150 years ago. There's also a collection of lifelike ceramic mushrooms created by Alma and Ernst Lorenzen of Lantz, as well as collections of tropical fish, butterflies, and seashells.

1355 Oxford St. In Dalhousie University next to the National Research Council building. © **902/494-3515**. www.dal.ca/~stanet/database/thomas.html. Admission free. Mon–Fri 8:30am–4:30pm. Metro Transit nos. 7, 9, 17.

Zwicker's Gallery ⭐ This gallery first opened its doors in 1886 to serve the officers of the British garrison and their wives, and was the focus of many artistic activities in Halifax. At the time, it was one of the few public institutions in the city dedicated to art appreciation. Today, the gallery remains a moving force in the Halifax art community. On exhibit are paintings, maps, prints, and engravings. Artists who have recently exhibited include Karen Kuluk, Shelley Mitchell, Nancy Stevens, Willem Verhulst, Hallie Watson, and Garry Young.

5415 Doyle St. © **902/423-7662**. www.zwickersgallery.ca. Admission free. Mon–Sat 10am–4pm. Metro Transit nos. 1, 10, 14.

3 Heritage Attractions

If there's a historically significant attraction worth your time, you'll find it in this section. Aside from government seats and one-time seaworthy schooners, Halifax has a number of beautiful churches, too. Most churches are open to the public; some also offer guided tours, others can only be toured at prearranged times. Specifics for each church are listed in the reviews in this section.

Bluenose II ⭐ *Kids* A replica of Nova Scotia's beloved racing schooner, which indeed never lost one competition, the *Bluenose II* is also the province's sailing ambassador, visiting ports around the world to take part in Tall Ship events and to encourage people to visit Nova Scotia. This 43.5-m (143-ft.) wooden replica was built in 1963 in **Lunenburg** ⭐, 45 minutes southwest of Halifax along the south shore (see "Side Trips from Halifax," chapter 10), where the original *Bluenose* was built in 1921. The original ship is immortalized on Canada's dime, and on a Canadian postage stamp released in 1929. If she happens to be in port during your visit, take a guided tour and get a bird's-eye view of the crew's small but exquisitely tidy quarters, the mess area (kitchen and eating area), and the wheel, sails, and rigging. Call ahead to check whether she's in port; she also spends time in her home port of Lunenburg.

1675 Lower Water St. Behind the Maritime Museum of the Atlantic. © **902/634-1963**. www. bluenose2.ns.ca/Lunenburg. Admission C$20 (US$13.35) adults, seniors and students, C$10 (US$6.65) children 2–12, free for children 1 and under. Jun 1–Sept 30 various times. Call for schedules. Metro Transit nos. 2, 4, 6.

HMCS *Sackville* ⊛ *Kids*   When you climb aboard the *Sackville*, one of the first things you question is how this small ship could play the part of a protector on the huge North Atlantic Ocean during a war. As you explore the inside of the ship, downstairs in the hold, even the white walls and ceiling of the mess cannot brighten the fact that 29 men had to eat, sleep, and spend their free time in this small area. Still, is the ship has a fascinating history, and children will enjoy climbing about and exploring. The *Sackville* was built at Saint John, New Brunswick, in 1941, and was one of more than 120 corvettes built in Canada during World War II. Corvettes soon became the workhorses of the North Atlantic, escorting convoys and attacking submarines. This particular ship escorted convoys from St. John's, Newfoundland to Londonderry, Ireland, from January 1942 to August 1944, and was engaged in several battles with submarines. She has been restored as a museum and floating memorial to the courage of all who served in Canada's navy.

1675 Lower Water St. At Sackville Landing wharf behind the Maritime Museum of the Atlantic. ⊙ **902/429-2132**. www.hmcssackville-cnmt.ns.ca. Admission C$3 (US$2) adults, C$2 (US$1.40) seniors, students, children all ages. June–Sept various times. Call for schedules. Metro Transit nos. 2, 4, 6.

Province House ⊛   Built in 1819, this National Historic Site is the seat of the Nova Scotia provincial government, Canada's oldest provincial Legislative Assembly, and the original home of Britain's first overseas self-government. Although Nova Scotia's is one of the smallest government houses in Canada, in the evolution of Canada, more history has been made inside its walls than in all the others combined. From the establishment of responsible government to Confederation debates; from the creation of the freedom of the press to the swearing in of Governors General, and Royal visits, this building has seen it all. The **Red Chamber** ⊛⊛, originally used by the Legislative Council until 1928 when it ceased to exist, is stately and beautiful. The ceiling is covered with exquisitely molded plaster garlands and plumes, while the panels around the doors and windows show a delicate pattern of pastoral scenes, buildings, and animals—some of the finest plaster workmanship in Canada. The room is now used for committee meetings, press conferences, and receptions. The **Legislative Assembly Chamber** ⊛ is at the opposite end of the building from the Red Chamber. Though not as elaborately decorated, it retains a sense of authority, especially when the House is in session. Head up to the rounded second-story gallery for visitors and press, and watch all the action of provincial parliament in session. If the House isn't in session when you visit, you'll be able to tour the floor of the chamber itself. Depending on your interests, this may be a better use of your time than watching unfamiliar politics.

1726 Hollis St. ⊙ **902/424-4661**. www.gov.ns.ca/legislature. Admission free. July–Aug Mon–Fri 9am–5pm; Sat–Sun 10am–4pm. Sept–June Mon–Fri 9am–4pm. Metro Transit nos. 7, 9, 2.

HISTORIC CHURCHES

The **Cathedral Church of All Saints** ⊛, 1320 Tower Rd. (⊙ **902/423-6002;** www.chebucto.ns.ca/Religion/COAST/index.html), is an imposing Gothic structure that stands over five stories high, 25.5m (86 ft.) wide, and 76.5m (255 ft.) long. It is the seat of the Anglican Archbishop of Nova Scotia and Prince Edward Island, and is well known in the city for its beautiful stained-glass windows and woodcarvings on the pulpit and chancel. Notice the 24 angels on the choir stalls, each hand-carved from oak. The cathedral received considerable damage from two wartime explosions; the first being the Halifax Explosion in 1917; the second, when a munitions magazine near Bedford Basin exploded in 1945. It was 1979 before the west end of the cathedral was completed in stone to replace the temporary wooden end. Parishioners are often on duty in the summer to answer any questions. There is ramp access on the west side (College Street). The cathedral is open from June 5 to August 25, Monday to Friday, from 9am to 5pm, and Saturday from 1pm to 4pm. During the rest of the year, you need to make an appointment to view the interior. Admission is free. Take Metro Transit nos. 7, 9, or 10.

How long do you think it takes to build a church? Well, **Our Lady of Sorrows Chapel** (★, 1259 South Park St., was built in 1 day. On August 31, 1843, more than 1,800 people came together to erect this charming little Catholic chapel that seats a mere 70 people. Though small itself, the church has a large stained-glass window dating from 1661, and wooden carvings that date from 1550, and were taken from a Flemish church. Sir John Sparrow David Thompson (1845–1894), Canada's fourth prime minister, and the first Roman Catholic to hold the office, is buried in the Holy Cross Cemetery, which surrounds the chapel. The chapel is open from April to October, Monday to Friday, from 8:30am to 4:30pm. Admission is free. Take Metro Transit nos. 1, 3, or 10.

Saint George's Round Church and Little Dutch (Deutsche) Church (★, 2222 Brunswick St. (© 902/423-2059), wins hands down for most unique design. The first St. George's, known as the "Little Dutch [*Deutsche*] Church," is in fact the second oldest church in Halifax. Built originally as a house, it was adapted for its present purpose in 1756. That's when it was moved by German settlers, known as "Foreign Protestants," to their burying ground in the northern suburb of the infant community, and thus became the first Lutheran church in Canada. The second Saint George's Church, on the corner of Brunswick and Cornwallis streets, was built in 1800 to accommodate the growing congregation, which became Anglican in 1827. Its patron was Edward, Duke of Kent (and father of Queen Victoria). The unique round design was influenced by the duke's love of round buildings in the classical style, and is the only remaining example of a 19th-century round wooden church in Canada. In 1994, over 40% of the structure was destroyed by fire, and a restoration has recently been completed. It's been designated a National Historic Site because of its architectural beauty and historical significance. Both churches are open from June to September, but you must call if you wish to book a guided tour. There are also exterior interpretation sites that you can view without an appointment. Admission is free. Take Metro Transit nos. 1, 5, or 82.

When construction of **Saint Mary's Basilica,** 1508 Barrington St. (© 902/423-4116), began in 1820, the design was for a much smaller Georgian-style church. When Halifax was designated an Archdiocese in 1852, the building was transformed, inside and out, to the grand Victorian-Gothic style. The highly adorned facade, with turrets and elaborately decorated windows, was designed by acclaimed New York architect Patrick Charles Keely, who designed more than 500 churches in North America. The beautiful spire rises 38m (128 ft.) above the roof of the basilica, and the outside front of the building resembles something out of *Cinderella*. There's a small museum inside, behind the altar. The basilica is open to the public from May 21 to September 1, daily from 7:30am to 6pm. **Note:** You must make an appointment to take a guided tour. Admission is free. Take Metro Transit nos. 2, 4, or 6.

Built in 1749, **St. Matthew's United Church** (★, 1479 Barrington St. (✆ **902/ 423-9209;** www.stmatts.ns.ca), is the oldest United Church building in Canada. The sanctuary was recently renovated and the grand pipe organ was completely rebuilt. It's open to the public in July and August, Tuesday to Saturday, from 10am to 5pm. Admission is free. Take Metro Transit nos. 2, 4, or 6.

St. Paul's Anglican Church (★, 1749 Argyle St. (✆ **902/429-2240;** www. stpaulshalifax.org), was built in 1749 (a rather odd and entertaining coincidence, given its street number). Not only is it the oldest Protestant church in Canada, but also it was Britain's first overseas cathedral, and is now a designated National Historic Site. It's a classic white Georgian building with lovely stained-glass windows. The original timbers were cut in Boston (still a British colony at the time) and shipped to Halifax. The burial vault underneath the church holds the remains of the illustrious British colonials of the period; St. Paul's is said to have more memorial tablets commemorating church members than any other church building in North America. The Halifax Explosion in 1917 left its mark, when a piece of flying debris was embedded in the wall over the memorial doors. St. Paul's was built with the help of an endowment from King George II. The Royal Pew, reserved for her Majesty the Queen and her appointed representatives, serves as an ongoing reminder of this. The church is open to the public Monday to Friday from 9am to 4pm. There are guided tours in summer. Admission is free. Take Metro Transit nos. 7, 9, or 18.

No visit to Halifax is complete without a turn around the **Old Burying Ground,** on the corner of Barrington Street and Spring Garden Road. The oldest existing stone marks the grave of John Connor, buried in 1754. Mr. Connor ran the first ferry across Halifax Harbour. It is also the final resting-place of Major General Robert Ross, the British general who burned Washington in the War of 1812. If you like history or old graveyards, you'll love this place. The Old Burying Ground is open from June to September, daily from 9am to 5pm. Admission is free.

4 Parks & Gardens

Halifax, known as the city of trees, has a variety of natural areas. Along with parks and gardens, there are shady boulevards to beat the summer heat, and green areas to enjoy a takeout lunch, or just kick back and read a book. Among the more unusual green areas are the **historic graveyards,** which are open to the public. They are outdoor museums documenting the history of the city's people. During June, July, and August, the grounds of the **Halifax Citadel** are a popular place for sunbathing and taking in an outdoor rock concert. For general inquiries, contact **Halifax Parks and Recreation Services** (✆ **902/490-4894**).

URBAN PARKS

The most popular and well-known park in the city is the **Halifax Public Gardens** (★★, on the corner of South Park Street and Spring Garden Road. Enjoy 17 acres of formal Victorian public gardens that have survived intact and relatively unspoiled in the heart of a modern city. The main entrance is at the corner of Spring Garden Road and South Park Street. The gardens are open from May through October. See "The Top Attractions" section, chapter 6, for a full review of the gardens.

The Commons (made up of the North Common and Central Common) is bordered by Robie, Cunard, North Park, and Trollope streets, as well as Bell

Road. Allocated in 1763 as grazing space for cattle and sheep, the Commons is considered the oldest park in Canada. It's open to the public year-round. The **North Common** sports 11 baseball diamonds, surrounded by a jogging track, with a beautiful water fountain in the center that is illuminated at night. When organized games are not scheduled, you'll often see an informal game of baseball, soccer, or football. In winter, the North Common is used for cross-country skiing. Mainly university students and adults use this area. The Commons are bisected by Cogswell Street. The **Central Common,** on the south side of Cogswell, is suited to young families: it has a swimming pool and spray-pool, a playground, and six tennis courts. Here, people also play cricket, soccer, basketball, touch football, field hockey, and rugby. Oh yes, you can in-line skate and skateboard here, too, on a specially paved area. Just a 10-minute walk up Bell Road from the Citadel, the Commons is a convenient stopping point for enjoying a picnic, playing a game of tag, or watching a game.

Victoria Park is located at the corner of Spring Garden and Tower roads and South Park Street. This park went through a facelift in 2002; the city replaced the asphalt walkways with bricks, created an **entertainment venue** in the open space in front of the Robbie Burns statue, and planted more shrubs and flowers.

Halifax's largest green area is **Point Pleasant Park** ★★, located in the south end of the city at the end of Tower Road. This park is an integral part of the city's present-day life, and of its history. In 1866, the Crown agreed to lease the lands of Point Pleasant Park to the people of Halifax for a term of 999 years at the most reasonable price of 1 shilling per year (about 10¢). Today, the park is used by Haligonians for hiking, cross-country skiing, jogging, picnicking, and walking their dogs. This is also one of the locations where Shakespeare by the Sea holds its open-air performances, in July and August. There are reams of pathways, uphill and down, through 186 acres of forest. Along these routes, you'll find decaying fortifications and remnants of gun batteries left from Britain's first defenses of Halifax, not to mention beautiful ocean views. Picnic areas with barbecues are dotted along the paths. Depending on what you want to see and do, you could spend anywhere from 1 to 3 hours here.

⎛Kids Time Out to Play

The Commons is a great place to take kids to get rid of some pent-up energy. There's always room to run on the North Common, then cross Cogswell Street to the Central Common for the swings and climbing apparatus. On hot days, little ones can cool off in the shallow spray-pool. The Commons is located northwest of the Halifax Citadel National Historic Site in the center of the city, bordered by Robie, Cunard, North Park, and Trollope streets, as well as Bell Road.

Cornwallis Park, also in the south end, is located across from **The Westin Nova Scotian Hotel,** on Barrington Street. The city has recently given this park new life. Along with open spaces, the play area has been expanded to include more equipment, and a heritage garden has been planted to commemorate the thousands of immigrants who passed through the nearby **Pier 21 Immigration building.**

In the city's north end, **Fort Needham Memorial Park** was originally part of the elaborate and layered defenses of the early city. Now, it's home to the **Halifax Explosion Memorial Bell Tower,** which overlooks the area devastated by the Halifax Explosion of December 6, 1917. It's located along Novalea Drive.

Another green area is located on the north side of Quinpool Road, just up from the Armdale Rotary. **Flynn Park** rambles up a hill sheltered by trees and dotted with picnic tables. Across busy Quinpool Road on the south side of the street is **Horseshoe Island Park,** which borders on the North West Arm. On Chebucto Road, between Mumford Road and Connaught Avenue, is **Saunders Park,** also the site of the original Halifax airport (closed in 1941). A memorial commemorates Donald Saunders, one of the airport's managers. Today, Saunders Park is an oasis for pedestrians and cyclists, along bustling Chebucto Road.

SUBURBAN AND RURAL GREEN SPACES

Hemlock Ravine Park ⍟ is located just outside of the Halifax Peninsula, on the west side of the Bedford Highway (route 2). This 197-acre park is actually a network of **five trails,** suitable for a variety of abilities, ages, and time allowances. The trails range from easy to steep and rugged. A map at the beginning of the trail system indicates each trail's level of difficulty. The trails are scattered with mushrooms in the fall and lady's slippers in the spring, along with blueberries, Indian pipe, lambkill, lichen, and ferns, in their seasons. The giant hemlock trees are impossible to miss—some of them are over 300 years old and 24.5m (80 ft.) tall. This is a great place for bird watching and observing wildlife. Be aware, however, that the signage throughout the trail network is inadequate in places, and the ravine can be slippery after a rainfall. Open fires are not permitted. To get to Hemlock Ravine Park, take the Bedford Highway, northeast past the Kearney Lake Road turnoff. Approximately 1km (.6 mile) farther on the east side is a round, white building, part of a former estate. Immediately opposite the white building is Kent Avenue. Turn west onto Kent Avenue and park in the parking lot on the left at the end of the street. Look for a pond a few meters (yards) to the west. This is the beginning of the park and trail system.

⌐Moments Julie's Pond

When Edward, Duke of Kent, arrived in Halifax in 1794 to serve as commander in chief of the Halifax Garrison, he was accompanied by his French mistress, Julie St. Laurent. He built an elaborate estate for her in what is now **Hemlock Ravine Park,** overlooking the shores of the Bedford Basin. (At that time, the land belonged to the Lieutenant Governor of Nova Scotia, Sir John Wentworth.) Now a public park, Hemlock Ravine Park boasts pathways that lead from the heart-shaped pond the duke created for Julie into an intricate five-trail system graced by towering hemlock trees. Only one building from the original estate remains today; the tiny, elegant music rotunda, perched on a hill between the Bedford Basin and the Bedford Highway.

Approximately 3km (1.8 miles) southwest of peninsular Halifax is **Sir Sandford Fleming Park** (also called The Dingle, meaning an Irish glen). The park was donated to Halifax in 1908 by Sir Sandford Fleming, creator of Standard

Time Zones, designer of Canada's first postage stamp, and engineer for the Canadian Pacific Railway. The 95-acre park has two major walking trails through four natural habitats: second-growth woodlands, a heath barren, a salt-water habitat, and a frog pond. Stop and visit the **Dingle Tower,** built of stone with two bronze lions at its foot, with a **great view of the North West Arm.** The tower was dedicated in 1912 to commemorate 150 years of representative government in Nova Scotia. The park is open year-round, while the tower is open June through August from dawn to dusk. Admission is free. To get to Sir Sandford Fleming Park, from the Armdale Rotary, follow Purcell's Cove Road (route 253) southwest. Watch for the wooden sign for the park on the east side of the road. Drive slowly, as the road to the parking area is narrow.

5 Festivals & Events

Halifax is home to several internationally acclaimed events, and if you are in the city during one of them, be sure to make your dinner reservations early as the city gets really busy.

The **Nova Scotia International Tattoo,** Halifax Metro Centre (© 902/451-1221; www.nstattoo.ca) runs for ten days each summer, beginning the last Friday in June until the following Sunday. It's an exciting, action-packed, color-ful display of dance, military maneuvers, pipe and drum bands, comedy, pageantry, and stunts, with over 2,000 performers from Nova Scotia and around the world. Tickets are C$26–$29 (US$17.35–$19.35) for adults and children 13 to 18, C$23–$27 (US$15.35–$18) for seniors and children 12 and under. **Prestige seats** are available for C$40 (US$26.70). For tickets call © 902/451-1221 or write to The Nova Scotia International Tattoo, Halifax Metro Centre, PO Box 955, 1800 Argyle St., Halifax, NS B3J 2V9.

The **Atlantic Jazz Festival** (© 902/492-2225; www.jazzeast.com/jazzfest. htm) is held at various locations throughout the city during early July. Profes-sional jazz entertainers from all over the world come together for concerts and improv sessions. The music is free daily from 12 noon to 6:00pm, on the du Maurier Stage, at the corner of Spring Garden Road and Queen Street, and there are evening concerts to fit every taste and budget in the clubs and bars through-out the city. Ticket prices range from C$10 (US$7) to C$30 (US$20). Advance tickets for all events go on sale in late May and are available from the **Neptune Theatre Box Office** (© 800/565-7345 or 902/429-7070). Tickets are also available on location until sold out. An **All Events Pass, Festival Jazz Sampler,** and **Jazz Encounters Sampler** are available.

The **Atlantic Film Festival** (© 902/422-3456; www.atlanticfilm.com) is an annual nine-day festival held in September celebrating the best in local and international film. Most of the films are shown at the **Park Lane Cinema,** Park Lane Shopping Centre, 5657 Spring Garden Road (© 902/423-4598; www. famousplayers.com/theatre.asp?TheatreID=38) and the **Oxford Theatre,** 6408 Quinpool Road (© 902/423-7488). Ticket prices range from C$9.50–$30 (US$6.35–$20) depending on the genre and length of film.

Shakespeare by the Sea (© 902/422-0295; www.shakespearebythesea.ca) presents Shakespearean classics in a whole new light. Most of the plays are presented outdoors in **Point Pleasant Park.** The highlight of the planned 2003 season is *Hamlet.* The special July 1 presentation of *A Midsummer Night's Dream* is performed at 4am on the Seawalk Stage at **Casino Nova Scotia,**

so that the climax of the play coincides with sunrise. The company also offers a family-oriented production each year. Several of the plays, including the family-oriented one, are allocated as donation performances; a donation of C$10 (US$6.70) per person is suggested. These tickets cannot be reserved in advance; you pay as you enter at the **Cambridge Battery in Point Pleasant Park.** Ticketed performances in 2003 include *Hamlet* and *A Midsummer Night's Dream.* Tickets can be reserved in advance by phoning the Shakespeare by the Sea office (© **902/422-0295**), or at the door. The price for *Hamlet* tickets is C$30 (US$20). At press time, the price for *A Midsummer Night's Dream* tickets had not been set. Call for more information. ***Note:*** Bring your own chairs or blankets, as a limited number of chairs are available, and for a C$2 (US$1.35) rental fee. It's also a good idea to bring a picnic lunch, bring babies in strollers, and keep dogs on leashes.

The **International Busker Festival** (© **866/773-0655** or 902/429-3910; www.buskers.ns.sympatico.ca) takes place in mid August and runs for eleven days. It's a combination of improv and carefully timed acts, ranging from comedy to music to magic to gymnastic feats. The festival takes place along the waterfront, beginning near **Historic Properties,** 1868 Upper Water Street, and meanders along the boardwalk for approximately 1.6km (1 mile). Although there is no official charge for the entertainment, you'll usually see an open instrument case or a hat passed so that you can show your appreciation. Along with the buskers (also known as street performers), there are beer tents and especially for children there are clowns and face painting.

If you happen to be in Halifax on December 31, and want to bring in the New Year with a bang, take in **New Year's Eve at the Grand Parade,** opposite City Hall, 1841 Argyle Street. The Halifax Regional Municipality puts on an evening of music, entertainment, and fireworks. It starts at 10:30pm and the fireworks follow the countdown at midnight. This is an all-ages, family-oriented event. Make sure you dress in plenty of layers and bring something warm to drink. For information and weather updates call © **902/490-6776**.

6 Especially for Kids

Many of Halifax's most popular attractions (see "The Top Attractions," earlier in this chapter) are ideally suited for families with children. Kids will have plenty to see and do at the **Art Gallery of Nova Scotia,** the **Halifax Citadel National Historic Site,** the **Maritime Museum of the Atlantic,** the **Museum of Natural History,** the **Pier 21 National Historic Site,** and the **Nova Scotia Sport Hall of Fame.** Traveling with your children creates special memories. To make sure they're happy ones, it's best to build time into your schedule for their interests and activities, keeping in mind their attention spans. If your children are preschoolers, shorter excursions are your best bet, with time for naps in between. Most children between 6 and 12 enjoy spending an hour at a museum—at least, one that has interactive displays and exhibits that interest them. Teens can spend all day at one spot if it's something they like, or only 5 minutes if it's something they don't—so be sure to involve them in the planning.

The mission of the **Discovery Centre** (★, 1593 Barrington St. (© **902/492-4422;** www.discoverycentre.ns.ca), is to make science and technology enjoyable and interesting to the public. It's a truly hands-on attraction, with experiment stations, computer quizzes, and optical illusions. There are two floors of activities, and a gift shop with scientific games, toys, and books. The center will keep your kids busy for a good 2 hours. Admission is C$6 (US$4) for adults, C$4 (US$2.70) for seniors, students, and children 2 to 18, free for children 1 and under. Open year-round Monday to Saturday from 10am to 5pm, Sunday 1pm to 5pm.

With a history of pirates and privateers, shipwrecks and sailors, Halifax has its share of ghost stories. Listen to some of them with your kids on one of the tours operated by **Halifax Ghost Walk** (© **902/466-1323** or 902/469-6716; macrev@ns.sympatico.ca). Tours are held from June to September approximately three times a week, rain or shine. Meet at the Old Town Clock, on Brunswick Sreet, at 8:30pm. The schedule varies, so be sure to call first. The tour costs C$9 (US$6) for adults, C$6.50 (US$4.33) for seniors and children 13 to 18, free for children 12 and under. Group tours can be arranged year-round. Another tour that children age 8 to 13 will especially enjoy (along with mom and dad) is that run by **Harbour Hopper Tours** (© **902/490-8687;** www.harbourhopper.com). Riding in an amphibious vehicle, high above average-size cars, you'll travel around the downtown streets and then take to the water for a trip around the harbor. Tours depart from 1675 Lower Water Street, **on the north side of the Maritime Museum of the Atlantic.** Tours are held from May to October from 9am to 9:30pm, and run every 30 to 45 minutes. The tour costs C$22.50 (US$15) for adults, C$21.50 (US$14.33) for seniors, C$19.95 (US$13.30) for students and children 16 to 18, C$13.95 (US$9.30) for children 6 to 15, free for children 5 and under. The family rate is C$65.95 (US$44).

Kids Nova Scotia Sport Hall of Fame

This is more than a museum, although it does contain exhibits representing 100 years of sports artifacts and photographs. There are lots of interactive displays—one that's especially fun lets you shoot hoops on a real basketball court or shoot pucks on a hockey rink. Challenge yourself by playing a computerized trivia game about the 300-plus Hall of Famers. Located at 1645 Granville St. (© **902/421-1266;** www.novascotiasport halloffame.com).

Ships inspire kids. Spend an hour on the **Halifax waterfront** ⭐ and gawk with your youngsters at the freighters, tug boats, Tall Ships, and cruise liners, plus sailboats, hovercraft, ferries, and naval ships.

For a special shopping treat, take your children to **Freak Lunchbox,** 1723 Barrington St. (© **902/420-9151**), a candy shop with such sucrose-laced offerings as caffeinated peppermints and imported chocolate bars. You can't miss the "Great Wall of Pez," with stacks of Pez candy and dozens of different Pez dispensers. Plus you'll find sugary memories from your own childhood on the shelves.

7 Organized Tours

A guided tour is a good way to get your bearings in Halifax and scout out spots you may want to return to later on your own. Spend a few hours traveling around the city by bus or van, or head out for a shorter tour on foot. The excursions in this section will take you to many of the top attractions covered earlier in this chapter.

HARBOR & OCEAN TOURS

Tours aboard the 39-m (130-ft.) sailing vessel *Silva* are operated by **Canadian Sailing Expeditions,** Lower Water St. at Queen's Wharf (*C* **902/429-1474;** www.canadiansailingexpeditions.com). This historical Tall Ship sailing experience is available in June on weekends, and from July to October daily, depending on the weather. Boarding times are 9:45am, 11:45am, 1:45pm, 3:45pm, and the tour lasts about 90 minutes. The cost of the tour is C$19.95 (US$13.30) for adults, C$18.95 (US$12.65) for seniors, C$19.95 (US$13.30) for children 13 to 18, C$13.95 (US$9.30) for children 5 to 12, free for children 4 and under.

Murphy's on the Water, 1751 Lower Water St. (*C* **902/420-1015;** www. murphysonthewater.com), offers a variety of tours from May to September. There's a 2-hour scenic harbor tour aboard the stern-wheeler *Harbour Queen,* which sails daily at 10am and 2pm. During the peak season in July and August, they also offer a 6:30pm sailing. The cost is C$19.95 (US$13.30) for adults, C$18.95 (US$12.65) for seniors, C$14.95 (US$10) for children 5 to 16. A family rate of C$65.95 (US$44) is available for 2 adults and up to 3 children under 16. The *Harbour Queen* also offers a **dinner cruise** Thursday to Sunday from 6:30 to 8:30 pm. The cost is C$39.95 (US$26.65) for adults, seniors, and children 16 to 18, C$29.95 (US$20) for children 15 and under. The **buffet meal** includes a choice of Beef Bordelaise or Haddock Roulade, with a wide variety of salads, vegetables, and dessert. Finally, you can party on the harbor aboard the *Harbour Queen,* and dance to the house band on Fridays and Saturdays from 9:30 pm to midnight. The cost is C$17.95 (US$12) per person. Alcoholic beverages are extra.

The 2½-hour nature and whale-watching tour on the *Haligonian III* offers an in-depth commentary on the marine life of the local waters. She sails from May to September daily at 10:30am, 1:30pm, 4:30pm, and also at 7:30pm during July and August. Tickets are C$26.95 (US$18) for adults, C$25.95 (US$17.30) seniors, C$16.95 (US$11.30) for children 5 to 16. There's a family rate of C$89.95 (US$60) for two adults and up to three children under 16.

Murphy's also provides a **Tall Ship cruise** aboard the *Mar II,* a two-masted, Ketch sailing vessel. The lunch cruise is a 90-minute tour of the harbor, with lunch provided, leaving at noon. Tickets are C$21.95 (US$16.65) for adults, C$20.95 (US$14) for seniors, C$16.95 (US$11.30) for children 5 to 16. The family rate is C$74.95 (US$50) for two adults and up to three children under 16. They also offer afternoon cruises at 2pm and 4pm; a cocktail cruise at 6:30 pm; a party cruise at 8:30 pm; and a moonlight cruise at 10:30 pm. Tickets for all of these cruises cost C$19.95 (US$13.30) for adults, C$18.95 (US$12.65) for seniors, C$14.95 (US$10) for children 5 to 16. The family rate is C$69.95 (US$46.65) for two adults and up to three children under 16.

If you want to make your way to **Peggy's Cove,** home of the most photographed lighthouse in North America—and perhaps the world—the **Peggy's Cove Express,** 1751 Lower Water St. (*C* **902/857-9319;** www.peggyscove.com), takes you round-trip by boat or bus from Cable Wharf to Peggy's Cove. The package, which includes some whale watching and a bowl of chowder wharf-side at Peggy's Cove, costs C$59.95 (US$40) per person. The tour leaves from Cable Wharf, at Lower Water Street, by boat at 10:30am, or by bus at noon. The return trip, by boat or bus, leaves Peggy's Cove at 4:30pm. See chapter 10 for a side trip to Peggy's Cove.

WALKING TOURS

Explore Halifax's rich tradition of pirates, haunted houses, buried treasure, and ghosts on the **Halifax Ghost Walk** (© 902/466-1323 or 902/469-6716; macrev@ns.sympatico.ca). Tours are held from June to September at 8:30pm on scheduled evenings, and last 90 minutes. Call to find out exact days. Tours begin at the Old Town Clock on Brunswick Street, and cost C$9 (US$6) for adults, C$6.50 (US$4.33) seniors and students, free for children 12 and under.

BUS, LIMO & RICKSHAW TOURS

Why not see the city in style—in a limo? **Black Cab London Taxi/Limo Tours**, 1869 Upper Water St. (© 800/928-7245, 902/425-2118 or 902/449-0299; www.blackcab.ca), shows you Halifax's connection to the *Titanic,* tours the area where the 1917 Halifax Explosion took place, and more. The company also offers a **historic pub tour** (Granite Brewery, Old Triangle Pub, and O'Carroll's), and a **Black Tie tour option,** as well. The Halifax tours are available year-round by appointment. However, tours from June to November run daily from 9am to 4pm, departing every hour on the hour from **Historic Properties,** at 1869 Upper Water St. Rates are C$19 (US$12.70) for adults, seniors, and children 13 to 18, C$14 (US$9.35) for children 12 and under. The pub tour leaves either from Historic Properties, or you can be picked up at a downtown hotel, at 6:30pm and 8:30pm. This tour costs C$29 (US$19.35) for adults over 21.

Black Heritage Tours (© 902/462-4495; www3.ns.sympatico.ca/black. heritage) offers educational and sightseeing tours, with an emphasis on the history of blacks in Nova Scotia. The owners are multi-generational African Nova Scotians. Tours are available from mid May to mid October and year-round by appointment. Guides will pick you up at your hotel and provide an in-depth tour of Halifax, Dartmouth, and outlying areas. The tour lasts approximately 3 hours. **Canadian Connection Tours** (© 800/864-7109 or 902/429-2543; cctc@ns.sympatico.ca) organizes tours of Halifax and other parts of Nova Scotia and will build a customized schedule based on what you want to see. Tour guides speak Japanese, English, and French.

If you don't mind a bit of a jerky ride, **Greater Halifax Rickshaw Service** (© 902/455-6677) offers a slower paced tour of the city from May through September. The system operates much like a taxi service where you can hail a rickshaw or call to have one pick you up. There's room for two in the rickshaw and rates are variable depending on distance and terrain. Guided tours are also available.

8 Outdoor Pursuits

BEACHES

While there are rocky beaches in Point Pleasant Park, and sandy beaches along the North West Arm and at Sir Sandford Fleming Park, it's not advisable to swim in the water due to pollution. For spots suitable for splashing around or doing a few laps, see the section on swimming, further on. Or see chapter 10, for a day trip along the eastern shore of the province and a variety of sandy ocean beaches.

BIKING

Halifax is in the process of designing bicycle lanes within the city. For now, the best place for cycling is the 39km (24 miles) of forested trails in beautiful **Point Pleasant Park.** *Note:* Bikes aren't allowed in the park on weekends and holidays.

The park's main gate is located at the end of Young Avenue, in the south end of the city.

If you're near the waterfront, and want to rent a bike, moped, or scooter, drop in to **Harbour Bike & Sea Rentals,** 1781 Lower Water St. (© **902/423-1185;** www3.ns.sympatico.ca/bikeandsea). The cost to rent a moped is C$14 (US$9.50) for 1 hour, C$46 (US$31) for a half day, and C$64 (US$43) for a full day. Bicycles are C$6 (US$4) for 1 hour, C$17 (US$11.50) for a half day, and $C25 (US$17) for a full day. Scooters cost C$7 (US$5) for 2 hours. You can also rent wheelchairs for C$3 (US$2) per hour, bicycle baby seats for C$5 (US$3.50) per day, strollers for C$3 (US$2) per hour, bicycle carracks for C$5 (US$3.50) per day, and binoculars for C$5 (US$3.50) per day.

CANOEING, KAYAKING & SAILING

The **North West Arm** is a beautiful body of water that is generally calm enough for kayaking and canoeing. The **Bedford Basin** is also a safe area for smaller craft. It's fine to sail in the open harbor, although you must be alert to other boats and ships, and aware of the weather.

You can rent canoes, kayaks, and sailboats while you're in Halifax. Several locations will also provide lessons. The **Armdale Yacht Club,** 40 Purcell's Cove Rd. (© **902/477-4617;** www.armdaleyachtclub.ns.ca), provides sailing instruction, plus mooring and supplies for visiting boats. The **Atlantic Yachting Academy** (© **902/457-3845;** http://strategis.ic.gc.ca/SSG/rb00232e.html) also offers sailing instruction.

St. Mary's Boat Club, 1641 Fairfield Rd. (© **902/490-4688**), on the North West Arm, offers sailing, kayaking, and canoeing lessons and rentals for all ages. There's also a play area near the club.

CROSS-COUNTRY SKIING

You can enjoy the pleasures of skiing cross-country on ungroomed trails at **Point Pleasant Park, Sir Sandford Fleming Park** (on the Loop Road Trail), and in **Hemlock Ravine Park.** Contact **Cross-Country Ski Nova Scotia** (© **902/ 425-5450 ext. 316;** www.crosscountryskins.homestead.com/crosscountry skins.html), for more information.

Cross-country skis, boots, and poles can be rented from **The Trail Shop,** 6210 Quinpool Rd. (© **902/423-8736;** www.trailshop.com), for C$20 (US$13.50) per day or C$35 (US$23.50) for a weekend. A C$75 (US$50) credit card deposit is required on each rental. The staff can give you instruction tips.

DOWNHILL SKIING

The nearest downhill facility is **Ski Martock,** RR#3, Windsor, NS B0N 2T0 (© **902/798-9501;** www.martock.com), with natural and man-made snow from mid-December to early April. It has day and night skiing and a variety of outdoor activities, making it one of the most popular winter locations for families in Nova Scotia. Plus, there's a lodge where you can warm your toes and satisfy your hunger. The best time to visit is early in the week, when you'll have a lot more room on the runs. It's also a good time to take group lessons, as the group will probably be much smaller than on weekends. There's also a snowboard park, cross-country skiing trails, and a new skating canal. The longest of the seven runs at the site is 1.6km (1 mile) with a vertical rise of 182m (600 ft.).

Lift tickets cost C$28 (US$19) for adults, seniors, and children 16 and up, C$16 (US$11) for children 7–15, free for children 6 and under. Learn-to-ski lessons cost C$35 (US$23.50) for a 1-hour private lesson.

Downhill skis, cross-country skis, snowboards, and other equipment can be rented for a full day for C$20 (US$13.50) for adults, seniors, and students 15 and up, C$16 (US$11) for children 15 and under.

To get to Ski Martock from Halifax, take highway 101 west toward the Annapolis Valley for approximately 50km (31 miles). Take exit 5A (the Windsor exit) and turn south onto Highway 14. Within a few minutes you'll see the signs for Ski Martock.

Ski Wentworth (★, PO Box 1202, Truro, NS B2N 5H1 (© **902/548-2089;** www.skiwentworth.ca) is approximately 1.5 hours north of Halifax. This is a large ski hill and the runs here are longer and more challenging than those at Ski Martock. The longest of the 23 trails is 3.7km (2.3 miles), with a vertical rise of 303m (1,000 ft.)—the most vertical drop in Nova Scotia. Be prepared for a crowd, especially on weekends, when people travel from all over Nova Scotia and New Brunswick to take in Wentworth's skiing. If at all possible, try to visit on a weekday.

Lift tickets for a full day cost C$35 (US$23.50) for adults, seniors, and students 12–18, C$29 (US$19.50) for children 6–11, free for children 5 and under. Rope tow tickets for the day cost C$7 (US$5) for adults, seniors, and children 5 to 18, free for children 4 and under. A full-day combination rental and lift package for skiing costs C$50 (US$33.50) for adults, seniors, and children 12 to 18, C$40 (US$27) for children 11 and under. The full-day snowboard combination package costs C$55 (US$37) for adults, seniors, and children 12 to 18, C$45 (US$30) for children 11 and under.

Learn-to-ski lessons are available for C$34.95 (US$24) per person and include a 90-minute lesson, ski equipment rental, and lift access. A beginner snowboarding lesson, equipment rental, and lift access is C$39.95 (US$27) per person.

Skis and snowboards are available for rent. A per-day package including skis, poles, and boots is C$25 (US$17) for adults, seniors, and children 12 to 18, C$22.50 (US$15) for children 6 to 11, C$20 (US$15) for children 5 and under. Per-day snowboard rentals (including boots) cost C$30 (US$20) for adults, seniors, and children 12 to 18, C$25 (US$17) for children 11 and under.

If you choose to stay the night, there is a lodge on site and other accommodations nearby, such as the **All Seasons Bed & Breakfast,** 14371 Hwy. 104 Wentworth Valley, NS B0M 1Z0 (© **888/879-5558** or 902/548-2994; www.bbcanada.com/1628.html), just a 3-minute drive from the ski hill. The **Wentworth Valley Inn,** 14962 Highway 4, Wentworth, NS B0M 1Z0 (© **877/548-2202** or 902/548-2202; http://home.istar.ca/%7Epaisley/index.html) is 1km (.6 mile) from the ski hill.

To get to Ski Wentworth from Halifax, take Highway 102 to Truro, then the exit for New Brunswick via Highway 104. Take exit 11 to Wentworth & Folly Lake. You can't miss the SKI WENTWORTH signs, or the runs themselves.

For more information on downhill skiing in Nova Scotia, contact **Alpine Ski Nova Scotia** (© **902/425-5450 ext. 349;** http://142.176.164.85/asns/).

GOLF

Nova Scotia has improved and increased the number of golf courses in recent years, now there's more than 60 courses throughout the province. The greater Halifax golf experience ranges from links with magnificent harbor views to tranquil rolling greens beside peaceful rivers.

Within the city peninsula, you can golf at the **Fairview Hills Golf Centre**, 425 Main Ave. (© **902/443-2230;** www.fairviewhillsgolf.com), a 9-hole, par-3 course with a pitch and putt, driving range, practice bunker, putting green, and mini-golf. Green fees are C$9 (US$6) for adults, C$6 (US$4) for seniors and children 15 and under. Club rental (3 clubs) is C$5 (US$3.50). The course is open from May to October, daily from 8am to dusk.

For something more challenging, take a 20-minute drive outside the city to the **Glen Arbour Golf Course** ⭐, 40 Clubhouse Lane, Hammonds Plains, NS B4B 1T4 (© **877/835-4653** or 902/835-4944; www.glenarbour.com), a new 18-hole, par 72 championship course designed by Graham Cooke, with a 9-hole, par-3 practice facility.

From July 1 to September 15, green fees are C$115 (US$77) for adults and seniors, C$45 (US$30) for children 12 to 18. From September 16 to the end of October, and from the beginning of May to June 30, green fees are C$75 (US$50) for adults and seniors, C$45 (US$30) for children 12 to 18. Play time from the beginning of May to the end of the season is 7am to dusk. Club rental is C$35 (US$23.50), shoes are C$15 (US$10).

In **Dartmouth,** the **Grandview Golf and Country Club,** 431 Crane Hill Rd. Westphal (© **902/435-3278** or 902/435-3767; www.nsga.ns.ca/GRAND/ GV.HTM), was designed by Bill Robinson, of Cornish & Robinson Golf Course Designers. Grandview is a championship-style course that has hosted a number of **Nova Scotia Golf Association Provincial Championships.** From Monday to Friday, green fees are C$49.75 (US$33.50); on Saturday and Sunday and holidays, they're C$53 (US$35.50) for all golfers. Children must be 10 years old to play. To get to the Grandview Golf and Country Club from Halifax, take the A. Murray MacKay Bridge to Dartmouth, to the Highway 7 exit, and proceed east.

The **Oakfield Golf & Country Club,** 6055 Highway 2, (© **902/861-2658** or 902/860-2124; www.nsga.ns.ca/oakfield/of.htm) is a semi-private 18-hole course that's about a 30 km (19 mi) drive northeast of Halifax. Oakfield was opened in 1962 and started out as an open course. Since then trees and shrubs have been planted and the difficulty of the course has been upgraded. Tee times are subject to availability as it is primarily a members club. Green fees are C$75 (US$50) for all golfers. Children must be 10 years old to play. To get to the Oakfield Golf & Country Club from Halifax, take the Bedford Highway, (route 2) through Bedford and follow the signs for Highway 2 and Waverly/Grand Lake. Or, take Highway 102 and take exit 7 to Grand Lake.

The **Granite Springs Golf Club,** 4441 Prospect Rd. (Route 333) Bayside, NS B3Z 1L6 (© **902/852-4653;** www.nsga.ns.ca/granite/gs.htm), is an 18-hole course about 40 minutes southwest of Halifax, **on the way to Peggy's Cove.** In May, green fees are C$35 (US$23.50) daily for all golfers; from June to September, green fees are C$50 (US$33.50) Monday to Thursday, and C$55 (US$37) Friday to Sunday and holidays for all golfers; in October, green fees are

C$40 (US$27) for all golfers. Children must be 10 years old to play. Club rentals are C$20 (US$13.50) per day.

About an hour west of Halifax is the **Osprey Ridge Golf Club** *★*, 270 Harold Whynot Rd., Bridgewater, NS B4V 2W6 (*☎* **902/543-6666;** www. ospreyridge.ns.ca). Nominated for *Golf Digest*'s "Best New Course in Canada" in 1999, the course was designed by Graham Cooke. The season runs from mid-April to early November, and the course is open from 6:30am until dusk. Green fees are C$56.35 (US$38) for all golfers. Children must be 10 years old to play. To get to the Osprey Ridge Golf Club from Halifax, take Highway 103 to Bridgewater, then take exit 12 and turn north. Turn east onto Pine Grove Road and continue to Harold Whynot Road. Turn south and continue to the club.

A beautiful 18-hole course plus a separate 9-hole course lies inland, northeast of Halifax, at the **River Oaks Golf Club,** Highway 357, Meaghers Grant, NS (*☎* **902/384-2033;** www.riveroaksgolfclub.com). The season runs from May 1 to October 31, and the course is open from 7am to 10pm. Green fees are C$35 (US$23.50) for all golfers Monday to Friday, C$38 (US$25.50) for all golfers Saturday and Sunday. Children must be 10 years old to play. To get to the River Oaks Golf Club from Halifax, take Highway 107 to route 357, then north 20km (12.5 miles) to Meaghers Grant.

Less than an hour north of Halifax is **Fox Hollow Golf Club,** Box 548, Stewiacke, NS B0N 2J0, (*☎* **902/639-2535;** www.nsga.ns.ca/fox/fh.htm). Peter Davies designed this 18-hole course, in a pastoral setting. The season runs from May 1 to October 31, and the course is open from 7am to dusk. Green fees are C$35 (US$23.50) for all golfers Monday to Thursday, C$37 (US$25) for all golfers Friday to Sunday. Children must be 10 years old to play. To get to the Fox Hollow Golf Club from Halifax, take Highway 102 to exit 11 to Highway 2, turn south and travel approximately 1 km (.6 mile).

For information on all available courses, contact **Golf Nova Scotia** (*☎* **800/565-0001;** www.golfnovascotia.com).

HIKING

Easy hiking on wide trails can be found in **Point Pleasant Park** *★*. There are 39km (24 miles) of trails winding through forests and along the ocean, and you can choose a trail depending on the time you want to spend hiking. To walk from one end to the other would take approximately 2 hours round trip, however there are many shorter trails. The entrance is at the south end of Young Avenue or Tower Road. Maps of the trails are available at the International Visitor Information Centre at the corner of Barrington and Sackville streets, plus there are large signs in the park showing the trails.

Shorter, but wilder and steeper hiking challenges are found at **Hemlock Ravine Park** *★*. This network of trails, five in all, has many starting points, ending points, and loops, for all types of hikers. There are some simple trails for groups and families, longer sections for a good workout, and more difficult trails for the serious hiker. Maps of the trails are usually available at the park entrance. Go north on the Bedford Highway, past the Kearney Lake exit, and look for Kent Avenue on the west side.

Across the harbor from Halifax is the **Trans Canada Trail.** It winds from Sullivan's Pond along Lake Banook and Lake Mic Mac to connect with the trails along the Shubenacadie Canal and in Shubie Park. There are 7km (4.4 miles) of wide path, accessible at a variety of locations, including Sullivan's Pond, the south end of Lake Banook, Graham's Grove, Fairbanks Center off Locks Road, and Shubie Park. Maps are available at the Visitor Information Centre at the Dartmouth Ferry Terminal at Alderney Gate.

ICE SKATING

Due to Halifax's temperate climate, outdoor ice surfaces in the peninsula area don't freeze safely enough for skating. Still, ice-skating—both figure skating and hockey—is popular, and there are a number of indoor arenas in the city where you can strap on a pair of skates in the winter.

Dalhousie Memorial Arena, 6185 South St. (© **902/494-8833;** www. athletics.dal.ca), offers varied skating programs throughout the week.

Other locations include the **Centennial Arena,** 27 Vimy Ave. (© **902/445-4080**); the **Halifax Forum,** 2901 Windsor St. (© **902/490-4614**); the **Halifax Metro Centre,** 1800 Argyle St. (© **902/421-8000**); and the arena at **Saint Mary's University,** Tower Rd. (© **902/420-5424**). It's a good idea to call ahead to verify posted skating times, as they can often change as a result of rescheduled local hockey games or rehearsals.

SWIMMING

Due to pollution in Halifax Harbour and the North West Arm, swimming is best done at your hotel or in city pools. Fortunately there are plenty of places to cool off, either with a quick dip in the summer, or after a workout during the winter months.

Centennial Swimming Pool, 1970 Gottingen St. (© **902/490-7219**), has the only 10-m (32.5-ft.) diving platform in the Maritimes, plus an Olympic-size pool. **Dalplex,** part of the Dalhousie University complex, 6260 South St. (© **902/494-3372),** has a 50-m (163-ft.) Olympic-size pool; 1-m (3-ft.), 3-m (10-ft.), 5-m (16-ft.) diving platforms; plus a Bubbler, creating lots of water bubbles for children's enjoyment, and a Tarzan rope. The **Needham Pool,** 3372 Devonshire Ave. (© **902/490-4633**), has an 18-m (60-ft.) pool, with a Tarzan rope and separate tot dock where smaller children can play safely. **The North-cliffe Center,** 111 Clayton Park Dr. (© **902/490-4690**), has a 25-m (80-ft.) pool, diving boards, slides, and tot docks.

There are two coed **YMCAs** in Halifax. One is located at 1565 South Park St. (© **902/423-9622**). The other is at 1239 Barrington St. (© **902/423-6162;** www.ywcahalifax.com). Be sure to call ahead to confirm times. For other inquiries, contact the **Halifax Regional Municipality Parks and Recreation Services** at © **902/490-4894.**

7

City Strolls

When Halifax was founded in 1749, it was compact and organized, and most people had to walk everywhere. In a way, nothing much has changed in 250 years. Sure, there are more streets, and lots of vehicles, but people still find walking to be the best way to get around the city. That is, if they want to discover the real Halifax, the city that has endured explosions and riots, and enchanted people from 18th-century royalty to 21st-century film stars.

Since peninsular Halifax is a relatively small area, most of the museums, landmarks, and other attractions are within walking distance of one another. The walking tours in this section cover the downtown core of the city, the waterfront area, and a collection of universities, parks, and interesting homes. The length of each walk varies from 30 minutes to 2 hours, but you can stretch them further if you stop off at any of the attractions along the way.

WALKING TOUR 1	HISTORIC HALIFAX

Start:	Neptune Theatre, 1593 Argyle St. Metro Transit nos. 7, 9, or 18.
Finish:	Historic Properties, 1869 Upper Water St.
Distance:	Approximately 1.5km (1 mile); 30 to 45 minutes.
Best Time:	In warm weather, between 9am and noon. In cold weather, 11am to 3pm.
Worst Time:	Whenever there is wind and rain, or when the sidewalks are icy.

Wherever you walk in Halifax, it seems you're never more than a block away from something historic. So forget the boredom of your high school history class—get out there and touch, see, and experience Halifax history.

The tour begins at:

❶ The Neptune Theatre

Theater has been the lifeblood of 1593 Argyle Street since 1915, when a vaudeville theater opened, called The Strand. After a serious fire in 1926, and a series of renovations and periods of redecorating, it reopened in 1928 as the Garrick Repertory Theater, only to close a year later due to the stock market crash of 1929. The next phase of its life, from 1930 to 1963, was spent as a cinema. **Neptune Theatre** (© **902/ 429-7070;** www.neptunetheatre.com) was born that year and claimed the

site as its own. It's undergone even more renovations since then, including a major C$12-million (US$8.6-million) reconstruction/renovation completed in 1997. Today, as in 1915, audiences enjoy the Neptune's entertainment (see chapter 9).

Walk down Sackville St. to Barrington St. and turn left. Continue to walk north along Barrington St. until you see:

❷ The Nova Scotia Centre for Craft and Design

Wealthy merchants built many of the buildings in this area in the late 1800s. No. 1672 belonged to George Wright, a local developer who was one of 33 millionaires on the maiden voyage of the *Titanic.* The talent of modern Nova Scotian craftspeople is on display at No. 1683, in the **Mary E. Black Gallery,** part of the Nova Scotia Centre for Craft and Design (see chapter 6).

Turn left on Prince St. and walk uphill to the corner of Argyle St. to:

❸ Carleton House
The large golden building, **Carleton House** is Halifax's oldest residential building (1759). Today, it is home to Dalhousie University's **Costume Studies Museum.**

Tips Four-Season Walking

Because Halifax is a maritime city and the climate is temperate, dressing in layers is a wise decision, as even the warmest days can have cool breezes, and the coldest days can become too warm for heavy coats if you're continually in the sun. City streets during the months of December through March can be messy with snow, slush and/or ice. Waterproof footwear with a good tread makes navigating safer and much more enjoyable.

Walk north along Argyle St. On your right is:

❹ St. Paul's Anglican Church
St. Paul's Anglican Church is the oldest building in Halifax (1750), and the first Protestant church in Canada (see chapter 6). It was Britain's first overseas "cathedral." Its burial vault holds the remains of important British colonials.

The church faces:

❺ The Grand Parade
This is a military parade ground from Halifax's earliest days, and still a central public gathering place. The Cenotaph in front of St. Paul's commemorates those who served in the two World Wars and the Korean conflict.

At the opposite end of the Grand Parade is:

❻ City Hall
This is a fine example of Victorian architecture, built in 1888 and now the seat of government for the Halifax Regional Municipality (H.R.M.).

Look up Carmichael St. to Citadel Hill, where you will see:

❼ The Old Town Clock
This is one of Halifax's most famous landmarks. Prince Edward, Duke of Kent, arranged for a turret clock to be manufactured for the Halifax garrison before his return to England in 1800. The clock officially began keeping time for the garrison and residents of Halifax in 1803. In its early years, the clock was used as a guardroom, as well as a residence for the clock's caretaker and his family.

Head to 1744 Argyle St., site of the Five Fishermen restaurant, and you will see the location of the:

❽ Former Victoria School of Art and Design
Built in 1817, the large wooden structure at the corner of Argyle and Carmichael streets was first a school—known as The Old National School—and the oldest school building still standing in Halifax. It later housed the Victoria School of Art and Design, founded in 1887 and now known as the Nova Scotia College of Art & Design. One of the patrons of the Victoria School was **Anna Leonowens,** whose earlier experiences as governess to the King of Siam's children formed the basis for the musical *The King and I.*

Walk across the Grand Parade and downhill on George St. for two blocks. Look one block straight ahead to the bottom of George St., where you will see:

9 The Celtic Cross

This large stone cross was dedicated to the original Irish settlers who came to Halifax in 1749. Unused to pioneer life and the harsh weather conditions, many of them died that first year.

Turn right onto Hollis St. On your left is the:

10 Art Gallery of Nova Scotia

This is the home of the province's impressive collection of regional, national, and international art. The fine Victorian-Italianate facade of the building dates back to 1864, when the 3.5-m (12-ft.) statue of Britannia looked down on an outdoor Farmers Market, active on this site for more than 100 years. (See "The Top Attractions" in chapter 6.)

TAKE A BREAK
Enjoy a cup of coffee or tea, a soft drink or juice, along with a sandwich or yummy dessert at the **Cheapside Café**, 1723 Hollis St. (© 902/425-4494), on the main floor of the Art Gallery of Nova Scotia.

On the other side of Hollis St. is:

11 Province House

Built between 1811 and 1818, this fine Georgian building was home to the first responsible government in the British Empire (see "Heritage Attractions" in chapter 6). A statue of **Joseph Howe**, a leader in this fight for democracy and twice-elected premier of Nova Scotia, stands in the courtyard.

On the northeast corner of Hollis and Prince sts. stands:

12 The Bank of Nova Scotia

There's a quirky tradition in this neighborhood of competing bank architecture. The Bank of Nova Scotia building is a registered historic building in the Art Deco style of the 1930s. Return to George Street and walk

back up to Granville, where you'll come to an imposing building on the corner of George and Granville streets, built in 1906, and once home to the **Bank of Commerce.** A block north, at the corner of Granville and Duke streets, is the highly decorated Italianate-style structure built in 1911 as the **Merchant's Bank.**

Just ahead is the attractive pedestrian plaza of:

13 The Granville Mall

When the original buildings were destroyed by fire in 1859, this block was completely rebuilt, producing one of the finest Victorian-Italianate facades in Canada. Today, modern hotel facilities, pubs, shops, and the **Nova Scotia College of Art and Design** (N.C.A.D.) share the unique spaces behind these facades. The entrance marked SHOPS OF GRANVILLE MALL leads into a network of arched brick passageways that connect the shops to the college. It's easy to imagine the scene a century ago: carts crowding the alleyway with merchandise from ports around the world.

Follow through to the exit onto Hollis St. Across the street and to the left is:

14 Morse's Tea Building

This large ironstone structure was built in 1841, and is now occupied by the Nova Scotia College of Art and Design (see chapter 6).

Cross Hollis St., then take the stairs leading down to Upper Water St. Take the crosswalk to the main courtyard of:

15 Historic Properties

The first restoration project of its kind in Canada, Historic Properties Privateers Wharf is living history at its best. Restored and redeveloped into offices and retail outlets in the early 1970s, this National Historic Site comprises 10 buildings, some dating back to the 1800s. Privateers Wharf was the center of activity on the Halifax waterfront, welcoming trading vessels and privateers alike. It was from Halifax that many of these privateers, licensed by the

Halifax Strolls

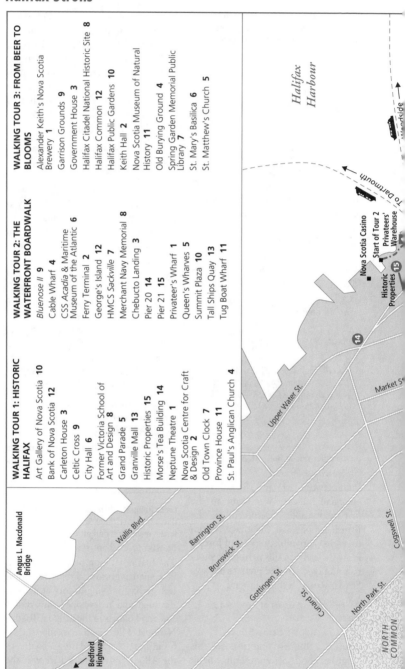

WALKING TOUR 1: HISTORIC HALIFAX

Art Gallery of Nova Scotia **10**
Bank of Nova Scotia **12**
Carleton House **3**
Celtic Cross **9**
City Hall **6**
Former Victoria School of Art and Design **8**
Grand Parade **5**
Granville Mall **13**
Historic Properties **15**
Morse's Tea Building **14**
Neptune Theatre **1**
Nova Scotia Centre for Craft & Design **2**
Old Town Clock **7**
Province House **11**
St. Paul's Anglican Church **4**

WALKING TOUR 2: THE WATERFRONT BOARDWALK

Bluenose II **9**
Cable Wharf **4**
CSS *Acadia* & Maritime Museum of the Atlantic **6**
Ferry Terminal **2**
George's Island **12**
HMCS *Sackville* **7**
Merchant Navy Memorial **8**
Chebucto Landing **3**
Pier 20 **14**
Pier 21 **15**
Privateer's Wharf **1**
Queen's Wharves **5**
Summit Plaza **10**
Tall Ships Quay **13**
Tug Boat Wharf **11**

WALKING TOUR 3: FROM BEER TO BLOOMS

Alexander Keith's Nova Scotia Brewery **1**
Garrison Grounds **9**
Government House **3**
Halifax Citadel National Historic Site **8**
Halifax Common **12**
Halifax Public Gardens **10**
Keith Hall **2**
Nova Scotia Museum of Natural History **11**
Old Burying Ground **4**
Spring Garden Memorial Public Library **7**
St. Mary's Basilica **6**
St. Matthew's Church **5**

Halifax Harbour

To Dartmouth

Nova Scotia Casino
Start of Tour 2
Privateers' Warehouse
Historic Properties **15**

Angus L. Macdonald Bridge

Bedford Highway

Wallis Blvd.

Barrington St.

Brunswick St.

Gottingen St.

Cunard St.

North Park St.

Cogswell St.

Upper Water St.

Market St.

NORTH COMMON

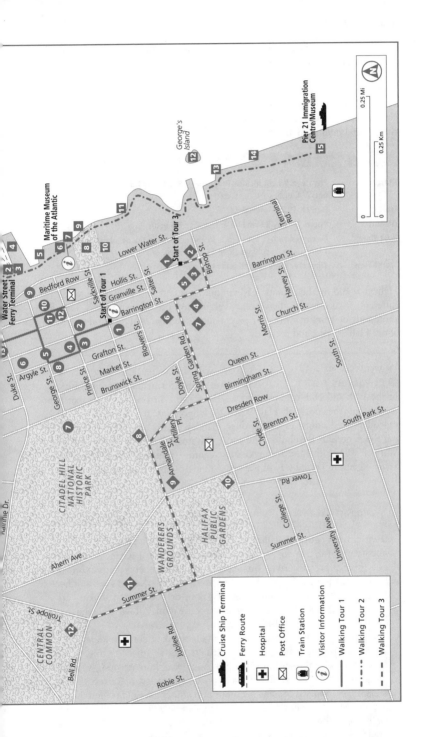

Maritime Museum of the Atlantic

Water Street Ferry Terminal

Lower Water St.

Start of Tour 3

Bedford Row

Hollis St.

Granville St.

Salter St.

Bishop St.

Barrington St.

Harvey St.

Church St.

Sackville St.

Start of Tour 1

Barrington St.

Blowers St.

Grafton St.

Market St.

Brunswick St.

Prince St.

George St.

Argyle St.

Duke St.

Morris St.

Queen St.

Birmingham St.

Dresden Row

Clyde St.

Brenton St.

South St.

South Park St.

Doyle St.

Sping Garden Rd

Spring Garden Rd

Artillery Pl.

Annandale St.

Tower Rd

College St.

Summer St.

University Ave.

George's Island

Pier 21 Immigration Centre/Museum

Terminal Rd.

Summer St.

CITADEL HILL NATIONAL HISTORIC PARK

WANDERERS GROUNDS

HALIFAX PUBLIC GARDENS

Martine Dr.

Ahern Ave.

Trollope St.

CENTRAL COMMON

Bell Rd.

Jubilee Rd.

Robie St.

Legend:
- Cruise Ship Terminal
- Ferry Route
- Hospital
- Post Office
- Train Station
- Visitor Information
- —— Walking Tour 1
- –·–· Walking Tour 2
- – – – Walking Tour 3

0.25 Km

0.25 Mi

British crown to raid enemy vessels, set sail and returned with their bounty. One of the most successful, Enos Collins, started the first bank in Nova Scotia, the Halifax Banking Company, in the iron-stone building to your left. Next to it is the oldest building in the group, the **Privateers' Warehouse,** built in 1813. Across the cobblestone courtyard is the original home of Pickford and Black, the international shipping company.

Walking Tour 1 ends here. If you want, continue on with Walking Tour 2, which begins where Walking Tour 1 leaves off.

WALKING TOUR 2   THE WATERFRONT BOARDWALK

Start:	Privateers Wharf, Historic Properties, 1869 Upper Water St. Metro Transit nos. 2, 4, or 6.
Finish:	Pier 21, 1055 Marginal Rd.
Distance:	Approximately 3.8km (2.3 miles); 2 to 2.5 hours
Best Time:	In warm weather, between 9am and noon, or in the evening between 7 and 10pm. In cold weather, 11am to 3pm.
Worst Time:	Whenever there is wind and rain.

Halifax would not be the city it is without its waterfront; everything would be different, right down to the weather. People have been drawn to this shore for thousands of years to work and play. Follow the boardwalk to find out more about Halifax, past and present.

The tour begins at:

❶ Privateers Wharf

In the 17th and 18th centuries, privateers used the port of Halifax to unload pirated booty, especially during the American Revolution and the War of 1812. Privateering was an accepted and respected way of waging war, and often the only means of defense for remote communities. It was also a method for many merchant Haligonians to become very rich. Today, there's still lots of activity on Privateers Wharf, in the restored 18th-century buildings, including that of modern-day merchant Haligonians.

⎛Fun Fact⎞ Stan Rogers and "The Last of Barrett's Privateers"

During the American Revolution and the War of 1812, privateers worked aboard privately owned warships, whose owners were given letters of marque (official permission) by their country to board enemy ships and take control of the cargo, crew, and ship. Most of the privateers were either fishermen, men who simply needed a job, or young men looking for adventure. Yet, although the crew made some money, it was only the ship owners who became really wealthy.

Privateering was immortalized by Canadian folk singer **Stan Rogers.** The chorus of his song "The Last of Barrett's Privateers," goes like this: "I was told we'd cruise the seas for American gold / We'd fire no guns, shed no tears, Now I'm a broken man on a Halifax pier, the last of Barrett's privateers." This song has become a kind of pub anthem in Halifax, and there's a good chance you'll hear the whole story while you're here. If you can't wait, view the complete words of the song at http://borg.cs.dal.ca/~tait/lyrics/folk_songs/barrets_privateers.txt. You may even want to learn them so you can sing along!

Turn right and walk along the boardwalk past shops and restaurants until you reach:

❷ The Ferry Terminal

This is the oldest continually operating saltwater ferry terminal in Canada (since 1752). The 12-minute ride between Halifax and Dartmouth is one of the best ways to view the skylines of both cities. Call ℂ **902/490-4000** or visit **www.region.halifax.ns.ca/metrotransit/index.html** for information on schedules and fares.

Just beyond the ferry terminal on your right is:

❸ Chebucto Landing

You'll see North America's oldest operating **Naval clock,** built in 1772. The clock looks down on the site of the landing of the first settlers to Halifax.

You are now in the most central area of the boardwalk. This is where the **International Busker Festival** takes place each August (see "Festivals & Events" in chapter 6), although there are often individual musicians and entertainers amusing passersby on any day of the year.

Also here is:

❹ Cable Wharf

Located here is a plethora of seasonal tour boat operators. You can take a cruise of the harbor, complete with dinner, or a water-taxi trip to Peggy's Cove. There's also deep-sea fishing, whale watching, sailing, and amphibious adventures to choose from (see "Organized Tours" in chapter 6). Take your pick! For a very special treat, take a 2-hour harbor cruise on the *Bluenose II,* if she is in port. Call ℂ **800/763-1963** or 902/634-1963, or log on to **www.bluenose2.ns.ca** for schedules and fares.

Continue south to:

❺ The Queen's Wharves

Established in 1995, these wharves provide moorings for visiting private sailing vessels. There's sure to be at least one romantic sailboat or classy yacht to admire.

TAKE A BREAK
Head inland from the wharf and cross Upper Water Street. Head north to **Sweet Basil Bistro,** 1866 Upper Water St. (ℂ **902/425-2133**). This classy little restaurant serves fresh pasta, seafood, and a whole array of salads. There's an outdoor patio in summer.

Head back to the boardwalk and keep walking south until you come to:

❻ The C.S.S. *Acadia*

Moored **behind the Maritime Museum of the Atlantic,** the C.S.S. *Acadia* was the first vessel designed and built to survey the coastal waters of Canada. During her career, which began in England in 1913, the *Acadia* pioneered hydrographic research in Canada's Arctic waters, and charted the coast of Newfoundland after that province joined Confederation in 1949. She is the only surviving ship to have served the Royal Canadian Navy in both World Wars, as well as the only vessel still afloat today to survive the 1917 Halifax Explosion. In 1982, she became part of the permanent collection of the **Maritime Museum of the Atlantic.**

Opened in 1948, the **Maritime Museum of the Atlantic** (ℂ **902/424-7490;** www.maritime.museum.gov.ns.ca) is the oldest and largest maritime museum in Canada and definitely worth a visit while you're in the city. It has been located on the waterfront since 1982, and houses fascinating exhibits on the S.S. *Titanic,* the Halifax Explosion, shipwrecks, the Navy, and Sable Island, to name only a few. (See "The Top Attractions" in chapter 6.)

A few steps farther on, at Sackville Landing, is:

❼ The H.M.C.S. *Sackville*

The only convoy escort corvette left in Canada, the H.M.C.S. *Sackville* has been restored as Canada's naval memorial. The **Bedford Basin** (Halifax's inner harbor) was the staging point for the great convoys of ships that brought relief and supplies to war-torn Europe during World War II, and corvettes like the *Sackville* protected them on their long and dangerous voyage. It's after these vessels that General Motors chose to name its most unique and powerful sports car, the Corvette.

Nearby is:

❽ The Merchant Navy Memorial

This memorial is dedicated to those who served in the Merchant Marine during the two World Wars. These sailors worked hard and often gave up their lives making sure that essential supplies were transported across the Atlantic Ocean to Britain during the fighting. The statue of a **lone sailor,** located close by, honors the thousands of seamen who passed through the port of Halifax.

Head south once again. If she's in port, the next ship you'll see is:

❾ The *Bluenose II*

This famous 43.5-m (143-ft.) schooner was built in 1963 in Lunenburg, a replica of the original *Bluenose* (1921–1946) depicted on the Canadian dime (see "Heritage Attractions" in chapter 6). When she is in port, you can book passage for a 2-hour harbor sailing tour. Call ✆ **800/763-1963** or 902/634-1963, or visit **www.blue nose2.ns.ca** for information on fares and schedules.

Continue south along the boardwalk and look inland to see:

❿ Summit Plaza

An arch and plaque commemorate the meeting of world leaders in Halifax during the 1995 G–7 Economic Summit. It was a little unusual for Haligonians to find areas of the downtown and waterfront closed off for security during the summit.

Just to the east past Summit Plaza, you'll see:

⓫ The Tug Boat Wharf

These boats are the manual laborers of the shipping industry, carefully maneuvering ships such as the mighty oil tankers gently into their berths. But they've had their 15 minutes of fame. Some were used in the film *K-19: The Widowmaker,* starring Harrison Ford, which was filmed in Halifax in 2001.

> **TAKE A BREAK**
> Head back inland again, through the parking lot to the corner of Salter and Lower Water streets. Look south to the Brewery Market, home of Alexander Keith's Nova Scotia Brewery, the Saturday morning Farmers Market, and the **City Deli Restaurant** (1496 Lower Water St. ✆ **902/425-3495**), offering a selection of sandwiches and soups for a light lunch.
> If you're looking for something more substantial, try the **Waterfront Warehouse** (1349 Lower Water St. ✆ **902/425-7610**). There's lots of seafood on the menu, served up in a nautical atmosphere.

Tips Healthy Hearts

Hearts in Motion is a marked walking trail located on the waterfront. Its purpose is to encourage a healthy lifestyle by enticing people to be more active. You can use it to measure your progress along your walking tour, or as an exercise program during your stay.

At this point, you can either continue with Walking Tour 2, or walk through the parking lot and across Lower Water St., then turn left and continue until you reach Alexander Keith's Brewery, where Walking Tour 3 begins.

If you opt to continue with Walking Tour 2, continue south along the boardwalk until you come to a lookout with a view of:

⑫ George's Island
This island played a key role in the harbor's defense system for almost 200 years. It has been named a National Historic Site, and its fortifications are currently undergoing restoration by the federal Department of Heritage. As we go to press, the site is scheduled to open to the public in 2003. Call ℭ **902/ 426-5080** for information, or log on to **www.parkscanada.pch.gc.ca.**

Continue south along the boardwalk for another 5 to 10 minutes until you reach:

⑬ The Tall Ships Quay
"Quay" is just another name for wharf, and is pronounced "kway." This wharf was built to host the **International Tall Ships** visit, in 2000, when more than 100 Tall Ships, from around the world gathered in Halifax. With any luck, there'll be a Tall Ship tied up at the dock when you visit.

Turn landward and you will see the **Electropolis Studios** (ℭ **902/429- 1971;** www.electropolis-studios.com), Eastern Canada's largest film production facility. In the summer, movies are projected onto the outside wall of the building for al fresco viewing (see chapter 9).

Look east again toward the water and you'll see:

⑭ Pier 20
This is Halifax's cruise ship docking facility. Halifax is quickly becoming a popular spot for international cruise lines, and you'll most likely see a ship in port if you visit between May and October.

If you walk the length of a cruise ship, you'll be standing near:

⑮ Pier 21 National Historic Site
This is Canada's Ellis Island. From 1928 to 1971, Pier 21 was Canada's "front door" to over a million immigrants, wartime evacuees, refugees, troops, war brides and their children. It has now been transformed into a highly interactive interpretive center that is a testament to Canada's profoundly emotional immigration experience (see "The Top Attractions" in chapter 6).

WALKING TOUR 3 | FROM BEER TO BLOOMS (ALEXANDER KEITH'S NOVA SCOTIA BREWERY TO THE HALIFAX PUBLIC GARDENS)

Start:	Alexander Keith's Nova Scotia Brewery, 1496 Lower Water St. Metro Transit nos. 2, 4, or 6.
Finish:	The Halifax Common.
Distance:	Approximately 4.2 km (5 miles); 2.5 to 3 hours (add another 2 hours if you plan to visit the Halifax Citadel National Historic Site).
Best Time:	In warm weather, any time. In cold weather, 11am to 3pm.
Worst Time:	Whenever there is wind and rain.

This walking tour winds through the center of downtown and ends up in the beautiful Halifax Commons. Along the way, you'll see 250-year-old headstones, Gothic-style churches, and the home of a famous brewmaster.

The tour begins at:

❶ Alexander Keith's Nova Scotia Brewery

This labyrinth of ironstone buildings has housed Alexander Keith's Breweries (📞 **902/455-1474;** www.keiths.ca) (see chapter 6) from the early 1800s to the present day. Inside is a combination of interesting shops and restaurants, a Saturday Farmers Market, and costumed interpreters to guide visitors through the smells and tastes of a working brew house. There is also an interpretive center and a company store. Enter **Brewery Market** at the North Arch, on Lower Water Street, and wander through the vaulted corridors where great horse-drawn wagons loaded with kegs of beer used to roll. Past the restaurants, potters' studio, and offices, take the stairs up to **Hollis Street.**

⸂ Fun Fact ⸃ Brewed to Last

India Pale Ale was originally brewed especially for the British troops in India. The quality of its ingredients and the preservative effect of hops kept it fresh on the long sea voyage down the coast of Africa, around the Cape of Good Hope, and into the Indian Ocean.

Exit and turn left. If the complex is closed, walk up Salter St. and turn left onto Hollis St., where you'll arrive at:

❷ Keith Hall

In the first half of the 19th century, many of Halifax's wealthiest citizens built elegant homes in this neighborhood. Past the brewery complex is Keith Hall, built as Alexander Keith's residence in 1863. Turn right up Bishop Street. This street appears much as it must have in the 1860s. Of particular interest is the **four-unit town house on the left,** built in 1862. This was a typical residence for the upper-middle-class city dweller of that era.

Continue to the corner of Barrington St. and turn right. Here stands stately:

❸ Government House

This is the residence of Nova Scotia's lieutenant governor. Though not open to the public, it is of interest. Built for Governor Sir John and Lady Francis Wentworth between 1799 and 1805, it is the oldest official government residence in Canada. Although Sir John was rather shy, Lady Francis was known for the boisterous parties she hosted in their mansion. She even invited Prince Edward (and his mistress)!

Across from Government House on Barrington St. is:

❹ The Old Burying Ground

This graveyard was used from 1749 to 1843. Visitors are encouraged to stroll through the grounds, where interpretive signs highlight graves of historical significance, including that of Captain James Lawrence, of the U.S.S. *Chesapeake*, who uttered the famous dying words "Don't give up the ship," during his confrontation with the British ship *The Shannon*, off Boston Harbor during the War of 1812. (Captain Lawrence was later reinterred in New York.) The large stone arch with the lion on top is the **Welsford Parker Monument,** erected in 1857 as a memorial to the Crimean War.

Exit the Old Burying Ground and walk north on Barrington St. On your right is:

❺ St. Matthew's Church

This church's history dates back to 1749, making St. Matthew's the oldest United Church in Canada. The large pipe organ has recently been rebuilt, and, with any luck, will be in use when you visit. Contact 📞 **902/423-9209** or **www.stmatts.ns.ca.** (See also "Heritage Attractions" in chapter 6.)

Up ahead, on the corner of Spring Garden Rd. and Barrington St. is:

❻ St. Mary's Basilica

Its graceful spire, rising almost 40m (128 ft.) above the roof, is the tallest polished (or "dressed," an architectural term that means the spire is covered with something—in this case, granite) spire in North America.

Walk up Spring Garden Rd. On your right is:

❼ The Spring Garden Memorial Public Library

Sir Winston Churchill appears to stride across the library's lawn, usually scattered with university students enjoying a break from lectures and munching fries from Bud the Spud's famous truck. It's not Sir Winston in the flesh, of course, but a statue of him, by noted sculptor Oscar Nemon. **Spring Garden Road**'s trendy shopping district begins just past the library. Pubs, cafes, and restaurants beckon with inviting aromas, and there's first-class entertainment, including jazz clubs and a movie theater with eight screens.

TAKE A BREAK
Try **Bud the Spud's famous french fries** for yourself— with ketchup, vinegar, and/or gravy. Pick a spot on the lawn of the Spring Garden Memorial Public Library, and relax. Bud and his wife Nancy have been selling their homemade fries at this location for 26 years. Spring Garden Road just wouldn't be the same without them.

Continue along Spring Garden Rd. and turn right onto Birmingham St. This street also has attractive shops and historic buildings. Take a gentle left and then right along Queen St., to where Queen St. and Dresden Row come together at Sackville St. Turn right onto Sackville St. Across the street is the main entrance to Halifax's famous fort:

❽ The Halifax Citadel National Historic Site

Better known to Haligonians as **Citadel Hill,** or just **The Citadel** (✆ 902/426-5080; www.parkscanada. gc.ca), the music and pageantry of the kilted 78th Highlanders and the precision of the Royal Artillery bring history to life here. Exhibits, an audiovisual presentation, and guided tours are available. Don't miss the firing of the noon gun—a daily ritual since the mid-1800s. While you're at the Citadel, take time to visit the **Army Museum** and see the collection of British and Canadian militaria. (See "The Top Attractions" in chapter 6.) Remember to add another 2 hours to this walking tour if you plan to visit the Citadel at this point.

Walk west back up Sackville St. to South Park St. On the north side you'll see:

❾ The Garrison Grounds

This is actually part of Citadel Hill and was used in the 1700s during peacetime as a campground for garrisons of soldiers, hence its name. It is now the area of Citadel Hill that is used for concerts, fundraisers and festivals during the summer months.

⌐ *Fun Fact* Fortified City

Although Halifax was one of the most fortified cities in the world from the late 18th through the 19th century, the fort you see today on Citadel Hill is in fact the fourth that has stood on the site. The massive, star-shaped Citadel took 28 years to build. It was supplemented with defense sites in Point Pleasant Park, on George's Island and McNab's Island, and at York Redoubt. Together, these sites are known as the **Halifax Defense Complex**. Whether through good management or good fortune, the fort's defenses were never tested; a shot has never been fired in combat.

Walk south on South Park St. until you reach Spring Garden Rd. On your right is the entrance to:

⑩ The Halifax Public Gardens

The 17 acres of lush trees, shrubs, and flowers is a wonderful place to explore and enjoy yourself from early May into November. Winding pathways lead past duck ponds, sparkling fountains, stately trees, and formal flower beds. There is also a charming red-roofed bandstand in the center of the gardens, where concerts are played on summer Sunday afternoons. (See "The Top Attractions" in chapter 6.)

TAKE A BREAK
Before you wander too far away from Spring Garden Road, stop into **Dio Mio Gelato Desserts Café**, 5670 Spring Garden Rd. (ⓒ **902/492-3467**). Their Italian ice creams are the smoothest around.

One block north of the gardens, along Summer St., is the headquarters of the provincial museum system, and:

⑪ The Nova Scotia Museum of Natural History

The museum (ⓒ **902/424-7393;** www.nature.museum.gov.ns.ca) houses artifacts and specimens that illustrate both the human and natural history of the province. Some particularly interesting exhibits are the dinosaur tracks and the Mi'kmaq artifacts. (See "The Top Attractions" in chapter 6.) Adjacent to the museum is the famous equestrian school of the **Halifax Junior Bengal Lancers.** You might just catch a glimpse of an outdoor practise session.

Back up Bell Rd. to the north is:

⑫ The Halifax Commons

This is Canada's oldest city park and a center for many sports events. From May to October there are baseball games and tournaments, soccer practices, and usually a Frisbee game between many a dog and master.

8

Shopping

Halifax is the regional shopping center of the Maritime provinces, and draws consumers from points in all three provinces to its malls, specialty shops, and big-box stores. The upside of this is variety and choice; the downside is the loss of small and unique retail stores in outlying areas. But the bottom line remains: Halifax has the best shopping in Atlantic Canada. There are large, multilevel, indoor malls, unique boutiques in historic buildings, bustling streets lined with cafes and shops filled with local arts and crafts, and a whole retail park of warehouse and big-box stores to wear out your credit cards.

1 The Shopping Scene

It's still illegal in Nova Scotia for large department, grocery, and clothing stores to open on Sunday. There are, however, a variety of smaller stores, including gift shops, fresh food markets, pharmacies, and corner stores that do throw open their doors on Sunday, usually from noon until 5pm.

From Monday through Saturday, most stores open at 9:30 or 10am. Closing times vary; independent outlets generally close between 5 and 6pm, while most of the malls stay open every evening until 9 or 9:30pm. *Note:* It's always best to call first, or check with your concierge, if you plan to shop after 5pm.

The Harmonized Sales Tax (HST) of 15% is added to your purchase at the checkout. Fortunately, for most retail purchases, nonresidents may apply for a tax refund (see "Fast Facts: Halifax" in chapter 3).

UPPER WATER STREET ✧

Historic Properties & Privateers Wharf, located on Upper Water Street, recalls an era dating back to Nova Scotia's seafaring past, and is one of the few concentrated shopping areas that is **open 7 days a week.** Shops are located in a number of buildings, with the main shopping area anchored by **Harbourside Market.** You'll find everything from fashion and housewares to Maritime artwork. **Granville Mall,** between Upper Water Street and Granville Street, is part of the Historic Properties complex. The shops here feature pewter, antiques, jewelry, giftware, and Christmas decorations. A lovely addition is that they open onto a cobblestone area with trees and benches.

SCOTIA SQUARE

This indoor mall is located on the corner of Barrington and Duke streets. It was the Mecca for shopping in the 1970s. Although less popular now, you'll still find fashions for the whole family—and shops specializing in jewelry, music, electronics, home decor, and books, plus a food court.

BARRINGTON PLACE SHOPS

Next to the Delta Barrington Hotel, **across the street from Scotia Square,** there are no less than 30 unique gift and clothing shops. A stroll along Barrington Street, once the main shopping area of the city, also presents good shopping opportunities.

HYDROSTONE MARKET ✪

This is a small, but truly European, shopping experience. Located in a one-block area of **Young Street,** in the north end of the city, the market has been restored to reflect its 1920s heritage. All the shops here are **open 7 days a week.** Along with antiques and French pastries, look for yarns, gourmet food, and fine crafts. While you're in the area, be sure to visit the **Hydrostone District,** a splendid example of a British-style garden suburb that was built following the Halifax Explosion in 1917 to replace housing that was flattened in the disaster.

QUINPOOL ROAD

This has been a traditional neighborhood shopping district since the 1940s, before it became a main artery to downtown. The road retains its vintage character, with its old-fashioned signs and storefronts; many of the shops are well-established family businesses. Aside from a variety of restaurants—Chinese, Greek, Indian, and Japanese—there are specialty shops selling sporting goods, cookware, children's clothes, and footwear. The Quinpool Road shopping district begins at the **corner of Robie Street and Quinpool Road** and continues west almost to **Connaught Avenue.**

SPRING GARDEN ROAD

This area is made up of a compact 9-block radius of shops and services, and is considered the trendiest shopping district in Halifax. It begins at the **intersection of Spring Garden Road and South Park Street,** and runs east to **Barrington Street,** including a number of side streets. There are more than 250 shops carrying everything from famous brand names to crafts made by local artisans. Along with the storefront boutiques, there are multilevel malls, with indoor parking. Spring Garden Road also has great food, boasting some of the city's best cafes, bistros, and restaurants, and it's home to **Bud the Spud ✪,** Halifax's famous french fry wagon. Look for it parked beside the Spring Garden Road Memorial Public Library, **between Brunswick and Grafton streets.**

If you need a break from shopping, stop in at the beautiful **Halifax Public Gardens** (see "The Top Attractions" in chapter 6). The main entrance is at the **corner of Spring Garden Road and South Park Street,** across from the **Lord Nelson Hotel,** another city landmark.

2 Shopping A to Z

ANTIQUES

Geddes Furniture and Antiques A popular, north-end spot with local antique hunters, this shop will also arrange delivery for visitors to other parts of Canada, New England, and New York. The knowledgeable staff is friendly, and there is usually a wide variety of fine antiques, both furniture and collectibles. 2739 Agricola St. ℂ **902/454-7171.** Metro Transit nos. 7, 12, 31.

Matthews Antiques & Collectibles This shop offers an eclectic collection of furniture, china and glass, toys, jewelry, and sports memorabilia, with some nautical items thrown in. Matthews also does restoration and appraisals. 2189 Windsor St. ℂ **902/429-4874.** Metro Transit nos. 17, 82.

Stoneleigh Antiques & Jewelry   This downtown shop has something for everyone, from porcelain to 19th-century furniture, bird carvings to teddy bears, and most things in between. There's also antique and unusual jewelry. They provide an appraisal service and shipping. 1870 Hollis St. © 902/429-2112. Closed November–May. Metro Transit nos. 2, 7, 9.

Urban Cottage Antiques and Collectibles   Located downtown in the heritage building on the corner of Duke and Granville streets, this shop carries a wide selection of antiques and used furniture, along with collectibles. 1819 Granville St. © 902/423-3010. Metro Transit nos. 7, 9, 18.

BOOKS
NEW
The Book Room (Finds (Kids   Not only is this Canada's oldest bookstore (163 years old), but the service is unsurpassed. Unlike many bookstores today, the staff is knowledgeable and can help you find what you're looking for. Along with bestsellers there are over 50,000 books for all interests and ages, including the best collection of Nova Scotia and Canadian books in Halifax. They also specialize in books and videos on the Halifax Explosion. The store will ship books worldwide. 1546 Barrington St. © 800/387-2665 or 902/423-8271. Metro Transit nos. 6, 7, 9.

Chapters/Indigo (Kids   A big-box chain store for book-lovers. They carry books on a wide selection of topics, from poetry to reference, plus great sale aisles. A growing selection of gift items is also offered. There's a special area for children, and a coffee shop. In Bayers Lake Park, 188 Chain Lake Dr. © 902/450-1023. In Mic Mac Mall, 41 Mic Mac Blvd. © 902/466-1640. www.chapters-indigo.ca. Metro Transit nos. 10, 54, 55.

Coles   A chain bookstore carrying bestsellers and other mainstream books and magazines. Halifax Shopping Centre. © 902/455-7205. www.chapters-indigo.ca. Metro Transit nos. 1, 3, 5.

Entitlement The Book Company   This is a great bookstore in which to browse—there's more than the usual mainstream titles, and you're sure to find something that fascinates. It also carries gift items, calendars, and journals. 5675 Spring Garden Rd. © 902/420-0565. Metro Transit nos. 1, 3, 10.

Frog Hollow Books (Finds   Owned by a book lover, this shop has a wide selection of books and is a real treat for bibliophiles. Visit during one of their many special events and experience a reading by a well-known author. Park Lane Mall. Spring Garden Rd. © 902/429-3318. Metro Transit nos. 1, 3, 10.

SmithBooks   A large bookstore chain, with a good collection of mainstream books for a variety of ages. Scotia Square, 2000 Barrington St. © 902/423-6438. www.chapters-indigo.ca. Metro Transit nos. 6, 7, 9.

Woozles (Kids   A delightful bookstore for and about children. They offer not only books, records, tapes, and toys, but also books on parenting and organized workshops for parents and children, individually and together. Check the website for details. 1533 Birmingham St. (off Spring Garden Rd.) © 902/423-7626. www.woozles.com. Metro Transit nos. 1, 3, 10.

USED
Back Pages (Value   This store specializes in rare books, as well as inexpensive used books. 1526 Queen St. © 902/423-4750. Metro Transit nos. 1, 3, 7.

Schooner Books Ltd. *(Finds)* This shop specializes in Atlantic provinces history and literature, early Canadiana, Canadian art, Canadian military history, illustrated books, fine bindings, and early children's books. You'll also find a general stock of good used and out-of-print books on a variety of subjects, plus a selection of antiquarian maps and prints relating to the Atlantic provinces. 5378 Inglis St. ℂ **902/423-8419.** Metro Transit nos. 9, 10, 18.

United Book Exchange For almost any topic, if you're just looking for an inexpensive read you'll find it here. It also carries used magazines and videos. 1669 Barrington St. ℂ **902/423-6980.** Metro Transit nos. 6, 7, 9.

CAMERAS

Atlantic Photo Supply This shop has been in business for more than 60 years, and the staff are very knowledgeable about their products. Aside from expert advice, they offer all styles of cameras, including video; camera supplies; and 1-hour developing. 5505 Spring Garden Rd. ℂ **902/423-6724** or 902/423-8820. www. atlanticphotosupply.com. Metro Transit nos. 1, 3, 10.

Camera Repair Ltd. If you're having problems with your camera, here's someone to help. This store is also an authorized service center for Canon and Pentax. 2324 Hunter St. (off Cunard St. between Robie and Windsor.) ℂ **902/423-6450.** Metro Transit nos. 5, 17, 82.

Carsand-Mosher Photographic Ltd. Here you'll find a huge selection of new and used camera equipment of all makes. Knowledgeable staff are on hand to assist with information or problems. 1559 Barrington St. ℂ **902/421-1980.** www. carsand.com. Metro Transit nos. 6, 7, 9.

CANADIAN ARTS & CRAFTS

Art Gallery of Nova Scotia (AGNS) A wonderful collection of folk art, jewelry, sculpture, pottery, textiles, woodwork, Mi'kmaq handcrafts, and original prints by Nova Scotian artists. The gallery also carries the full product line from the celebrated Maud Lewis Collection. Born in the town of Digby, about 200km (120 miles) southwest of Halifax, Maud Lewis (1902–1970) charmed art connoisseurs and professed philistines alike with her colorful, homespun paintings of life in rural Nova Scotia. Not only that, her work sparked what became an international craze for folk art. Your visit to Halifax isn't complete without a little piece of Maud—the AGNS has everything from placemats to mouse pads for sale. It's a little kitschy, sure, but we just can't help falling under Maud's spell.

There's also the **Art Sales and Rental Gallery** at the AGNS to consider. Choose a piece of original art from the works of more than 150 Maritime artists. It may even turn out to be a "before they were famous" collector's item. New works are added every 2 weeks. 1723 Hollis St. ℂ **902/423-1772.** www.agns.gov.ns.ca. Metro Transit nos. 2, 7, 9.

Bogside Gallery Here you'll find a wide variety of artwork from some of Atlantic Canada's finest artisans. There's everything from pewter to pottery, paintings to wooden art, and more. Hydrostone Market. 5527 Young St. ℂ **902/453-3063.** www.shop-halifax.com/hydrostone. Metro Transit nos. 7, 12, 31.

Carrefour Atlantic Emporium This shop carries handcrafts, original art, and literature from artists who hail from Atlantic Canada, Canada's First Nations, and the Canadian North. Privateers Wharf, Historic Properties, 1869 Upper Water St. ℂ **902/423-2940.** Metro Transit nos. 2, 7, 9.

Hall of Frame/Second Gallery   Walls and walls of modern and traditional paintings, drawings, original prints and photographs greet you in this shop. All are created by well-known Nova Scotia artists.   6301 Quinpool Rd. ✆ **902/423-6644.** Metro Transit nos. 6, 14, 32.

Handsmith   An eclectic collection of ceramics, wood, jewelry, metal, and fabrics by Canadian artisans.   Historic Properties, 1869 Upper Water St. ✆ **800/344-9553.** Metro Transit nos. 2, 7, 9.

Harbour Swan   Here you'll find a wide selection of locally handcrafted pottery, bird decoys, lamps, glass, toiletries, designer wear, and souvenirs. World-wide shipping is available.   Privateers Wharf, Historic Properties. 1869 Upper Water St. ✆ **902/420-9399.** Metro Transit nos. 2, 7, 9.

Jennifer's of Nova Scotia (*Finds*   A Maritime tradition, every item for sale in this shop is produced locally. Over 125 Nova Scotian craftspeople showcase their work here, including pottery, woolens, jewelry, clothing accessories, pewter, and woodwork.   5635 Spring Garden Rd. ✆ **902/425-3119.** www.jennifers.ns.ca. Metro Transit nos. 1, 10, 14.

Nova Scotian Crystal (*Finds*   For a unique, sometimes expensive, souvenir of your visit, be sure to check out Canada's only maker of fine mouth-blown, hand-cut crystal. Visit the glassworks to see how the crystal is made and then the showroom to see beautiful stemware, vases, and bowls. A special item is their annual Christmas ornament; a new design is created each year. Worldwide shipping available.   5080 George St. ✆ **902/492-0416.** www.novascotiancrystal.com. Metro Transit nos. 2, 4, 7.

Painter's Palate Art Gallery   A great place to pick up original paintings of Maritime scenes and Halifax landmarks. The gallery also features flower studies and still lifes.   Spring Garden Place, 5640 Spring Garden Rd. ✆ **902/425-4619.** Metro Transit nos. 1, 10, 14.

CHOCOLATES & SWEETS

Freak Lunchbox (*Moments*   Treat yourself and visit this new candy shop that carries everything from candy brands you loved as a child to caffeinated pep-permints to chocolate candies with bugs inside. True to its name, it is decorated with paintings of old Freak Show signs. There's also a "Great Wall of Pez," for Pez fanatics.   1723 Barrington St. ✆ **902/420-9121.** Metro Transit nos. 6, 7, 9.

Sweet Jane's   For everything your sweet tooth craves, try Sweet Jane's. You'll also find unique cards and stationery, lunch boxes, and other gifts. Sweet Jane's is more than candy, it's a really sweet shopping experience.   5431 Doyle St. ✆ **902/425-0168.** Metro Transit nos. 1, 3, 10.

DEPARTMENT STORES

The Bay (Hudson's Bay Company)   Canada's own original department store, the Bay began as a fur-trading post more than 300 years ago. It carries house-wares and clothing for all ages.   7067 Chebucto Rd. ✆ **902/453-1211.** www.hbc.com. Metro Transit nos. 2, 4, 5.

Sears   Sears carries a large and comprehensive collection of household items, including appliances, furniture, electronics, dishes, and clothing.   Halifax Shopping Centre, 7001 Mumford Rd. ✆ **902/453-1752.** www.sears.ca. Metro Transit nos. 1, 2, 4.

DISCOUNT SHOPPING

A Buck or Two *(Kids)*   A great place for families to pick up items they forgot, or inexpensive toys and activities to keep the kids amused on rainy days. Parklane Mall, 5657 Spring Garden Rd. ℂ **902/425-4977**. Metro Transit nos. 1, 10, 14.

Zellers   A smaller-scale, though still comprehensive, department store. The Village at Bayers Rd., 7071 Bayers Rd. ℂ **902/454-5801**. www.hbc.com/zellers. Metro Transit nos. 2, 3, 4.

FASHION
ADULTS

Brio   Brand-name swimsuits, plus dance, fitness, and skating apparel. Although expensive, this is one of the best places in the Maritimes to find these products. 5411 Spring Garden Rd. ℂ **902/423-1741**. Metro Transit nos. 1, 10, 14.

Cleve's Sporting Goods   This is a popular stop for parents and teens as they carry a large selection of brand-name sports apparel from bathing suits to ski wear, baseball caps to sneakers, and everything in between. Prices are reasonable, with some good sales. 5524 Spring Garden Rd. ℂ **902/420-1649**. Warehouse Outlet, 204 Chain Lake Dr. ℂ **902/450-5353**. Metro Transit nos. 1, 10, 14.

Colwell's   This is the traditional, classic clothing store for women and men in Halifax. You will find elegant dresses and business suits, as well as more casual wear, by such designers as Jones New York, Arnold Brant, Tomboline, Peter Nygard, Timberland, and Tilley, to name a few. Expect to be pampered; the quality of service goes back 100 years, and includes in-store tailors, appointment shopping, and delivery service. Barrington Place Shops, 1903 Barrington St. ℂ **902/ 420-1222**. Metro Transit nos. 6, 7, 9.

Dugger's Men's Wear   This large, attractive store carries stylish yet comfortable clothing. You'll find everything from casual weekend wear to business suits, and the brand names include Tommy Bahama, Strellson suits (designed in Europe), and the Hugo Boss Golf Collection. A popular stop for up-and-coming and successful businessmen. 5476 Spring Garden Rd. ℂ **902/425-2525**. www.newedge.net/duggers. Metro Transit nos. 1, 10, 14.

Enchanted Forest   A trendy shop for ladies from size 0 (inexplicably) to 18, including petite sizes. Salespeople are helpful and fun, and they can assist you in choosing and accessorizing outfits—from casual and funky to classic and elegant. They carry European and Canadian designer labels. 5475 Spring Garden Rd. ℂ **902/422-5337**. Metro Transit nos. 1, 10, 14.

Heroine *(Finds)*   A small shop in size but huge in uniqueness and quality, and the favorite of Halifax's best-dressed women. Owner Jody Manley is passionate about clothing and this is obvious in her store. She carries only Canadian labels (Muriel Dombret, Comrags, David Dixon, Phillip Dubuc, Brenda Beddome, Olena Zylak) and most of the clothes are hand cut, not factory made. The styles are primarily elegant business casual, and styled to fit a woman's body, sizes 6–14. Jody uses direct marketing to promote the lines she carries. Several times throughout the year, at the beginning of each fashion season and during holidays, she brings the designers to her shop to meet her clientele. Be sure to call about special events when you're in town. You can also make private appointments and arrange custom orders. Jody also carries custom-designed jewelry and a small line of men's clothing. The shop is decorated in minimalist style, very New York, with clean lines. 1656 Granville St. ℂ **902/420-0328**. Metro Transit nos. 7, 9, 18.

Me & Max *(Finds)*   Owner Linda Casey-Mishimagi has worked in the international fashion industry for over a decade and brings this expertise to her shop. Linda believes that quality and design will create a timeless wardrobe, and she and her helpful staff work to help you create the look you want, whatever your size. The European-style boutique carries upscale clothing by Max Mara, Weekend, Marina Rinaldi, and Burberry, in sizes 12–20. You'll also find quality gold and silver jewelry. 5491 Spring Garden Rd. © **902/425-7171**. www.meandmax.ca. Metro Transit nos. 1, 10, 14.

Mills Brothers   Another clothing institution in Halifax, this business has been around since 1919. Mills is made up of 12 shops under one roof, carrying everything from brand-name clothing, quality suits and formal wear, to casual clothing, plus famous fragrances and cosmetics, hosiery, lingerie, outerwear, and accessories. There's also a gift shop. Mills Brothers also makes deliveries. 5486 Spring Garden Rd. © **902/429-6111**. www.millsbrothers.com. Metro Transit nos. 1, 10, 14.

Mitchell Furs and Outerwear   Because this shop specializes in outerwear, it has the best selection in Halifax. Mitchell's carries full-length and shorter furs, fur-lined coats, and leather coats and jackets. There's a wide selection of wool and cashmere coats, and microfiber coats and jackets. 6247 Quinpool Rd. © **902/422-8591**. Metro Transit nos. 6, 14, 32.

Renaissance   Renaissance carries casual clothing for the whole family by Polo Ralph Lauren, Mexx, Part Two/Inwear, Tommy Hilfiger, Calvin Klein, and OshKosh, to name a few. It also carries footwear. Your shopping is made even more enjoyable by the rustic atmosphere of the heritage building in which the store is located. 1549 Barrington St. © **902/422-3509**. Metro Transit nos. 6, 7, 9.

The Tannery by DJ's   If you're into leather boots, be sure to check out DJ's. It has a friendly staff and a wide selection of men's and women's brand-name footwear to choose from. There's also quality luggage and accessories. Corner of Spring Garden and Queen sts. © **902/429-4934**. Metro Transit nos. 1, 10, 14.

Unicorn   A shop in a beautifully restored firehall, Unicorn has a historic atmosphere, and carries men's and women's clothing and footwear. Clothes are casual to dressy. Look for designer women's shoes from the likes of Stuart Weitzman, Sacha Lond, and Ramon Tenza. 1579 Grafton St. © **902/423-4308**. Metro Transit nos. 2, 7, 9.

CHILDREN
Bib n' Tucker Children's Shop   All the brand names your offspring could want—Deux Par Deux, Tommy Hilfiger, Columbia, Gumboots, Marese, Absorba, and Elvira Valie. Available in sizes from infants to 16. 6423 Quinpool Rd. © **902/423-6474**. Metro Transit nos. 6, 14, 32.

Kidz by Hansel & Gretel/Shirt Shack   Here you'll find a wide variety of quality children's clothing, along with a selection of souvenirs and touristy-type t-shirts. From infant sizes to pre-teen. Scotia Square Mall, 5251 Duke St. © **902/ 423-8759**. Metro Transit nos. 2, 4, 6.

FOOD & MARKETS
Great Ocean Natural Food Market   Along with vitamins and health supplements, Great Ocean has a bulk food section with groceries and organic produce. There's also a deli where you can grab a quick and nutritious lunch. 6485 Quinpool Rd. © **902/425-7400**. Metro Transit nos. 6, 14, 32.

Halifax City Farmers Market *(Finds)* *(Value)*   North America's oldest market is open only on Saturdays, but well worth the visit if you're in town. The market is located in the Alexander Keith's Brewery building and is, just as in bygone days, bustling with vendors and visitors from 7am to 1pm. You will find everything from homemade breads and deli food to handmade crafts and pickles. In season there are fresh berries, maple syrup, Christmas trees and decorations, flowers, and herbs. Through it all marches a parade of regular and transient musicians—from fiddlers to string quartets. 1496 Lower Water St. © **902/492-4043.** Metro Transit nos. 2, 7, 9.

The Harbourside Market   This rustic, waterfront building houses such a variety of food vendors that you're sure to find something to please. There's a food market, a takeout, a deli, an Italian counter, and a seafood section. There's even a microbrewery. This market is open 7 days a week. Historic Properties, 1869 Upper Water Street. © **902/422-3077.** Metro Transit nos. 2, 7, 9.

Newfoundland Grocery Store *(Finds)*   Now you can feast like the Newfoundlanders do, and discover what you've been missing: seal flippers, cod tongues, partridge berries, and more. The friendly staff will introduce you to the delicacies, as they've been doing for over 50 years. 6061 Willow St. © **902/423-6209.** Metro Transit nos. 5, 17, 82.

GIFTS & SOUVENIRS

Aitkens Pewter   You'll find a variety of Atlantic Canadian pewter, but note especially the ornaments depicting Halifax historic buildings—they make great souvenirs and take-home gifts. The store is open 7 days a week. Privateers Wharf, Historic Properties, 1869 Upper Water St. © **902/423-4563.** Metro Transit nos. 2, 4, 6.

Four Feet on the Ground Giftware *(Finds)* *(Kids)*   Whether you are a pet owner who loves animals up close and personal, or someone who prefers to love them from afar and visit your friends with pets, don't miss this shop. You will find dishes, collars, clothing, treats, and everything imaginable for your pet. Plus there's animal-theme fine jewelry, dishes, throws, place mats, rugs, home decor and more for the animal lover. There's no other store with this variety in the Maritimes. They specialize in dogs, but also carry items featuring cats, horses, and other animals. The shop is located next to the Carnegy Animal Hospital in Clayton Park, 5 minutes' drive outside the Halifax Peninsula. 7 Langbrae Drive, Suite 4. © **902-457-0117.** www.fourfeetontheground.com. Metro Transit nos. 2, 4, 33.

House Warmings   A compact, two-level shop tucked in the south courtyard of the Alexander Keith's Brewery building. It carries a selection of candles, glassware, and garden accent items. Prices are reasonable. Inside the Brewery Market, 1496 Lower Water St. © **902/425-1777.** Metro Transit nos. 2, 7, 9.

Murphy's Company Store   This is a great spot for souvenirs—including Nova Scotian handicrafts, T-shirts, and Anne of Green Gables collectibles. 1751 Lower Water St. Cable Wharf (beside the Ferry Terminal). © **902/420-1015.** www. murphysonthewater.com/mcs.html. Metro Transit nos. 2, 7, 9.

Paper Garden   If you're a paper lover, this is the shop for you. There's fine stationery, beautiful hand-made paper, journals, tapestries, pens, candle wax, and more. Browsing here is a very tactile shopping experience. Barrington Place Shops, 1903 Barrington St. © **902/423-3182.** Metro Transit nos. 2, 7, 9.

Pewter House   Here you'll find a wide variety of locally crafted and imported pewter, along with tableware—napkins, place mats, and tablecloths. The shop also carries items with a nautical theme. 1875 Granville St. ℭ **902/423-8843.** Metro Transit nos. 2, 7, 9.

HOME DECOR

Ambience Home Accents *(Finds*)   Here you'll find mainly Canadian and locally made home furnishings and accessories, including papier-mâché framed mirrors, teak chairs, handmade wooden boxes, and beautiful hand-painted silk pillows and wraps. 5431 Doyle St. ℭ **902/423-9200.** Metro Transit nos. 1, 3, 10.

Attica   Attica specializes in modern furniture and accessories by local and international designers and artists. Of special interest are the one-of-a-kind designs by award-winning co-owner Christopher Joyce. Items for sale are notable for their clean lines, sophistication, and overall minimalist sensibility. 1652 Granville St. ℭ **902/423-2557.** www.attica.ca. Metro Transit nos. 2, 7, 9.

Bass River Chairs   This is a local Nova Scotian company known for its kitchenware and hardwood furniture. Bass River chairs also carries fabric accessories and specialty foods. The Historic Properties location is open 7 days a week. Halifax Shopping Centre, 7001 Mumford Rd. ℭ **902/454-2424.** Historic Properties, 1869 Upper Water St. ℭ **902/492-8387.** www.bassriverchairs.com. Metro Transit nos. 2, 4, 6.

Thornbloom *(Finds*)   This store stocks fine bed linens, kitchenware, furniture, giftware, and home accessories. It's definitely worth a visit; just being there is a pampering experience. Spring Garden Place, 5640 Spring Garden Rd. (corner of Spring Garden Rd. & Dresden Row). ℭ **902/425-8005.** http://shop.timwebworks.com/thb_carl/default.asp. Metro Transit nos. 1, 10, 14.

JEWELRY

Destiny Jewelry   Family owned and operated, this store specializes in sterling silver jewelry incorporating semi-precious stones. It also stocks giftware and home decor items. Barrington Place Shops, 1903 Barrington St. ℭ **902/482-7464.** Metro Transit nos. 2, 7, 9.

Fire Works Gallery   Jewelry lovers beware—you'll adore this shop. Custom-designed jewelry, hand engraving, and filigree work, using gold, platinum, diamonds, and colored gemstones created in the on-site studio. You'll also find jewelry by other artisans, and estate jewelry. 1569 Barrington St. ℭ **902/420-1735.** www.fireworksgallery.com. Metro Transit nos. 2, 7, 9.

James Bradshaw, Goldsmith   Bradshaw designs are solid and angular, yet simple and elegant, and always recognizable. The shop sells only Bradshaw's creations, with a selection of rings, wedding rings, bracelets, earrings, brooches, and pendants, all in gold, some with stone insets. 1551 Birmingham St. ℭ **902/425-0121.** www.jamesbradshawgoldsmith.com. Metro Transit nos. 1, 3, 10.

Touch of Gold   This shop has won national and international awards for custom-designed jewelry. It is also the exclusive dealer for Rolex watches in Nova Scotia. 5640 Spring Garden Rd. ℭ **902/423-5600.** Metro Transit nos. 1, 3, 10.

The Vault *(Finds*)   Popular with some of Canada's most fashionable women, this shop is the exclusive location in Atlantic Canada for designs by Holly Yashi, Kenny Ma, Ayalabar, and Zoppini of Italy. Spring Garden Place, 5640 Spring Garden Rd. ℭ **902/425-3624.** Metro Transit nos. 1, 3, 10.

KITCHENWARE

The Cookhouse   Don't let the name mislead you, this shop carries all the latest gourmet kitchenware along with pots and pans, small appliances, and everything else you need for your kitchen.   6451 Quinpool Rd. ℂ **902/431-5022**. Metro Transit nos. 6, 14, 20.

The Swedish Chef's Shop   For the professional or wannabe, this shop carries products and inspiration. You'll find cookbooks, chef's clothing, and high-quality cookware. Advice from the Swedish Chef is free.   The Hydrostone Market, 5515–5547 Young St. ℂ **902/454-4636**. www.shop-halifax.com/hydrostone. Metro Transit nos. 7, 12, 80.

MALLS & SHOPPING CENTERS

Bayers Lake Business Park is 11km (7 miles) (or a 15-minute drive) from downtown Halifax, and is the largest concentration of retail space in Atlantic Canada. This is the home of the big-box stores—**Costco** (ℂ **902/876-8700**), **Wal-Mart** (ℂ **902/450-5570**), **Kent Building Supplies** (ℂ **902/450-2000**), **Office Depot** (ℂ **902/450-5241**), **Chapters/Indigo** (ℂ **902/450-1023**), and **Future Shop** (ℂ **902/450-7200**) are all represented here. You'll definitely need a vehicle to find your way through the over 232 hectares (580 acres) of light industrial and commercial activity, but there's lots of parking, and Metro Transit provides hourly service from the city. To get to Bayers Lake Business Park from Halifax, take the Bicentennial Highway (route 102) at exit 3. Or take Metro Transit no. 12 or 21.

The main shopping center in the **Halifax Shopping Centre Annex,** 7001 Mumford Rd. (ℂ **902/453-1752**; www.halifaxshoppingcentre.com), has two floors and 150 shops, anchored by Sears department store, Sobeys groceries, and Lawton's Pharmacy. This mall has lots to offer aside from clothes, jewelry, books, household needs, and food. The customer service center provides complimentary strollers, wheelchairs and walkers, free gift-wrapping during special holidays, baby changing and feeding facilities, and plenty of parking. There's also a **visitor information center,** and someone to help you carry your parcels to your car. The center is open Monday to Saturday from 9:30am to 9pm. The Halifax Shopping Centre and the Halifax Shopping Centre Annex are located in the west end of Halifax, with the main entrance to both on Mumford Road, and a secondary entrance to the Halifax Shopping Centre on Bayers Road, just past the corner of Bayers Road and Connaught Avenue toward route 102. Or take Metro Transit no. 1, 2, or 3.

Located on Spring Garden Road, **Park Lane,** 5657 Spring Garden Rd. (ℂ **902/420-0660**; www.shopparklane.ca), is a trendy mall comprising three floors of specialty retailers. Ladies apparel to work in, gowns to be seen in, men's wear, lingerie, giftware, home furnishings, art, and shoes are all part of the mix. On the first level, there's an eight-screen movie theater and a food court with a variety of cuisine, including Chinese, Italian, and Indian. Park Lane is open Monday, Wednesday, and Saturday from 9:30am to 6pm; Thursday and Friday from 9:30am to 9:30pm. There's indoor parking, and metered parking on the street. Take Metro Transit no. 1, 10, or 14.

Spring Garden Place, 5640 Spring Garden Rd. (ℂ **902/420-0675**; www.springgardenplace.com), is located on the corner of Spring Garden Road and Dresden Row. It's on two levels, and features clothing and jewelry shops, a

Canadian-made leather and fur store, a bakery, and **Ryan Duffy's Steak & Seafood** restaurant, one of Halifax's best steak eateries (see chapter 5). The lower level includes a **Garden Market,** open 7 days a week, with fresh produce and gourmet cuisine. The mall is open Monday to Wednesday from 9am to 6pm; Thursday and Friday from 9am to 9pm; Saturday from 9:30am to 5:30pm. There's indoor parking with an hourly charge, as well as metered parking on the street. Take Metro Transit no. 1, 10, or 14.

The **Village at Bayers Road,** 7071 Bayers Rd. (© 902/453-2630), formerly the Bayers Road Shopping Centre, offers a wide variety of specialty shops and national chain stores. It was the shopping mall of choice for consumers outside of Halifax for years because of its location close to the major entrance highway to the city. The development of malls in Bedford and Dartmouth has diminished the consumer traffic, resulting in areas of the mall being made over into office space. It's open Monday to Friday from 9am to 9pm; Saturday from 9am to 6pm. There's free parking. Take Metro Transit no. 2, 4, or 12.

MUSIC & MUSICAL INSTRUMENTS

Halifax Folklore Centre (Finds)   Located in a 130-year-old home, this unique shop carries a large selection of vintage guitars and violins, plus new and used musical instruments, including Celtic harps, mandolins, and banjos, as well as amplifiers, basses, and bodhrans (Irish goatskin drums). There's also a selection of unusual gifts, plus Celtic and Maritime music books. 1528 Brunswick St. © 902/422-6350. Metro Transit nos. 1, 2, 4.

OUTDOOR EQUIPMENT

The Trail Shop   Nova Scotia's leading outdoor store has knowledgeable, experienced staff willing to share that experience. You'll find everything you need from basics to accessories for hiking, camping, climbing, trekking, and paddling. The Trail Shop also rents sports equipment, including kayaks and skis. 6210 Quinpool Rd. © 902/423-8736. www.trailshop.com. Metro Transit nos. 6, 14, 20.

SPECIALTY

Christmas by the Sea   Atlantic Canada's largest year-round Christmas shop carries gifts and decorations from around the world: Fontanini nativities, mouth-blown, hand-painted European glass ornaments, and locally designed nautical decorations. Worldwide shipping is available. 1880 Hollis St. © 902/429-6090. www.christmasbythesea.com. Metro Transit nos. 2, 4, 7.

TARTAN WEAR

Bounty Boutique   Here you'll find a large selection of kilts along with giftware and souvenirs. The store is open 7 days a week.   Historic Properties, 1869 Upper Water St. © 902/425-6696. Metro Transit nos. 2, 4, 6.

Plaid Place   Plaid Place specializes in men's highland dress and made-to-measure tartan items. But you'll also find a ready-made selection of tartan skirts, kilts, ties, and scarves, Scottish sweaters, pottery, and jewelry. There are even tartan blankets and throws. If you have Scottish heritage, you'll be intrigued by the store's complete selection of clan accessories, from mugs to key chains. Barrington Place Shops, 2000 Barrington St. © 902/429-6872. www.plaidplace.com. Metro Transit nos. 2, 7, 9.

TOBACCO

Jon Alan's Cigar Emporium   An experience in itself. Visit this large walk-in humidor with more than 600 types of cigars, including a particularly good selection of Cuban varieties. The store also carries cigar accessories, such as ashtrays, cases, cutters, and lighters. 5523 Spring Garden Rd. (Corner of Dresden Row and Artillery Place, just off Spring Garden Rd.) ℭ 902/425-7665. www.jonalans.com/emporium/emporium. html. Metro Transit nos. 1, 3,10.

MacDonald Tobacco & Gifts   You'll find imported tobacco, luxury cigarettes, and Cuban cigars in a humidified walk-in cigar room. The shop also specializes in nautical brassware. In Barrington Place Shops, 1903 Barrington St. ℭ 902/ 423-6647. In Casino Nova Scotia, 1983 Upper Water St. ℭ 902/425-6777. www.tobaccoand gifts.com. Metro Transit nos. 2, 7, 9.

TOYS

Discovery Centre Gifts Shop ⟨Kids⟩   There are toys, experiments, books, microscopes—in short, lots of items to make science fun. Be sure to take your kids and yourself to the **Discovery Centre** (see "Especially for Kids" in chapter 6) as well. 1593 Barrington St. (Corner of Sackville & Barrington sts.) ℭ 902/492-4422. www. discoverycentre.ns.ca. Metro Transit nos. 2, 7, 9.

WINE & SPIRITS

Nova Scotia Liquor Corporation (NSLC)   Most Haligonians purchase their wine, spirits, and beer at these outlets, located throughout the city. You'll find the best selection here. In the Halifax Shopping Centre, ℭ 902/455-4352. Metro Transit nos. 1, 2, 4. 2559 Agricola St. ℭ 902/429-5645. Metro Transit nos. 5, 82. 1120 Queen St. ℭ 902/ 425-7218. Metro Transit nos. 3, 7, 18. www.nsliquor.ns.ca.

Port of Wines   A division of the NSLC, this store carries a wide selection of specialty wine and liquor. This is the place to shop if you're looking for something special, such as a 25-year-old single-malt scotch, or a vintage wine. In Scotia Square Mall, 2000 Barrington St. ℭ 902/422-4206. In the Quinpool Centre, 6169 Quinpool Rd. ℭ 902/423-7126. Metro Transit nos. 6, 14, 20. www.nsliquor.ns.ca/services-port-of-wine.asp.

9

Halifax After Dark

Halifax has a reputation as a rowdy garrison town that likes to party. But the city also has a more refined side, with such offers as the theater and the symphony. As the entertainment center of the Maritimes, the city brings in well-known names in the music industry, and with thousands of university students to amuse, there are always concerts and comedy shows.

Urban legend has it that the city has the most bars and nightclubs per capita in the country—there are over 50 in the downtown core alone. Live music is offered in almost every bar and lounge, especially on weekends. From jazz to country, Celtic to pop, Halifax hums.

For those who aren't content to remain stationary while listening to those tunes, head out to a dance club. Most are open until 2am; some stay open until 3:30am. You can even party like the British soldiers did 150 years ago—at Alexander Keith's brewery.

FINDING OUT WHAT'S ON For up-to-date information on what's happening in town, consult the Thursday edition of the *Chronicle-Herald,* or pick up a copy of *The Coast,* a free weekly newspaper that publishes nightlife listings. *Where Halifax* is usually available in hotel rooms and has listings of current events, including entertainment.

GETTING TICKETS Halifax is a small enough city that you shouldn't have much trouble accessing tickets on short notice—even for the same day. Your concierge will likely be able to obtain them for you. Halifax does not have an umbrella ticket agency, but for information on sporting and entertainment events at the **Halifax Metro Centre** call their info line at ☎ **902/451-1202** or their box office at ☎ **902/451-1221.** For information about and tickets to the Nova Scotia Symphony, as well as live theatre and other live entertainment at the **Rebecca Cohn Auditorium**, call ☎ **800/874-1669** or **902/494-3820.** Another popular Halifax venue is the **Neptune Theatre,** ☎ **800/565-7345** or **902/429-7300.**

1 Performing Arts

Halifax doesn't have the variety and depth of entertainment that you'll find in Toronto or New York. The **Halifax Metro Centre,** 1800 Argyle St. (info line ☎ **902/451-1202;** box office 902/451-2332; www.halifaxmetrocentre.com; Metro Transit nos. 2, 7, 9) is the largest entertainment facility in the city, seating up to 10,000 people. The Centre hosts the annual International Tattoo, and is the venue for big-name entertainers such as Garth Brooks and touring productions including the Broadway musical *Cats.* **The Rebecca Cohn Auditorium,** 6101 University Ave. (☎ **800/874-1669** or 902/494-3820; www.dal.ca/~cohn/box.html; Metro Transit nos. 3, 7, 17) is part of the Dalhousie Arts

Centre. "The Cohn," as it is known by Haligonians, is an intimate 1,000-seat theater, including the 200-seat balcony. Recent acts performing here have included Roch Voisine, the Royal Winnipeg Ballet, and Bruce Guthro. It is also home to Symphony Nova Scotia, and the Dalhousie Theatre Department series.

THEATER

Grafton St. Dinner Theatre   If you like laughter with your food, this dinner theater presents lighthearted musical comedies that will go down as easy as the edibles. The main course is chosen from prime rib, chicken Kiev or poached salmon, and special dietary requirements can be handled with 48 hours notice. An appetizer and dessert are also included. Past productions by the cast include: *Eat, Drink, and Be Murdered,* with music and characters set in the 1950s; *The Cheatin' Heart Café;* and *Ain't We Got Fun,* with a 1930s atmosphere and music. Tickets cost C$36.95 (US$24.65) for adults, C$33.75 (US$22.50) for seniors, C$18 (US$12) for children 11 and under, except for Saturdays, when children's tickets are full price. Shows run Tuesday through Sunday, starting at 6:45pm and finishing at approximately 10pm. 1741 Grafton St. ℭ **902/425-1961.** www.graftonstdinnertheatre.com. Metro Transit nos. 2, 7, 9.

Halifax Feast Dinner Theatre   In this combination of musical theatre and dining there's some interaction with the characters, but most of the production is presented on stage. Your choice of main courses includes such fare as chicken, salmon, roast beef, and vegetarian plates. The 2003 season productions include: *My Big Fat Cape Breton Wedding,* from February to June (Greek-wedding movies have nothing on this!); *The Olden Girls,* from June to November, where four golden oldies hit the road on a bus tour of the Maritimes and audience members get to share in their hilarious adventures, and *The MacBunkers Christmas,* in November and December, modeled after TV's famous Bunker family. Tickets are C$34.50 (US$23) per person and reservations are required. Shows run Wednesday to Saturday, beginning at 7pm and finishing at approximately 10pm. Maritime Centre, corner of Barrington and Salter sts. ℭ **902/420-1840.** www.feastdinnertheatre.com. Metro Transit nos. 2, 7, 9.

Neptune Theatre   As the city's premier theater, Neptune has brought world-class performances to Halifax for decades, and with its recent major renovations the historic building is also world class. It includes Fountain Hall—a 479-seat main stage, and the intimate du Maurier Theater—a 190-seat secondary stage, plus rehearsal halls. The main season runs from September to May, with a shorter summer season. 1593 Argyle St. ℭ **902/429-7300.** www.neptunetheatre.com. Metro Transit nos. 2, 7, 9.

Rebecca Cohn Auditorium   As part of the Dalhousie Arts Centre, "the Cohn" is home to the Dalhousie Theatre Department's presentations, as well as visiting performances. Dalhousie Arts Centre, 6101 University Ave. ℭ **800/874-1669,** or 902/494-3820 for tickets, ℭ **902/494-7081** info line. www.dal.ca/~cohn/box.html. Metro Transit nos. 3, 7, 17.

Shakespeare by the Sea (*Value*) (*Kids*)   This series of outdoor productions takes place during July and August at various venues in the city, including Point Pleasant Park and the Citadel. Shakespeare by the Sea is a fabulous way to experience the Bard. Various locations. ℭ **902/422-0295.** www3.ns.sympatico.ca/sbts. Point Pleasant Park Metro Transit no. 9.; Citadel Metro Transit no. 6.

CLASSICAL MUSIC

Symphony Nova Scotia   You'll find a variety of classical presentations, from Baroque to Pops and more. Internationally acclaimed guest and host conductors lead the 37-member orchestra through 65 performances during their September to May season. A holiday tradition is the annual performance of *The Nutcracker*. Dalhousie Arts Centre, 6101 University Ave. *©* **800/874-1669** or 902/494-3820 for tickets, *©* **902/494-7081** info line. www.symphonynovascotia.ca. Metro Transit nos. 3, 7, 17.

CONCERT SERIES

St. Cecilia Concert Series   A series of classical instrumental and vocal performances featuring local, national, and international talent. The season runs from September to June at various venues in the city. *©* **902/420-4805**. www. stcecilia.ca.

DANCE

Halifax Dance   This dance school and facility is located in the Brewery Market. Local and touring performances are presented throughout the year, and performers also participate in other city productions, including *The Nutcracker* with Symphony Nova Scotia. The Brewery Market, 1496 Lower Water St. *©* **902/422-2006**. www.halifaxdance.ns.ca. Metro Transit nos. 2, 4, 7.

Live Art Productions   Live Art Productions is an innovative art organization that has been presenting cutting-edge dance and performance art in Halifax for over 20 years. Performances are held at various venues, including the Sir James Dunn Theatre and the du Maurier Theatre. *©* **800/874-1669** or 902/494-3820 for tickets, 902/494-7081 info line. www.chebucto.ns.ca/Culture/Liveart.

2 The Club & Live Music Scene

If you want to party, you've come to the right place. Halifax has had a reputation for boisterous nightlife for 2½ centuries. Whether you want to clap your hands to Celtic music, kick up your heels, or relax with jazz, there's lots to choose from right in the downtown. Weekends usually mean lineups at all the popular locations, so you might want to arrive a little early, or at least prepare yourself mentally for a wait. Cover charges vary from location to location, and from night to night. Most are C$6 (US$4) or under.

DANCING

The Argyle   This is the place to be on Thursday night for the college crowd. Dancing and drinking are the activities, so depending on your age, get there early (there are huge lineups), or avoid it at all costs. 1575 Argyle St. *©* **902/ 492-8844**. Metro Transit nos. 2, 7, 9.

Boomers Lounge & Eatery   For the mature (read over 35) visitor, this is a pleasing spot to go dancing. You'll enjoy the mood, and the music of the '50s, '60s, and '70s. 1725 Grafton St. (At George St.) *©* **902/425-5260**. Metro Transit nos. 2, 7, 9.

New Palace Cabaret   If you like to feel the beat in your bones, this is the place to go. In other words, loud, pulsating music and dancing until 3:30am. 1721 Brunswick St. *©* **902/429-5959**. Metro Transit nos. 2, 4, 6.

Pacifico Bar & Grill   This popular club has one of the city's biggest dance floors, and the music is a variety of current pop and older familiar dance tunes. The clientele is both couples and singles, in the 20–35 age group. The bar also has billiards, a big-screen TV, and, in case you work up an appetite with all that dancing, a full-menu restaurant. 1505 Barrington St. ℂ **902/422-3633.** Metro Transit nos. 6, 7, 9.

The Velvet Olive This is a good place for dancing, with local DJs early in the week and live bands from Wednesday to Saturday. Along with great cocktails, and tasty Thai food, The Velvet Olive is known for its good-looking bartenders. 1770 Market St. ℂ **902/492-2233.** www.velvetolive.com. Metro Transit nos. 2, 7, 9.

(*Fun Fact* **The Dome**

More commonly, even affectionately, known as "the liquordome" by locals, this is practically a block of interconnected drinking establishments, including **The Attic**, 1741 Grafton St. (ℂ 902423-0909); **My Apartment**, 1740 Argyle St. (ℂ **902/422-5453**); **Cheers**, 1743 Grafton St. (ℂ **902/421-1665**); and **Lawrence's**, 1726 Argyle St. (ℂ **902/425-8077**). Each location has its own personality, so you'll have to stroll through to find the one that suits yours. There's food, live bands, and dancing in each of the clubs—and there are more bars than you can count. You might even consider dropping bread crumbs so you don't get lost in the maze. Be prepared for weekend lineups at every door, but when you finally get in you can stay until 3:30am. Visit the website: www.thedome.ca. Metro Transit nos. 2, 7, 9.

JAZZ & BLUES

Bearly's House of Blues & Ribs A popular spot for live blues and bluegrass music. There is live jazz on Tuesday nights, the Karaoke Nights on Wednesdays are popular with the university crowd, and live blues music is featured each night from Thursday to Saturday. Expect a casual and friendly atmosphere with comfortable chairs and low lights. Bearly's House also has home-cooked meals and a variety of Greek specialties. 1269 Barrington St. ℂ **902/423-2526.** Metro Transit nos. 6, 7, 9.

FOLK/CELTIC

Lower Deck Good Time Pub This is a popular spot for Maritime Celtic music and a lot of silly good times. The pub serves Maritime food including such popular standbys as sausage and sauerkraut. Privateers Warehouse, Historic Properties. Upper Water St. ℂ **902/425-1501.** Metro Transit nos. 2, 4, 6.

The Old Triangle Irish Alehouse You'll love the atmosphere of this rustic pub. It's divided into three areas—the music room with excellent traditional Celtic entertainment; the pourhouse; and the snug, which has tiny, private rooms that in the olden days were the only part of a pub ladies were allowed to visit. Simple but delicious Irish cuisine is served in all three areas. 5136 Prince St. ℂ **902-492-4900.** www.theoldtriangle.com. Metro Transit nos. 6, 7, 9.

The Split Crow A traditional spot favored by office workers during the week and the older crowd on weekends, with an occasional influx of university students. Most are drawn by the good Celtic entertainment, the rest by the reasonable pub food. Granville Market, Historic Properties, 1855 Granville St. ℂ **902/422-4366.** www.thesplitcrow.com. Metro Transit nos. 6, 7, 9.

ECLECTIC

The Marquee Club and Hell's Kitchen   This popular club brings in a lot of Canadian touring bands, along with bands from the local music scene. In Hell's Kitchen (appropriately located below the main floor club) you can enjoy excellent pizza and Thursday-night live jazz entertainment. It's dimly lit and rather small, with a beautiful stainless steel bar. 1037 Gottingen St. ✆ **902/429-3020.** Metro Transit nos. 1, 7, 10.

Tribeca   In 2002 this club came under new ownership, had a name change, and was beautifully redecorated. Now it has a fresh, open, New York feel to it. There's a variety of live music, and the food has been described as "Martha Stewartish" with such things as crab cakes, shrimp on angel-hair pasta, and tasty lamb burgers. 1588 Granville St. ✆ **902/492-4036.** Metro Transit nos. 6, 7, 9.

3 The Bar Scene

The bar scene is healthy in Halifax, with so many choices that I doubt you will have the opportunity to do more than scratch the surface. Two streets—**Argyle Street** and **Spring Garden Road**—offer the highest concentration, and with the majority of the bar population in these two places, sometimes things get loud and crowded, but not usually dangerous. The reviews below will help you narrow your choices to the ones you'll most likely enjoy.

BARS & LOUNGES

The Bitter End   This is a wine and martini bar, but it's better known as the best place in town to get a Caesar—the liquid variety, not the salad, although they do serve food as well. The club was expanded in 2002, but it still has a cozy and classy atmosphere. 1572 Argyle St. ✆ **902/425-3039.** Metro Transit nos. 2, 7, 9.

Cellar Bar & Grill   This is an affordable neighborhood bar with a warm atmosphere and good food. 5677 Benton Place. ✆ **902/492-4412.** Metro Transit nos. 1, 10, 17.

Tips 1663 Argyle Street

Halifax has a confusing way of incorporating a variety of clubs under one roof and calling them by different names. You can enter one club, and without even realizing you left, be drinking in another. Such is the situation at 1663 Argyle Street. It is home to the **Economy Shoe Shop** (✆ **902/ 423-7463**), an artsy eatery and lounge; **Diamond** (✆ **902/423-5503**), a jukebox joint for the younger crowd; the **Belgium Bar** (✆ **902/423-7463**), a beer garden in a bright atrium; and **Backstage** (✆ **902/423-8845**), an upscale bar for grown-ups. Confusing as it is, it's the hot spot in the trendy Spring Garden Road district. You might even catch a glimpse of an "on location" movie star while you're sipping your beverage of choice. Metro Transit nos. 2, 7, 9.

The Fireside   Think shabby chic and relaxation—deep sofas, cozy armchairs, intimate tables, and the best martinis in the city. 1500 Brunswick St. Just off Spring Garden Rd. ✆ **902/423-5995.** Metro Transit nos. 1, 10, 17.

Mexicali Rosa's   Here's where you'll find a variety of margaritas and Mexican food, with a definite Central American flair.   5680 Spring Garden Rd. ✆ **902/422-7672.** Metro Transit nos. 1, 10, 17.

Stayner's Wharf Bar & Grill   It's worth having a beer or meal here just to check out the photographs of personalities and events that decorate the walls. Call ahead to find out when there is live music entertainment.   5075 George St. (Next to the Ferry Terminal.) ✆ **902/492-1800.** Metro Transit nos. 6, 7, 9.

PUBS

Maxwell's Plum   This British-style pub is best known for its large selection of imported draft and single-malt scotch whiskey, served along with hearty pub grub.   1600 Grafton St. ✆ **902/423-5090.** Metro Transit nos. 2, 7, 9.

Peddlers' Pub   You'll find more food variety than drinks here, but you might want to check out their weekday $1.99 supper specials.   Granville Mall. ✆ **902/ 423-5033.** Metro Transit nos. 6, 7, 9.

Thirsty Duck Pub & Eatery   This pub has been around for a while, and its clientele, originally university students, have aged along with it. The food is decent and cheap, and there's a rooftop patio in the summer.   5472 Spring Garden Rd. ✆ **902/422-1548.** Metro Transit nos. 1, 10, 17.

Your Father's Moustache   A current popular spot for the university crowd, it's also a good place to hear local live entertainment. It also has an extensive menu.   5686 Spring Garden Rd. ✆ **902/423-6766.** Metro Transit nos. 1, 10, 17.

BREW PUBS

Granite Brewery   This brew pub has great beers and amazing food, and there's an authentic British-pub feel to the stone-walled tavern. Be sure to try the signature "Peculiar" beer, which is brewed on the premises.   1222 Barrington St. ✆ **902/423-5660.** www.granitebrewery.ca. Metro Transit nos. 7, 9, 18.

John Shippey's Brewing Company   This spot has superb waterfront views with outdoor seating from May to September, and indoor seating year round. Specialty brews and eight craft ales are brewed on-site.   Historic Properties, 1869 Upper Water St. ✆ **902/423-7386.** Metro Transit nos. 2, 4, 6.

Rogue's Roost Brew Pub & Eatery   This is a microbrewery and ale house, featuring five of its own brews for you to sample. Good food. Lots of windows on Spring Garden Rd. The Roost also includes a restaurant.   5435 Spring Garden Rd. ✆ **902/492-2337.** Metro Transit nos. 1, 10, 17.

CIGAR BARS

Jon Alan's Cigar Bar   An upscale establishment that offers over 600 varieties of cigars, six dozen varieties of single-malt scotch, and an extensive martini list. 5523 Spring Garden Rd. (Corner of Dresden Row and Artillery Place.) ✆ **902/422-5267.** www. jonalans.com/emporium/emporium.html. Metro Transit nos. 1, 10, 17.

Tom's Little Havana Café   A quaint spot that's usually packed, but still a good place to chat and enjoy a fine cigar and a drink. The staff are really friendly. 5428 Doyle St. (Just off Spring Garden Rd.) ✆ **902/423-8667.** Metro Transit nos. 1, 10, 17.

HOTEL BARS

Most of these bars cater mainly to their own clientele, usually an older group. If you're looking for a quiet drink and conversation, though, they're a fine choice. At the **Fife & Drum,** in the Casino Nova Scotia Hotel, 1919 Upper Water St.

(© 902/428-7805; Metro Transit nos. 2, 4, 6), you'll find traditional Maritime entertainment in a Scottish-style pub. They serve a wide selection of draft and scotch. **The Promenade Lounge,** in the Westin Nova Scotian, 1181 Hollis St. (© 902/421-1000; Metro Transit nos. 7, 18, 19), is a relaxing upscale bar. **Sam Slick's,** in the Delta Halifax Hotel, 1990 Barrington St. (© 902/492-6443; Metro Transit nos. 2, 7, 9), is a cozy little lounge, with a tasty luncheon buffet and late-night snacks.

A Halifax mainstay that has been newly decorated is the **Victory Arms Pub,** in the Lord Nelson Hotel, 1515 South Park St. (© 902/420-9781; Metro Transit nos. 1, 10, 17). It serves a traditional British pub menu, with Guinness on tap. **Willows Wine Bar and Bistro,** in the Holiday Inn Select Halifax Centre, 1980 Robie St. (© 902/423-1161; Metro Transit nos. 7, 17, 80), serves international wines by the glass, and offers live music on the weekends.

TAVERNS

Midtown Tavern   This old Halifax sports tavern has been around for years and is a "real man's" kind of bar. But there's great food, great prices, draft specials, friendly service, and an interesting array of regulars. 1684 Grafton St. © 902/422-5213. Metro Transit nos. 2, 7, 9.

Sea Horse Tavern   This is the oldest tavern in Nova Scotia, but under new ownership it has started to draw the university crowd. 1665 Argyle St. © 902/423-7200. Metro Transit nos. 2, 7, 9.

GAY & LESBIAN PUBS & BARS

Eagle Dance Bar, Pub and Eatery   You can enjoy dancing, drinking, and eating, every day until 2am. There's also a generous brunch on the weekends. 1567 Grafton St. © 902/425-1889. Metro Transit nos. 2, 7, 9.

Reflections Cabaret (Finds   This is a popular location for both gay and straight clubbers. This bar has a large dance floor and is one of the hottest nightclubs in the city. 5184 Sackville St. © 902/422-2957. www.reflectionscabaret.com. Metro Transit nos. 7, 9, 20.

(Fun Fact Under the Stars

Just as dining on the patio during the day is an added treat, drinking under the stars adds a whole new dimension to a party. Somehow the expanded space seems to expand the experience, making it happier, funnier, more memorable. Halifax pubs and lounges have reached up to their roofs and out onto the sidewalks to give their customers this added pleasure. Some of the best patio and rooftop locations are: **The Split Crow** patio, 1855 Granville St. (© 902/422-4366); **The Thirsty Duck** rooftop, 5472 Spring Garden Rd. (© 902/422-1548); the **Economy Shoe Shop** patio, 1663 Argyle St. (© 902/423-7463); the **Argyle** rooftop, 1575 Argyle St. (© 902/431-9402); and **The Old Triangle Alehouse** patio, 5136 Prince St. (© 902/492-4900). All are open until 2am. Unfortunately, the umbrellas and flower pots are put away in October and not seen again until May, leaving only five months to drink in the experience.

4 Other Diversions

CASINOS

Casino Nova Scotia   Here you'll find gaming galore, from craps to roulette to almost 700 slot machines. When you finally need food there are three on-site restaurants to choose from, including **T.G.I. Friday's;** fine cuisine at **Bacchus** (see chapter 5); and live entertainment and pub food in the **Schooner Room.** Past headliners on the Casino mainstage have been Dionne Warwick, Michelle Wright, and John Gracie. The dress code is smart casual, but you'll see lots of jeans and sweats during the day, and it's not much fancier at night. Players must be 19 or older to enter, and it's open 24 hours a day. 1983 Upper Water St. ℂ 902/425-7777. www.casinonovascotia.com. Metro Transit nos. 2, 4, 6.

CINEMA

Alfresco Filmfesto (Finds (Kids)   How's this for a unique family experience—relaxing on the grass beside the harbor, watching a classic film under the stars. The films are projected on the wall of the Electropolis building (5091 Terminal Rd.) on scheduled Thursday and Friday nights from June through August. Chairs are available if you get there early, and screenings are free, or you can make a donation. The show starts at dusk. 5091 Terminal Rd. ℂ 902/422-3456. www.atlanticfilm.com. Metro Transit nos. 7, 18, 19.

The Atlantic Film Festival (Value)   During nine days in September, dozens of regional, national, and international films are available to the public at a number of venues throughout the city. After more than 20 years, this is still one of the premier film festivals in the country. ℂ 902/422-3456. www.atlanticfilm.com.

IMAX   Immerse yourself in the experience by watching from a steep-stacked theater seat surrounded by a six-stories-high and seven-stories-wide movie screen. Imax Empire 18, 190 Chain Lake Dr., Bayers Lake Business Park. ℂ 902/876-4629. Metro Transit nos. 12, 21.

MAINSTREAM THEATER RELEASES

Check out Hollywood's latest offerings at multi-screen theaters throughout the city. **Empire Theatres** has two locations—190 Chain Lake Dr. (ℂ 902/422-2022; Metro Transit nos. 12, 21) and 6408 Oxford St. (ℂ 902/422-2022; Metro Transit nos. 1, 18, 58). **Famous Players** is located in the **Park Lane Mall,** 5657 Spring Garden Rd. (ℂ 902/423-4598; Metro Transit nos. 1, 10, 17).

COFFEE HOUSES

Coburg Coffee House is located at 7085 Coburg Rd. (ℂ 902/429-2326; Metro Transit nos. 1, 18, 58) and is popular with the Dalhousie university crowd because it's in their backyard. The **Dandelion,** at 5986 Spring Garden Rd. (ℂ 902/446-3331; Metro Transit nos. 1, 10, 17), is decorated with funky folk art and is another university stop. **Java.Net Café,** 5982 Spring Garden Rd. (ℂ 902/422-7302; Metro Transit nos. 1, 10, 17), allows you to surf while you sip. **Perks** has really good coffee at two locations, the first is right by the Ferry Terminal, at 1781 Lower Water St. (ℂ 902/429-9380; Metro Transit nos. 2, 4, 6) and 6098 Quinpool Rd. (ℂ 902/429-1856; Metro Transit nos. 6, 14, 20). The **Second Cup** has a whole variety of flavored coffees (try the Amaretto Almond), and beans (ground or whole) that you can buy to take home. It's located at 5425 Spring Garden Rd. (ℂ 902/429-0883; Metro Transit nos. 1, 10, 17), with big windows so you can people watch while you relax.

Steve-O-Reno's has been voted the best coffee in town. Plus they have a yummy Thai noodle salad, and other healthy and natural foods. It draws an artsy crowd and university students. You'll find it at 1536 Brunswick St. (© **902/429-3034;** Metro Transit nos. 1, 2, 4). See chapter 5 for a full review. **Timothy's Coffees of the World** has a worldwide selection of good coffees and there are two locations, at 1791 Barrington St. (© **902/429-6397;** Metro Transit nos. 2, 7, 9) and 5475 Spring Garden Rd. (© **902/423-1651;** Metro Transit nos. 1, 10, 17). A lot of people like to read while they drink their coffee, and the **Daily Grind** has a great selection of magazines and newspapers, as well as sandwiches, breads, and delicious carrot cake. It's at 5686 Spring Garden Rd. (© **902/429-6397;** Metro Transit nos. 1, 10, 17).

POOL HALLS

Pool and billiards are back "in" and the city has a variety of locations. The most popular is **Breakers** (1661 Argyle St. © **902/422-8003;** Metro Transit nos. 2, 7, 9), right next door to the Economy Shoe Shop, another popular nightspot. Breaker's is fully licensed and there's a private room for parties or special events. **Dooly's Billiards** (1657 Barrington St. © **902/429-2627;** Metro Transit nos. 2, 7, 9) is an upscale chain of pool halls, with fireplace and comfortable stuffed chairs. **Gatsby's** (5675 Spring Garden Rd. © **902/429-9999;** Metro Transit nos. 1, 10, 17) has two tables, and a games room. There's food service to 2am. **The Oasis Pub & Eatery** (5675 Spring Garden Rd. © **902/422-2227;** Metro Transit nos. 1, 10, 17) has a casual atmosphere, four large-screen TVs, pool tables, shuffleboard, and dartboard—but it is a little grungy. **The Planet Bar & Diner** (5435 Spring Garden Rd. © **902/423-8225;** Metro Transit nos. 1, 10, 17) has lots of tables and good pub food. Private rooms are available, and there's an outdoor patio open in summer. **The Tickle Trunk** (5680 Spring Garden Rd. © **902/429-2582;** Metro Transit nos. 1, 10, 17) has pool tables, live entertainment, and board games.

LATE-NIGHT BITES

Depending on what your stomach can handle after midnight, there are a few locations from which to choose. Most are within walking distance of the clubs, but even in friendly Halifax you should not walk alone.

Alfredo Weinstein & Ho   If you can handle spicy food after a night on the town, here you have the choice of Italian, Deli, and Chinese, all on the same menu. If you want a real feast try the signature dish, Oriental Steak Pizza with sliced steak, onions, mozzarella, cheddar, and Ho's oriental sauce. There's also sandwiches or stir-fries for the less hardy stomach. It stays open until 4am on Fridays and Saturdays. 1739 Grafton St. © 902/454-9344. Metro Transit nos. 7, 9, 2.

Apple Barrel 24Hr Restaurant   This spot is open whenever the hunger pangs strike, and you can order something greasy like French fries, or a plainer sandwich—or something sweet, if you can stomach dessert at 4am. 1726 Grafton St. (At the Prince George Hotel.) © 902/425-0500. Metro Transit nos. 7, 9, 2.

La Cave *(Finds*   If it's something sweet you're after, there's no better place than this. What better way to complete a night on the town than to go underground for a piece of decadent cheesecake. Settled in a cozy cave or booth, or next to the fireplace in the main dining area, savoring an orange-chocolate cheesecake, you'll experience a perfect ending to a night on the town. From Sunday to Wednesday it's open until 2am, but Thursday to Saturday until 4:30am. 5244 Blowers St. © 902/429-3551. Metro Transit nos. 7, 9, 18.

Freeman's Little New York Freeman's is the uptown equivalent of the Apple Barrel, except it only stays open until 5am, which is most likely late enough. Freeman's serves Italian specialties and pizza, along with Canadian cuisine. Takeout is also available. 6092 Quinpool Rd. ℂ **902/429-0241.** Metro Transit nos. 6, 14, 20.

Gatsby's This spot has fast, friendly service with good prices. The spinach lasagna is worth trying, and their carrot cake is also excellent. It's open until 2am, and mid May to October there is an outdoor patio. 5695 Spring Garden Rd. ℂ **902/429-9999.** Metro Transit nos. 1, 10, 17.

Marquee Club and Hell's Kitchen If it has to be pizza and nothing but pizza, the best after midnight is at the Marquee Club and Hell's Kitchen. The Marquee Club is on the main floor, and Hell's Kitchen is downstairs (how appropriate). They're open until 3:30am. 1037 Gottingen St. ℂ **902/429-3020,** Metro Transit nos. 1, 10, 17.

The Pita Pit For something not quite so heavy, and perhaps a little more nutritious, a pita filled with savory vegetables and sprouts will go down quite easily. It's open until 4am on weekends. 1586 Argyle St. ℂ **902/429-8080.** Metro Transit nos. 2, 7, 9.

10

Side Trips from Halifax

If you have access to a vehicle and an extra few days, there are some wonderful side trips from Halifax to add to your itinerary. For 1-day trips, visit nearby **Dartmouth** and **Peggy's Cove.** Two days will give you time to visit the **Annapolis Valley,** the **South Shore, Yarmouth, Truro** and **Parrsboro,** and the **Eastern Shore.** You'll need 3 days to visit **Cape Breton Island** and tour the Cabot Trail.

1 Dartmouth

Dartmouth is so close to Halifax that travelers often overlook it. This is unfortunate, because Halifax's sister city has its own identity and offerings.

ESSENTIALS
GETTING THERE It's relatively easy and you have lots of choices. You can follow Barrington Street north to the A. Murray MacKay Bridge and cross to reach Dartmouth. There is a 75¢ toll for the bridge, which is paid on the Dartmouth side. This will take approximately 10 minutes if it's not during the morning or afternoon rush hour. Or follow route 2 from Halifax through **Bedford** to route 7, which takes you to Dartmouth; a more picturesque drive that winds along the **Bedford Basin** but takes at least 30 minutes.

You can also take a **Metro Transit** bus along either route. Take Metro Bus nos. 84 or 89 to travel to Dartmouth across the A. Murray MacKay Bridge, and Bus nos. 80 or 82 to travel to Bedford, then change to nos. 66, 84, or 85 to reach Dartmouth.

Finally, you can catch the **ferry** across the Halifax Harbour from **Upper Water Street** and land about 15 minutes later at **Alderney Gate** in Dartmouth.

VISITOR INFORMATION Obtain information and maps on **Dartmouth** at **Alderney Gate Landing,** 60 Alderney Drive, at the ferry terminal (© **902/490-4433**), or at **MicMac Mall,** 21 MicMac Blvd. (© **902/461-9939**). Take Hwy. 111 from the A. Murray MacKay Bridge to exit 5.

WHERE TO STAY
Coastal Inn Concorde ★ The clean, comfortable rooms at the Concorde all include kitchenettes, and are in fact quite spacious. Many have a view of Halifax Harbour. Nearly half of the units are one-bedroom suites; the deluxe suites include a whirlpool bath and sauna. If you'd rather not do your own cooking, the **Concorde Inn restaurant** serves home-style fare, or there are several other eateries nearby. The inn's bright red roof makes it easy to locate.

379 Windmill Rd., Dartmouth, NS B3A 1J6. © **800/565-1565** or 902/465-7777. Fax 902/465-3956. www.coastalinns.com. 56 units. C$75–$99 (US$45–$60) double; C$89–$149 (US$54–$90) suite. Packages available. Extra person C$10 (US$6.70). Children 16 and under stay free in parents' room. AE, DC, MC, V. Free parking. **Amenities:** Restaurant (Canadian); business center; limited room service; laundry service; dry cleaning. *In room:* A/C, TV, dataport, kitchenette, hair dryer available on request.

Side Trips from Halifax

Comfort Inn ⚹   This Comfort Inn is located close to the MacKay Bridge. It provides basic, clean accommodations, with a 100% satisfaction guarantee— if there's a problem with your room that cannot be fixed to your satisfaction immediately, the room is free for the night. There is no restaurant on-site, but the inn does serve a continental breakfast for an extra C$3 (US$2) charge.

456 Windmill Rd., Darmouth, NS B3A 1J7. ℭ **800/228-5150** or 902/463-9900. Fax 902/466-2080. www.choicehotels.ca. 81 units. April 1–Oct 31 C$95–$150 (US$57–$90). Nov 1–March 31 C$69–$99 (US$46–$66). Packages available. Extra person C$8 (US$5.35). Children 17 and under stay free in parents' room. AE, DC, MC, V. Free parking. Pets accepted with some restrictions. *In room:* A/C, TV w/pay movies.

Maranova Suites Hotel ⚹ *Kids*   This is a good spot for families, as all the units have been recently renovated and are equipped with kitchenettes. All also have sitting areas and balconies. One-bedroom and two-bedroom suites are also available. Some units have great views of the harbor looking towards Halifax. Complimentary day passes to the Dartmouth Sportsplex are available to keep

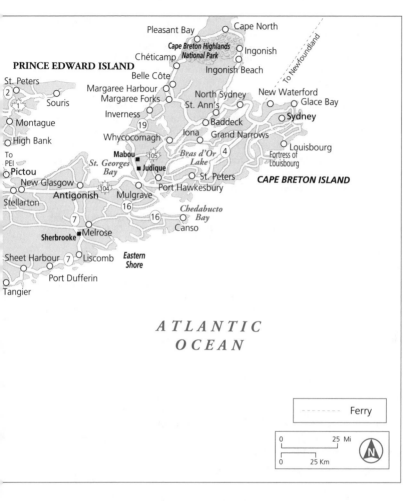

the kids occupied. The hotel is a 5-minute walk to the ferry terminal, where the pedestrian-only ferry takes you directly to the Halifax waterfront.

65 King St., Dartmouth, NS B2Y 4C2. © **888/798-5558** or 902/463-9520. Fax 902/463-2631. www.mara novasuites.com. 64 units. C$81–$240 (US$49–$144). Packages available. Children 17 and under stay free in parents' room. AE, DC, MC, V. **Amenities:** Restaurant (North American), lounge; business center; coin-op washers and dryers; dry cleaning. *In room:* A/C, TV w/pay movies, kitchenette.

Park Place Ramada Plaza Hotel ★ *Kids* This is a full service, luxury hotel featuring spacious, comfortable rooms and suites and an indoor waterslide and spa. There are special coloring contests for children under 10 in the restaurant and free cookies and milk for bedtime snacks on the weekend, plus children under 5 eat free at the restaurant if accompanied by an adult that purchases a meal. Check with the front desk for details. The hotel is just a 15-minute drive from the Halifax International Airport, and only a 10-minute drive from downtown Halifax via the A. Murray MacKay Bridge.

240 Brownlow Ave., Dartmouth, NS B3B 1X6. ℭ **800/561-3733** or 902/468-8888. Fax 902/468-8765. www.ramadans.com. 178 units. March–Nov C$125–$160 (US$75–$96). Dec–Feb C$79–$119 (US$53–$79.50). Packages available. Extra person C$15 (US$10). Children 17 and under stay free in parents' room. AE, DC, MC, V. Free parking. Pets accepted. **Amenities:** Restaurant (North American), lounge, bar; indoor pool; exercise room; sauna; laundry service; dry cleaning. *In room:* A/C, TV w/pay movies, dataport, coffeemaker, hair dryer, iron.

Prince Albert B&B ★ *(Kids)* This is a fresh little bed-and-breakfast, suitable for couples or small families. It is located in downtown Dartmouth, a 10-minute walk from the ferry from Halifax. Each suite has its own bathroom and large sitting room with an additional pullout couch or futon. There's a microwave and fridge in each suite for light meals. Your hosts, Diane and Eva Aikens, are happy to give you directions to local shopping and points of interest on both sides of the harbor. The B&B is only a 7-minute hike to the walking trail at lovely Lake Banook.

81 Prince Albert Rd., Dartmouth, NS B2Y 1M1. ℭ **902/469-0362.** www.bbcanada.com/4145.html. 2 units. C$65–$115 (US$39–$69). Rates include full breakfast. V. Free parking. *In room:* TV/VCR, fridge, coffeemaker.

WHERE TO DINE

MacAskill's Restaurant ★ SEAFOOD The first thing you will notice once you're inside MacAskill's is the great view of the harbor, the Halifax waterfront, and the skyline. The next thing you'll notice is the comfortable elegance of the restaurant's decor. The leather chairs in the cozy lounge are a perfect place to watch the sunset. The menu continues the enjoyment with a good variety of choices including the excellent Chicken in Filo, a MacAskill's original: boneless chicken breast, stuffed with mushroom duxelle, then baked in a filo pastry and served with a basil veloute. The Scallops "Pernod" is also a good choice, with Atlantic scallops sautéed with shallots and flambéed in Pernod, finished with fresh herbs, seafood veloute and cream, served on a bed of rice. The desserts are worth mentioning, particularly the Dessert Sampler, a combination of Swiss lemon mousse, cheesecake of the day, and German torte.

88 Alderney Dr. ℭ **902/466-3100.** Reservations recommended on weekends. Main dinner courses C$15–$30 (US$10–$20). AE, MC, V. Mon–Sat 5pm–10pm.

La Perla Dining Room ★ *(Finds)* NORTHERN ITALIAN This authentic Italian restaurant is across the harbor from Halifax in Dartmouth's oldest commercial building. The extensive menu is made up of traditional Italian recipes using fresh ingredients and spices. The antipasti include a variety of interestingly prepared snails, squid, mussels, frogs' legs, and a hot Italian sausage simmered with onions, pine nuts, mushrooms, and sweet vermouth. The list of pasta and main courses is long and the dishes delicious, featuring such offerings as Petto di Pollo al Dragoncello, grilled chicken breast served with sweet potato hay, tarragon cream sauce, and Zinfandel poached pear; Scallopini di Vitello al Astice, a veal scallopini simmered with lobster, sherry, cream, and a hint of curry and served with potato and vegetable; and Trota in Crosta di Noce con Salsa di Arancia, pan-seared pecan-crusted trout with an orange bourbon butter sauce, served with rice pilaf. The pleasant decor does not measure up to the menu, but once the food is served it doesn't matter. The easiest way to get to La Perla is to take the ferry from Halifax. Then you simply exit the ferry terminal building at the Alderney Library exit and you will see La Perla directly across the street.

73 Alderney Dr. ℭ **902/469-3241.** Reservations recommended on weekends. Main courses C$15–$30 (US$10–$20). AE, MC, V. Mon–Fri 11:30am–10pm; Sat–Sun 5pm–10pm.

EXPLORING THE AREA

Settled in 1750, **Dartmouth** has grown as a bedroom community to Halifax, and as an industrial location. Even so, it strives in its development to maintain a balance with nature. It is known as the City of Lakes—there are 23 within the city limits—and Dartmouth promotes a variety of water sports as well as walking trails and camping areas around the lakes. One landmark worth noting is the **World Peace Pavilion,** located in the park adjacent to **Alderney Gate** (60 Alderney Drive). Conceived by a group of students and built in 1995, it was opened by the spouses of the G–7 members. On display are dozens of rocks and bricks from historical and important sites all over the world: the Great Wall of China, the Parthenon in Greece, the Outback in Australia, and the Berlin Wall. All were sent to the pavilion as a testament to peace.

A visit to the **Shubenacadie Canal** is fun and educational for adults and children. Aside from enjoying the many beautiful walking trails along the canals, you'll learn the history of the Shubenacadie waterway, a system of rivers and lakes that at one time formed the shortest route between Halifax Harbour and the Bay of Fundy. The Mi'kmaq used it for centuries, and in the early 1800s local businessmen decided to connect the waterway and use locks so that ships could be transported along the route. They abandoned the canal in 1870 when railroads became a more popular method of transporting goods. The canal is at 54 Locks Road. To get there, follow Main Street and take the exit for Braemar Drive and Shubie Park (route 318). Braemar Drive becomes Waverly Road; Locks Road is on your left.

Black Cultural Centre for Nova Scotia ★ (Finds) This center is an inspiring treasure chest of stories and history about blacks in the Halifax Regional Municipality. The complex houses a library, auditorium, and exhibit rooms. There's information on black migration to Nova Scotia, the history of slavery in the province prior to 1800, little known stories about the Underground Railroad leading slaves to freedom in Nova Scotia, displays on community and religious life, and records of military service. There's also data about the importation of the Jamaican Maroons as workers in 1796, and their subsequent deportation to Sierra Leone in 1800. There's an inspiring display of black inventors and black heroes. The centre is housed in a large, two-story wood/brick building on a three-acre lot in Cherrybrook, the oldest community of people of color in the Halifax Regional Municipality.

1149 Main St. At Cherrybrook Rd. © **800/465-0767**. www.bccns.com. Admission C$5 (US$3.35) adults, C$3 (US$2) seniors & students, free for children 5 and under, C$15 (US$10) families. June 1–Sept 1 Mon–Fri 9am–5pm; Sat 10am–4pm; Closed Sun. Sept 2–May 31 Mon–Fri 9am–5pm. Closed Sat–Sun. Travel along Alderney Drive to a sharp left, where it becomes Prince Albert Rd. Follow this street until you see the exit for Highway 7 and Main St., on the right. Follow Main St. past the Nova Scotia Community College, on your right, and the Forest Hills exit, on your right, all the way to Cherrybrook.

Quaker House This two-story, wooden frame house was built in 1785 and is one of the oldest homes in the area. It originally belonged to William Ray, a barrel maker who came to Dartmouth as part of a community of Quakers. (From Nantucket Island, the Quakers traveled to the Dartmouth area to establish a whale fishing industry. Although they remained for less than two decades, their culture had an important impact on the development of the area and they assisted in securing the Dartmouth Common Land for public use.)

The Quaker House is restored and furnished to reflect its time period and is representative of the Nantucket Island domestic architecture from which it is derived. Guides dressed in simple Quaker garb provide tours and information, and there is a backyard herb garden open to visitors. On Wednesday afternoons there are traditional craft demonstrations.

57 Ochterloney St. © **902/464-2253**. www.dartmouthheritagemuseum.ns.ca/quaker.html. Admission C$2 (US$1.35). June 4–Aug 31 Tue–Sun 10am–1pm and 2pm–5pm. Closed Mon. Closed Sept 1–June 3. The house is approximately three blocks up Ochterloney St. from Windmill Rd.

2 Famous Peggy's Cove

Nova Scotia has dozens of picturesque lighthouses sprinkled along its shores. The lighthouse at Peggy's Cove is just one of them, and undoubtedly the most famous one. Like most other lighthouses in the province, it's located at the end of a long, narrow, winding road through a small fishing village. Yet Peggy's Cove and its lighthouse continue to draw visitors from all over to visit its gift shops, photograph the lighthouse, and clamber over the rocks at the edge of the sometimes angry, sometimes gentle Atlantic Ocean.

Because it's so famous, Peggy's Cove is also a tourist trap—especially in the summer, and also during the shoulder seasons. So, if you choose to visit Peggy's Cove any time from May to October, you'll also be visiting with many, many others. Is it worth the trip? Yes, but realize that if you're looking for that idyllic Nova Scotia moment with nothing but you, the lighthouse, the ocean, and maybe a few gulls overhead, you're probably not going to find it, because hundreds of other people have come to Peggy's Cove that day searching for the same thing.

Opt to visit in the off-season, though be prepared for inclement weather and much colder temperatures.

ESSENTIALS

GETTING THERE   If you're traveling by car, take the Bicentennial Highway (Route 102) out of Halifax and take exit 1A to the South Shore onto route 103. About 5km (3 miles) down the road, you'll see exit 2 to Peggy's Cove; take route 333 along the **Lighthouse Route.** It is approximately 43km (26 miles) from Halifax and should take about 40 minutes.

You can also travel to Peggy's Cove by bus or boat. The **Peggy's Cove Express,** 1751 Lower Water St. (© **902/857-9319;** www.peggyscove.com), takes you round-trip from Cable Wharf to Peggy's Cove. The package includes transportation by land and/or sea. If you go by boat, you'll have the opportunity to do some whale watching along the way. The package also includes a bowl of chowder wharf-side at Peggy's Cove, and costs C$59.95 (US$40) per person. The boat leaves from Cable Wharf at Lower Water Street, in Halifax, at 10:30am; the bus leaves from the same location at noon. The return trip by boat or bus leaves Peggy's Cove at 4:30pm.

VISITOR INFORMATION   The **Visitor Information Centre,** 109 Peggy's Point Rd. (© **902/823-2256;** http://explore.gov.ns.ca), is located in the de Garthe Gallery, in Peggy's Cove.

WHERE TO STAY & DINE

Oceanstone Inn and Cottages ★★ (Moments   This is a unique and beautiful location just moments from Peggy's Cove. There is a combination of 10 houses and cottages, some right on the ocean shore, others set back and surrounded by trees, with a view of the ocean. The cottages have fresh flowers, fireplaces, fully equipped kitchens, and one, two, or three bedrooms. If you prefer not to cook, there is a fine dining restaurant in the main lodge. This is definitely a spot to pamper yourself.

8650 Peggy's Cove Rd., Indian Harbour, NS B3Z 3P4. ℂ 902/823-2160. Fax 902/823-1282. www.ocean stone.ns.ca. 10 units. May 15–Oct 15 C$75 (US$50) double; C$90 (US$60) suite; C$175 (US$117) cottage (sleeps 3); C$235 (US$157) cottage (sleeps 5); C$325 (US$217) cottage (sleeps 6). Oct 16–May 14 C$65 (US$43.50) double; C$75 (US$50) suite; C$145 (US$97) cottage (sleeps 3); C$180 (US$120) cottage (sleeps 5); C$250 (US$167) cottage (sleeps 6). Packages available. AE, DC, MC, V. **Amenities:** Limited water-sports rentals. *In room:* Kitchen in 5 units.

Peggy's Cove Bed & Breakfast ⭐ (Finds) This restored fisherman's home on the oceanfront has a wonderful view of Peggy's Cove and the lighthouse from the windows and large deck. Along with an upstairs lounge and an outdoor hot tub, the B&B is within walking distance of Peggy's Cove attractions. It was formerly owned by the well-known painter William deGarthe.

19 Church Rd., Peggy's Cove, NS B0J 2N0. ℂ 800/725-8732 or 902/423-1102. Fax 902/423-8329. www. welcome.to/salt.sea. 3 units. July 1–Aug 25 C$125 (US$91) double; C$135 (US$97) deluxe; C$145 (US$105) superior. June 15–30 & Aug 26–Sept 15 C$115 (US$84 double; C$125 (US$91) deluxe; C$135 (US$97) superior. Oct 15–June 14 C$95 (US$69) double; C$105 (US$76) deluxe; C$115 (US$84) superior. Rates include full breakfast. Packages available. Extra person C$15 (US$10). AE, MC, V. **Amenities:** Jacuzzi. *In room:* No phone.

Sou'Wester Restaurant With a seating capacity of close to 200, this large family restaurant serves traditional, home-style meals and specializes in lobster and seafood chowder. The food is good and the prices are reasonable. The large windows overlook the Peggy's Cove lighthouse.

178 Peggy's Cove Rd. ℂ 902/823-2561. Main courses C$10–$16 (US$7–$11). MC, V. Mid May–Dec 8am–sunset; Dec–mid May 9am–6pm.

EXPLORING THE AREA

Peggy's Cove was settled in 1811. Since then it has been, and still is, a working fishing village. The current lighthouse was built in 1914, and during World War II the Royal Canadian Navy used it as a radio station. Today the permanent population hovers around 200, but during the summer months the village hosts thousands of visitors every day.

Don't go to Peggy's Cove without your camera, but do go early in the day, or you'll only have photos of crowds to take home. Be sure to follow posted signs and stay within the safe areas, particularly close to the water. Wear a sweater or jacket as the weather along the shore is often chilly.

There are other things to do in Peggy's Cove besides photograph the lighthouse. Erected in memory of the 229 people who died in the Swissair plane crash 8km (5 miles) off Peggy's Cove in 1998, the stark **Swissair Flight 111 Memorial** is worth seeing. The oval monument has three vertically carved "sights," sightlines that direct the eye to the area of the ocean where the plane crashed. The smooth roundness of the memorial distinguishes it from the rugged boulders scattered along the barren shore. The **William E. deGarthe Memorial Monument** ⭐, 109 Peggy's Point Rd. (ℂ 902/823-2256; www.lostatsea.ca/ degarthe.htm) is a 30-meter (100-foot) wide stone memorial to Nova Scotia fishermen carved by William E. deGarthe, a marine artist and sculptor. He carved the mural in the late 1970s on a granite outcropping behind his summer home. It depicts fishermen at work, their wives and children, a guardian angel watching over the fishermen, and the legendary "Peggy" of Peggy's Cove (see the sidebar "Who Was Peggy, Anyway?"). DeGarthe was 70 years old when he carved this masterpiece, which his wife later donated to the province. The opportunity to see this mural is worth fighting the traffic and tourists. Look for it opposite the Visitor Information Centre (109 Peggy's Point Road).

3 The Annapolis Valley

The Annapolis Valley is known for its yearly bounty of fruits and vegetables—apples, berries, you name it. Nowadays, it's becoming known for its wines as well. Along with having the opportunity to taste gold-medal winners that your friends have probably never heard of, you'll see some of the most beautiful scenery in the province. September is the best time to visit the Annapolis Valley, when the fruit, vegetable, and grape harvest festivals are underway. You might even get the chance to crush some grapes yourself.

ESSENTIALS

GETTING THERE   If you are driving, take Highway 102 (Bicentennial Drive) north out of Halifax for approximately 15km (9 miles) until you reach the exit for Highway 101 and the Annapolis Valley, **near Bedford.** It's about 50km (31 miles) to **Grand Pré,** where you take exit 10 to route 1 (west).

You can also travel to the Annapolis Valley by chartered minivan or bus. **Atlantic Canada Yourway Tours,** 6256 Windcrest Terrace, (© **902/453-1411;** www.globalserve.net/~alaing) offers tours in an air-conditioned minivan that seats 1 to 6, from May 1 to October 31, for C$35 (US$23.35) per hour. Plan for at least four hours; eight would be better. **SMT (Eastern) Ltd. & Acadian Lines,** 1161 Hollis St. (© **902/454-9321;** www.smtbus.com/acadian.htm) provides daily service to **Wolfville.** The price of a return ticket is C$32.20 (US$21.50) for adults, C$24.15 (US$16.10) for seniors and students with valid ID, C$16.10 (US$10.75) for children 5 to 12, free for children 4 and under. The bus leaves the VIA Rail building, at 1161 Hollis Street, at 6:30pm and arrives in Wolfville at 8:05pm. There are also buses leaving Halifax from Monday to Friday at 8am, and Friday and Sunday at 2:15pm. The bus leaves Wolfville daily at 1:20pm, also Monday to Friday at 10:45am, Friday at 6:05pm, and Sunday at 8:20pm. The trip takes approximately 95 minutes.

VISITOR INFORMATION   If you're looking for general information on the Annapolis Valley, a good place to start is the **Evangeline Trail Tourism Association,** 5518 Prospect Rd., New Minas (© **902/681-1645;** www.evangeline trail.com). They can provide you with maps and up-to-date listings of events in the valley. There's also the town of Kentville, just west of Wolfville, and their visitor information center is at the **Kentville Business and Visitor Centre,** 125 Park St. (© **902/678-7170).**

For information on the town of Wolfville, visit the **Wolfville Visitor Centre** (© **902/542-7000)** located on the east end of Main Street at Willow Park, approximately 7km (4.4 miles) from Highway 101, exit 10.

WHERE TO STAY & DINE

Blomidon Inn ⭐   This sea captain's mansion was built in 1882 and is now owned by meticulous hosts Jim and Donna Laceby. The guest rooms on the second and third story of the inn are decorated in the Victorian style, with antique furniture and four-poster or canopy beds, private bathrooms, and some with sitting rooms included. 12 of the 26 units have Jacuzzis. 2 have fireplaces. All units are non-smoking. The main floor consists of the lobby and two beautiful sitting rooms with fireplaces and decorated with antique furniture.

The dining room is also on the main floor and the menu is creative and advocates fresh Annapolis Valley produce. The roasted pork tenderloin coated in a savory herb crust and served with a wild blueberry and apple compote and fresh vegetables is delicious. As is the Seafood Mistrel, a colorful combination of scallops, lobster, mussels, and salmon, cooked in fennel and saffron broth and served with vegetables and fresh homemade fettuccini.

Surrounding the inn is an extensive garden with seating areas, fishponds, a cottage garden in memory of Jim's grandmother, and a vegetable garden where fresh produce and herbs are grown for the kitchen.

127 Main St., PO Box 839, Wolfville, NS B0P 1X0. © 800/565-2291 or 902/542-2291. Fax 902/542-7461. www.blomidon.ns.ca. 26 units. June 20–Sept 30 C$119 (US$79.35) double; C$149 (US$99.35) superior; C$169 (US$112.70) suite. May 1–June 19 & Oct C$109 (US$72.70) double; C$129 (US$86) superior; C$149 (US$99.35) suite. Nov–Apr C$89 (US$60) double; C$119 (US$80) superior; C$129 (US$86) suite. Rates include continental breakfast. Packages available. Extra person C$12 (US$8). AE, MC, V. Free parking. Approximately 6km (4 miles) from exit 10 on Highway 101. **Amenities**: Restaurant (Canadian); outdoor tennis court. *In room:* A/C, TV.

Old Orchard Inn ★ (Kids)

Though called an inn, this establishment is a sort of hybrid between a motel and a resort. Besides its panoramic view of the Minas Basin and Cape Blomidon in the distance, it has lots of activities to amuse adults and children alike, including an indoor pool and an outdoor playground and tennis courts. Guest rooms are spacious, if not particularly unique in any way, and the bathrooms are clean. The two dining room/lounge areas have the best ambience. The Acadian Room, with its large stone fireplace and windows-with-a-view is cozy and comfortable, while the Blomidon Room makes you feel as though you've strayed into a European castle complete with stone walls and rough-hewn timbers. The menu specialties emphasize local seafood and fresh produce. In summer, enjoy the outdoor sundeck or walks on the ridge and dykes surrounding the property. The 29 cabins are set off from the main complex.

153 Greenwich Road South, Wolfville, NS B0P 1X0. © 800/561-8090 or 902/542-5751. Fax 902/542-2276. www.oldorchardinn.com. 100 units, 29 cabins. C$115 (US$77) double; C$135 (US$90) king. Cabins C$90 (US$60) double; C$95 (US$63.35) triple. Packages available. Extra person C$10 (US$6.70). Children 16 and under stay free in parents' room. AE, DISC, MC, V. Free parking. Cabins closed Nov–Apr. From Highway 101, take Exit 11 south. Pets accepted. **Amenities**: Restaurant (Canadian), lounge; indoor pool, 2 outdoor tennis courts; sauna; secretarial services; massage; laundry service. *In room:* A/C, TV w/pay movies, hair dryer.

Paddy's Pub & Rosie's Restaurant (Value)

Here's an Irish pub, a restaurant, and the valley's only craft brewery, all under one roof. If you're hungry, be sure to order the delicious Irish stew; the Chicken Sesame Salad is also a winner. But if you're in the mood for snacking, they also serve pub standards like nachos and wings. The craft beers are brewed on site. Choose from the Irish Cream ale (thick, with a somewhat muddled flavor), the Valley Ale (crisp), the Raven ale (dark and hardy), plus others that are brewed on a somewhat irregular basis. Try to visit on a Wednesday night when there's live Irish music and entertainment. The staff is friendly and the restaurant/pub is comfortable and relaxing, with a definite Irish theme in the decor.

320 Main St., Wolfville. © 902/542-0059. Main courses C$7–$16 (US$5–$11). AE, MC, V. Sun–Wed 11am–11pm; Thur–Sat 11am–12:30am. Approximately 8km (5 miles) on route 1 from exit 10 on Highway 101.

Restaurant Le Caveau ★ (Finds)

This fine dining restaurant is tucked into the **Domaine de Grand Pré vineyard complex** and serves northern European cuisine with a Swiss influence. The menu changes regularly and makes use of whatever fresh produce is in season. Main courses include venison as well as salmon, beef, chicken, pork, seafood, veal, and lamb. The Pork Schnitzel served in a mushroom sauce with homemade noodles and vegetables is delicious. During their "harvest festival," held in September, they serve a wonderful Vintner Rosti—a combination of noodles, vegetables, sausage, and wine, that should not be missed. From May to October, enjoy your meal on the outdoor patio under a huge grapevine arbor. There's a Grand Pré wine to suit every dish; simply ask the staff for a recommendation. While you're in the restaurant, take a moment to view the round corner table—a cross section of a huge tree trunk polished to a high gloss. It would take hours to count all the rings.

11611 Highway 1, Grand Pré. ✆ **902/542-7177**. www.grandprewines.ns.ca. Reservations recommended. Main courses C$7–$20 (US$4.60–$13.35). AE, MC, V. Wed–Sat 11:30am–2pm and 5:30–8pm; Sun & Holidays 5–8pm. Closed Mon–Tue. Closed Jan 1–Mar 19. Approximately 2km (1.2 miles) on route 1 from exit 10 from Highway 101.

⟮*Finds*⟯ The Cape Blomidon Lookoff

One of the best views in Wolfville is Cape Blomidon to the north. Mi'kmaq legend says this was the home of Glooscap, a god responsible for transforming the landscape and animals into their present-day forms. To get to the Lookoff (✆ **902/582-3022**), travel 8km (5 miles) from exit 10 (from Highway 101) along route 1; in Greenwich, take route 358 north for approximately 14km (8.7 miles) to the Lookoff parking lot. A clear day offers a panoramic view of the Annapolis Valley and the Minas Basin: a colorful quilt of apple orchards, vineyards, forests, and streams, as far as the eye can see.

EXPLORING THE AREA
GRAND PRÉ

Traveling along route 1 through Grand Pré is like traveling back in time. Things slow down, colors seem richer, and you want to linger. Acadians first settled this area in the 1600s. Later, after the Deportation (the British forced the Acadians out of Nova Scotia in 1755), the British settled the area with Planters (New Englanders).

Grand Pré National Historic Site ⟨★⟩ ⟮*Kids*⟯   Now cloaked with vines, this church was built in 1922 to commemorate and preserve the history of the Acadians who lived in the area in the 17th and 18th centuries. The church stands among weeping willows on 14 acres of sweeping grounds. A statue of the fictional Acadian heroine, Evangeline, immortalized in Longfellow's poem of the same name, also graces the outside. Inside, the displays depict the early Acadians' success with the fertile farmland, their association with the Mi'kmaq, and their relationship with the British and the French, which led to their deportation from Nova Scotia by the British in 1755. Visit the authentic blacksmith shop onsite. Plan to spend 45 minutes.

2241 Grand Pré Rd. ✆ **902/542-3631**. www.grand-pre.com. Admission C$2.50 (US$1.65) adults, C$2 (US$1.35) seniors, C$1.10 (US$0.75) children 6–16, free for children 5 and under, C$7 (US$4.65) families. Daily 9am–6pm. Closed Nov–May. Highway 101 west from Halifax, take exit 10, north on route 1, travel 1.5km (1 mile) to Grand Pré Rd., turn north.

Tangled Garden   A stroll though this garden is a treat for any gardener or nature lover. Enter through the vine-covered pagoda and you get the first hint of where the name originated. The stone and grass covered walkways lead you through beds of perennials, past sheds and shade trees to the vegetable and herb gardens. Smell the herbs, listen to the birds, and enjoy the beauty. The gift shop stocks jellies and vinegars made from organically grown herbs in the garden and prepared without preservatives or coloring, in addition to original artwork by the owners. Look for wooden sculptures and mixed-media abstract works. Plan to spend 30 minutes to an hour.

11827 Hwy 1. © **902/542-9811.** www.tangledgarden.ns.ca. Admission free. Daily 10am–6pm. Closed Jan–March. Less than 1km (0.6 miles) from exit 10 from Highway 101.

WOLFVILLE

Wolfville has been voted one of the best places to retire in Canada—but don't make the mistake of thinking everyone here is a senior citizen. There are as many Acadia University students in the town from September to May as there are permanent residents, and this keeps things lively with sports events, as well as music and theater. Wolfville has more than its share of historic homes, and there is a variety of retail shops and restaurants along the six-block main street (called Main Street, funnily enough).

Finds The Atlantic Theatre Festival in Wolfville ★★

This festival has earned a reputation for tackling a wide variety of classics with flair and serious talent. Look for works by Stephen Sondheim, Noel Coward, and Anton Chekov. The season runs from late June to early September. Tickets range from C$26.50 (US$17.70) to C$40.30 (US$26.90). For information on the upcoming season and showtimes, contact the box office: 356 Main St. Wolfville (© **800/337-6661** or **902/542-4242;** www.atf.ns.ca).

K. C. Irving Environmental Science Centre and the Harriet Irving Botanical Gardens ★★ *Value*   This leading-edge science center and 6 acres of botanical gardens opened in 2002. A stroll through the botanical gardens introduces you to a variety of habitats, including the Acadian forest, bogs, and meadows, plus an enclosed formal Victorian Garden highlighting indigenous plants. Connected to the gardens, the science center is a state-of-the-art facility with research laboratories, greenhouses, an auditorium, and conference facilities. The highlight of the building—for visitors, at least—is the **Orangerie,** a spacious, high-ceilinged room furnished with Internet-ready computer terminals and comfortable chairs that invite reading, study, or simply contemplation. One end wall of the many-windowed room features a huge fireplace, while a waterfall cascades down the other wall, near the entranceway. Allow at least two hours to fully explore the complex.

University Ave. © **902/585-1757.** www.acadiau.ca/blueprint/irving/index.htm. Admission free. Gardens open daily 7:30am–sunset (weather permitting). Science Centre open daily 8am–10pm. Turn south on University Ave. from the western end of Main St., the complex is on the west side at the top of the hill.

The Wines of Domaine de Grand Pré ⭐

Touring local vineyards is a great way to explore and get to know the Annapolis Valley. Follow the signs with the grape cluster on them. **Domaine de Grand Pré,** 11611 Highway 1 (© 866/479-4637 or 902/542-1753; www.grandeprewines.ns.ca) is our favorite. Tidy rows of grapevines running up a long hill; a tall geometric fountain next to a lovely courtyard; a grape leaf and cluster motif in the cobblestones underfoot. When you arrive at Domaine de Grand Pré, you soon realize you've arrived somewhere special. There's an outdoor patio and European-style pergola that beckons in fine weather. There's also the on-site restaurant, **Restaurant Le Caveau** (see "Where to Stay & Dine" earlier in this section). The gift shop and tasting room are beside the courtyard, and stocks Domaine de Grand Pré's wines, along with cheeses, artwork, and other items. Free tours are available from May to October. (If your tour includes a tasting, there is a C$7 (US$4.70) charge.) The vineyard's harvest festival takes place annually in mid September; it's a delightful opportunity to try stomping grapes and sample wine while enjoying wonderful food and music. The vineyard is open to the public June through October, Monday through Saturday from 10am to 6pm, Sunday from 11am to 5pm. Tours are held daily at 11am and 3pm. To get to the vineyard, take Highway 101 west out of Halifax and take exit 10 to route 1, Grand Pré and Wolfville.

Other vineyards worth visiting:

- **Habitant Wines Ltd.,** 10318 Highway 221 (© 877/262-9463).
- **Saint Famille Wines,** 11 Dudley Park Lane (© 800/565-0993 or 902/798-8311; www.st-famille.com).

4 The Historic South Shore

This is the Nova Scotia you've seen advertised: fishing villages, lighthouses, colorful boats at anchor along the shore, and the schooner *Bluenose II.* From Halifax to Yarmouth, the coast is dotted with communities whose livelihood depends primarily on the sea.

ESSENTIALS

GETTING THERE   If you have a vehicle, leave Halifax on Highway 102 and take exit 1A west to Highway 103. Drive for approximately 80km (50 miles) to exit 10 and follow route 3 south to **Mahone Bay.**

Lunenburg is 103km (64 miles) southwest of Halifax and can be reached by following Highway 103 and taking exit 11 west on route 3.

Bridgewater is approximately 108km (67 miles) southwest of Halifax along Highway 103, take exit 12.

To reach **Liverpool,** follow Highway 103 to exit 19, approximately 154km (96 miles) southwest of Halifax.

Atlantic Canada Yourway Tours, 6256 Windcrest Terrace, (© **902/453-1411;** www.globalserve.net/~alaing) offers tours in an air-conditioned minivan that seats 1 to 6, from May 1 to October 31, for C$35 (US$23.35) per hour. Plan for at least eight hours to visit some (not all) of the attractions. An overnight trip would be better. **DRL Group,** (℃ **877/450-1987** or 902/450-1987; www.drlgroup.com/coachlines) provides daily bus service to Mahone Bay, Lunenburg, and Liverpool. The bus leaves Halifax at 6:25pm and arrives in Mahone Bay at 7:45pm, Lunenburg at 8pm, and Liverpool at 9:15pm. Return tickets are C$24 (US$16) to Mahone Bay, C$28 (US$19) to Lunenburg, and C$42 (US$28) to Liverpool.

VISITOR INFORMATION Stop in to the visitor information centers in each town for information on local events, but remember that most are closed from mid October to mid May.

In **Mahone Bay,** the visitor information center is located at 165 Edgewater St. (℃ **902/624-6151;** www.mahonebay.com), near the three churches.

As you enter **Lunenburg** along route 3, follow Dufferin St. to Linden Ave., which turns into Bluenose Drive. The visitor information center (℃ **902/634-8100;** www.explorelunenburg.ca) is located along the waterfront.

Liverpool's visitor information center is at 28 Henry Hensey Dr. (℃ **902/354-5421**).

WHERE TO STAY & DINE

Boscawen Inn & McLachlan House ⭐ Built in the late 1800s, the Boscawen has a wonderful view of Lunenburg Harbour. In a town full of historic homes, the inn is the town's best example of the Queen Anne Revival style. The rooms are spacious, and all have private bathrooms, although one isn't actually in the room, but further down the hallway. Each guest room is beautifully decorated with antiques and quilts. Some have four-poster or canopy beds. Smaller rooms are decorated with more of a country flair. Try to get a room on the south side with a view of the harbor, although the north-facing rooms have decent views of the municipal park. *Note:* The stairs to the third floor are steep, and it's quite a hike up there from the entrance.

McLachlan House is below and across the street from the inn, and has two rooms and two suites, but you'll have to cross the street for breakfast. The upstairs formal dining room opens on to an outside deck that has one of the best views of the harbor in town. It's a lovely spot to sip a beverage in the evening, or simply spend an hour reading. There's a more casual restaurant downstairs, complete with a grand piano and bar.

Note: Each room is priced separately; for example, a double four-poster bed, on the ground floor, facing the harbor, is C$95 (US$64). A queen four-poster bed, on the first floor with an excellent view of the harbor, a sitting area in the turret, and a large bathroom with Jacuzzi and fireplace, is C$185 (US$123.50). There are 10 units between C$80–$100 (US$54–$67), 5 units between C$105–$115 (US$70–$77), and 5 units between C$150–$185 (US$100–$124).

150 Cumberland St. PO Box 1343, Lunenburg, NS B0J 2C0. ℃ **800/354-5009** or 902/634-3325. Fax 902/634-9293. www.3.ns.sympatico.ca/boscawen. 20 units. C$80–$185 (US$54–$124) double. Rates include continental breakfast. Extra person C$15 (US$10). AE, DISC, MC, V. Free parking. From Highway 103 take exit 11 and follow route 3 to Dufferin St. Follow Dufferin to Lincoln St., while on Lincoln turn left onto Duke and then right onto Cumberland St. **Amenities:** 2 restaurants (Canadian); bar; laundry service. *In room:* TV, hair dryer.

Lane's Privateer Inn (*Value*) This establishment is attractive and clean, has friendly, helpful staff, and good rates. The home of one of Liverpool's most famous privateers, Capt. Joseph Barss, built in 1789, is also part of the complex. The present inn is run by the Lane family, and is now in its third generation of

operation. All of the units were renovated in 2000, with new beds, air condi-
tioners, and decor. The king and queen rooms have sitting areas. The inn overlooks the beautiful Mersey River; outside are spacious grounds with flowerbeds
and shrubbery. The unassuming restaurant serves good seafood and pasta. The
cozy pub has a pool table and dartboard.

27 Bristol Ave. PO Box 509, Liverpool, NS B0T 1K0. ℰ **800/794-3332** or 902/354-3456. Fax 902/354-7220.
www3.ns.sympatico.ca/ron.lane. 27 units. C$87 (US$58) double; C$99 (US$66) queen; C$115 (US$77) king.
Rates include continental breakfast. Extra person C$12 (US$8). Children 15 and under stay free in parents'
room. AE, DISC, MC, V. Free parking. From Highway 103 take exit 19 and follow route 3. Turn left onto
Bristol St. **Amenities:** Restaurant (Canadian), lounge; limited water-sports rentals. *In room:* A/C, TV.

Quarterdeck Beachside Villas & Grill ★ *Finds* These accommodations are
so close to the ocean, you might get a little seasick. The charming two-story
villas are located along a white sand beach; you can watch the tide roll in and
out from the front window or upstairs balcony. The first floor of the villa
includes a dining area, sitting area equipped with a propane fireplace and TV,
bathroom, and kitchen with a full-size refrigerator, stove, microwave, and other
necessities for preparing meals. Upstairs are two bedrooms, each with a balcony
overlooking the beach and ocean, plus another bathroom. These accommodations are ideal for both summer and winter vacations. Although the licensed
dining room is casual, the menu is not (try the planked salmon). Enjoy the
sound of waves crashing in the background while you dine.

Summerville Beach, PO Box 70, Port Mouton, NS B0T 1T0. ℰ **800/565-1119** or 902/683-2998. Fax 902/683-
2547. www.quarterdeck.ns.ca. 13 units. C$129–C$319 (US$86–$213). Packages available. AE, DISC, MC, V.
Free parking. 3km (2 miles) from exit 20 off Highway 103. **Amenities:** Restaurant (Canadian); limited water-
sports rentals; bike rental; limited room service; babysitting. *In room:* TV w/pay movies, kitchen, fridge,
coffeemaker, hair dryer.

EXPLORING THE AREA
MAHONE BAY
The charming village of Mahone Bay, whose three waterfront churches have
been photographed by the thousands, was settled in 1754. The town is small but
packed with interesting architecture, as well as artisan and craft shops.

Mahone Bay Settlers Museum ★ This museum holds a wealth of stories
and data on the Mahone Bay area, and the museum building itself is a piece
of history. Known as the "Begin House," it was built in 1855 and features the
infamous architectural detail called the "Lunenburg Bump." The displays inside
include more information about the unique local architecture, and the early
settlement of Mahone Bay by "foreign Protestants." One exhibit explores the
Begin family connection to the museum, the *Bluenose*, and to the local community. Particularly interesting is the Inglis/Quinlan collection of antiques and
tablewares that give you a good sense of life in eighteenth and nineteenth century Mahone Bay. Head upstairs and explore the Wooden Boat Gallery, located
in the former sail-making loft of Benjamin Begin. The museum has a research
facility with information on the families who settled the area, including ships'
lists, and graveyard listings. For children, there's an assortment of activities,
including themed coloring sheets, scavenger hunts, and a variety of books and
puzzles. Give yourself two hours to visit this fascinating museum.

578 Main St., Mahone Bay. ℰ **902/624-6263**. www.ns.sympatico.ca/mbsm. Admission free. Jun–Aug
Tues–Sat 10am–5pm; Sun 1–5pm. Closed Sept–May. Follow route 3 into the village and turn left onto
Main St.

SHOPPING   Amos Pewter, 589 Main St. (© **902/624-9547;** www.amos pewter.com), has artisans onsite, and visitors can watch them at work. Along with jewelry and ornamental pieces, they have been designing and producing Christmas ornaments since 1975, and these are wonderful collectibles. They feature children with toys, elves, and often birds. It's a great place to shop for a reasonably priced, quality collectible from Nova Scotia.

Suttles & Seawinds, 466 Main St. (© **902/624-6177;** www.suttlesand seawinds.com) is also a distinctive shop, with quilts and clothing designed and manufactured locally. Back when Nova Scotia was being settled, and quilt making was much more common, a suttle was the name for the scraps of material women would save and eventually sew into their quilts. Owner Vicki Lynn Bardon wanted to continue this tradition of quilt making, hence the store's name. Suttles & Seawinds has branches in Halifax and Toronto, but this shop in Mahone Bay is where it all started.

LUNENBURG

Lunenburg was settled in 1753 by German and Swiss Protestants, and is the home of Nova Scotia's famed schooner, the *Bluenose.* If you're lucky, the *Bluenose II* replica will be in port and you will be able to take a tour. Later, a walk along the waterfront will introduce you to the many shops and balconied restaurants offering fresh seafood.

Fisheries Museum of the Atlantic ★★ *Kids*   Even if you're not a museum type, you'll likely enjoy your visit here. Our family allotted one hour for a visit and left before we wanted to—three hours later! The museum's collection is impressive and varied: It has the largest collection of artifacts and stories on the original *Bluenose,* an aquarium, called the Millennium Aquarium, with examples of local saltwater fish species, and then there's the *Theresa E. Connor,* an original banks schooner located at the wharf. There's a multitude of displays and activities concerning the offshore and inshore fisheries, including the opportunity to talk with some experienced fishermen. The **Life in Fishing Communities exhibit** is an inside look at the lifestyle of fishing families and includes interactive displays of rug hooking and quilting. Children will especially enjoy the launching of a miniature *Bluenose* schooner several times a day. You'll all enjoy the instructional and entertaining videos shown throughout your time there.

68 Bluenose Dr., Lunenberg. © **902/634-4794**. www.fisheries.museum.gov.ns.ca. Admission C$8 (US$5.35) adults, C$6.50 (US$4.35) seniors & students, C$2.50 (US$1.70) children 6–17, free for children 5 and under, C$19 (US$12.70) families. May 4–Oct 27 daily 9am–5:30pm; Oct 28–May 3 Mon–Fri 8:30am–4:30pm. Closed Sat–Sun Oct 28–May 3. From Highway 103 take Exit 11, follow route 3 to Lunenburg; follow museum signs and look for the bright red buildings.

 The Bluenose

This two-masted schooner has become a symbol of Nova Scotia and her fishermen. Built in 1921 in Lunenburg, she worked as a fishing schooner but also raced to fame, and was never beaten. The image of the *Bluenose* is found on the Canadian dime, a Canadian stamp, and famous photographs by Angus MacAskill. A replica of the original *Bluenose,* called, not surprisingly *Bluenose II,* was built in Lunenburg in 1963 and acts as a floating ambassador for the province. This *Bluenose* has never raced.

LIVERPOOL

Liverpool is famous for its eighteenth-century privateering, and you can get up close to the privateers' history with the lighthouse at **Fort Point Lighthouse Park** ⭐, located at the end of Main St., (© **800/655-5741;** www.regionofqueens. com). After you explore the inside of the lighthouse, you can investigate the interpretive panels, models, and audiovisual presentations about privateers outside.

Perkins House Museum   This is definitely worth a stop to get to know more about Simeon Perkins, Liverpool's leading citizen in the late 1700s. He was a merchant and shipowner whose boats fished off Labrador and traded in the West Indies. He was also a colonel of the local militia, probate judge, Justice of the Court of Common Pleas, and a Member of the Legislative Assembly. Take the time to read some samples of Perkins' meticulous diaries, which bring alive the accounts of life in a colonial town. Remember too that this house, built in 1766, entertained governors, privateer captains, and itinerant preachers. If only the walls could talk.

105 Main St., Liverpool. © **902/354-4058**. www.perkins.museum.gov.ns.ca. Admission C$2 (US$1.35) adults, C$1 (US$0.67) seniors & children 6–17, free for children 5 and under, C$5 (US$3.35) families. June 1–Oct 15 Mon–Sat 9:30am–5:30pm; Sun 1pm–5:30pm. Closed Oct 16–May 31. From Highway 103 take exit 19 and follow route 3. Turn left onto Bristol St., follow to the end and turn left onto Main St.

5 Truro, the Hub of Nova Scotia & the Fossil Cliffs at Parrsboro

Truro is a historic town in the center of Nova Scotia, near the beginning of the **Bay of Fundy.** It has long been a hub of Nova Scotia; first with the railway, and later the highway. If prehistory is your thing, be sure to leave time for a visit to Parrsboro and its dinosaur tracks, located another 90 minutes' drive past Truro.

ESSENTIALS

GETTING THERE   If you're traveling by car, take the divided Highway 102 to Truro, for approximately 100km (60 miles) and then take exit 13 or 14A to tour the town.

VIA Rail, 1161 Hollis St. (© **800/561-3952** or 902/494-7900; www.via rail.ca) leaves Halifax every day (except Tuesday) at 12:45pm and arrives in Truro at 2:05pm. The return train leaves Truro at 2:50pm and arrives in Halifax at 4:10pm, so unless you just want to enjoy a train ride, you'll have to stay overnight. The cost of a round-trip ticket is C$38 (US$25.35) for adults, C$34.20 (US$22.80) for seniors, university students with ID, and children 11 to 16, C$19 (US$12.70) for children 2 to 11, free for 1 year and under as long as they don't take up a seat.

SMT (Eastern) Ltd. & Acadian Lines, 1161 Hollis St. (© **902/454-9321;** www.smtbus.com/acadian.htm) provides daily service to Truro. The bus leaves Halifax Truro at 7am, 8:15am, 12:45pm, 1:30pm, 4pm, and 6:30pm. The return bus from Truro to Halifax leaves at 8:20am, 12:15pm, 1:20pm, 4:25pm, 5:05pm, 9:55pm, and 10:50pm. Tickets cost C$30.47 (US$20.32) for adults, C$22.85 (US$15.24) for seniors and students, C$15.23 (US$10.15) for children 5–12, free for children 4 and under provided they can sit on a parent's lap. **Atlantic Canada Yourway Tours,** 6256 Windcrest Terrace, (© **902/453-1411;** www.globalserve.net/~alaing) offers tours in an air-conditioned minivan that seats 1 to 6, from May 1 to October 31, for C$35 (US$23.35) per hour. Plan for at least eight hours to visit both Truro and Parrsboro.

When you're ready to head for Parrsboro, look for route 2 and the **Glooscap Trail.** The route hugs the shore of **Cobequid Bay** and is definitely off the beaten track. It will take you over an hour (it's 90km (54 miles) from Truro) to reach Parrsboro, but the time will pass quickly while you enjoy the scenery, the bay, and the villages you'll pass through from time to time. There are no trains or regular buses that travel to Parrsboro. We suggest you rent a vehicle if you plan to visit Parrsboro.

VISITOR INFORMATION   The **Truro Visitor Information Centre** (② **902/ 893-2922**) is located in the center of town at **Victoria Square,** on Court Street. (Follow Willow Street or Robie Street to the lights at Prince Street.) In Parrsboro, the **Tourist Information Centre** is located on the **main street next to the Bandstand.** Make sure you ask about the tide times while you're here, as the Bay of Fundy has the highest tides in the world and they rise very quickly.

WHERE TO STAY & DINE

John Stanfield Inn ⊙   The John Stanfield Inn was built for the late Senator John Stanfield and his wife Sarah in 1902. This Queen Anne–period house has been restored to its original condition with huge archways, a beamed ceiling, and hand-carved fireplace mantels. Each of the 10 rooms is decorated with period furniture and has a full bathroom. The rooms with queen beds also have a Jacuzzi and/or fireplace. It's a wonderful location for a romantic getaway, or to celebrate a special anniversary. The inn also has a licensed, fine dining restaurant that serves delicious seafood (the Fisherman's Harvest includes a large variety of in-season seafood) plus English-style roast beef and sautéed chicken breast. The only downside of the establishment is its inauspicious location behind a modern motel.

437 Prince St., Truro, NS B2N 1E6. ② 800/561-7666 or 902/895-1505. www.johnstanfieldinn.com. 10 units. June 16–Sept 30 C$179 (US$119.35) double; C$199 (US$132.70) queen. Oct 1–June 15 C$129 (US$86) double; C$189 (US$126) queen. Rates include continental breakfast. Packages available. AE, DISC, MC, V. Free parking. From Halifax via 102 take exit 13, follow connector to lights at Willow St., turn left on Willow, straight through next set of lights, left onto Prince St. at next set, hotel is on the right. **Amenities:** Restaurant (North American); indoor pool; secretarial services; coin-op washers and dryers. *In room:* A/C, TV, dataport, coffeemaker, hair dryer, iron.

Maple Inn ⊙   The inn is set on a quiet street less than a ten-minute walk from shopping and live theatre; another five minutes will take you to the Fundy Geological Museum. The inn itself is two century-old homes that have been renovated and connected. The rooms are individually decorated, some with wooden antique furniture, others with iron bedsteads; all are attractive and welcoming. The largest unit is a quaint third-story suite with a king-size canopy bed for the adults, a separate room with twin beds for the kids, a private Jacuzzi, and a sitting room with TV. A delicious full breakfast is served in the bright dining room. You can relax and chat in the sitting room by the fireplace, or, during the summer, unwind on the front verandah and watch the hummingbirds sip nectar from the hanging flower baskets.

2358 Western Ave., PO Box 457, Parrsboro, NS B0M 1S0. ② 877/627-5346 or 902/254-3735. www3.ns.sympatico.ca/mapleinn. 8 units. C$90 (US$60) double; C$105 (US$70) queen; C$145 US$96.70) suite. Rates include full breakfast. Packages available. Extra person C$15 (US$10). MC, V. Free parking. From Highway 102 take exit 14A and follow route 2 west 90km (56 miles) into Parrsboro, where it becomes Eastern Ave. Follow this street until you reach Western Ave., turn right. *In room:* TV in 4 units, no phone.

Stowaway Restaurant   This restaurant has take out, it delivers, or you can relax in the dining room. Order up a serving of fried chicken, meat and potatoes, or fish and French fries, but save room for their homemade pies. There's also a bakery onsite where you can pick up something yummy to take back to your room, or to munch while you drive. Children's menus are available.

69 Main St., Parrsboro. ℂ **902/254-3371**. Main courses C$7–$15 (US$5–$10). Feb 1–Dec 31 Daily 9am–9pm. Closed Jan. Follow route 2 into Parrsboro where it becomes Eastern Ave., turn left onto Main St.

EXPLORING THE AREA
TRURO

Known as the **Hub of Nova Scotia** for over 100 years, **Truro** was the center for train connections throughout the province; then, as highways became more important, the town became the central point for road networks. French Acadians first settled the area in 1703, but after their expulsion by the British in 1755, New Englanders came to farm and fish the rich area. The town is famous for the development of kerosene oil, the first ribbed-knit underwear (Stanfield's), the first condensed-milk factory, the first school of agriculture, and the first railway workers' union in Canada. Presently, the town's population is 13,000, and it's an important center of transportation, manufacturing, agriculture, trade, and education.

If you want to stretch your legs, visit Truro's 1,000-acre **Victoria Park** (𝄐 (ℂ **902/893-6078**). The park has walking trails, waterfalls, and the 200-step, 80° incline known as **Jacob's Ladder.** Climbing it proves a real aerobic workout. To get to Victoria Park, from Highway 102, take exit 13 to Willow Street. At the next lights, take Arthur Street to Young Street, and turn right. At the next intersection, turn left on Brunswick Street. The entrance to the park is on the right at Park Road, off of Brunswick Street.

As you drive around Truro, you'll see large **wooden sculptures** along the streets. For a century, Truro streets were lined with majestic elm trees that have recently been attacked by Dutch elm disease. As a way of retaining some of the history of these trees, the town commissions artists to carve them into historic figures or symbols. To date there are over 30 sculptures completed. For a brochure detailing the history of these carvings, stop in at the visitor information center at Victoria Square.

Colchester Historical Society Museum and Archives   This museum is housed in the old Science building of the Provincial Normal College, later called the Nova Scotia Teachers College (NSTC). It was built in 1900 and provided space for a laboratory, greenhouse, manual training rooms, and a museum. In the 1970s, after the NSTC closed, the building was renovated to house the collections of the Colchester Historical Society Museum and Archives. The first floor is used for permanent and traveling exhibits of home life and industry in Colchester County, of which Truro is a part. The second floor contains the archives and research area. School records, personal diaries, collections of photographs, political posters, and old newspapers are just a few of the items on display. The third story is used for meeting space for the society's programs and lectures.

29 Young St. ℂ **902/895-6284**. www.genealogynet.com/Colchester. Admission C$2 (US$1.35) adults, seniors, students & children 12–18, C/US$0.50 children 11 and under. Tue–Fri 10am–noon and 2–5pm; Sat 2–5pm. Closed Sun–Mon. From Highway 102 take exit 13 and turn north on Willow St. At the next set of lights bear right onto Arthur St. and follow this street until you reach Young St. Turn left.

Little White Schoolhouse Museum   If you, or someone you know, ever attended a one- or two-room schoolhouse, you'll enjoy visiting this one. Originally known as the Riverton School, the building is representative of schoolhouses in Nova Scotia from the mid-1800s to the 1950s. On display are artifacts and books used during those periods—slates, desks, primers, and more. Students and teachers who attended or taught in one-room schoolhouses are invited to register as alumni. There's a picnic area nearby where you can relive recess and lunch hours.

20 Arthur St. ℭ **902/895-5170**. Admission free. Jun–Aug Mon–Sat 10am–6pm. Sept–May Tues 9am–noon, or by appointment. From Highway 102 take exit 13 and turn north on Willow St. At the next set of traffic lights turn right onto Arthur St. The schoolhouse is immediately on your right.

 The International Tulip Festival in Truro

Each year in mid May, Truro bursts into bloom. Over 350,000 tulips, in a rainbow of shades, are planted each fall by volunteers and businesses. In May you'll see them along the street, in parks, in front of retail shops, in home gardens, and anywhere a spot can be found. To celebrate their bloom the community hosts a weekend of events for residents and visitors.

PARRSBORO

This area has been known for its rocks and minerals for hundreds of years. In 1604, Samuel de Champlain collected amethyst from these shores when the French were exploring along the coast. A hundred and fifty years later, Parrsboro was a busy shipbuilding center. Today, the town maintains its special charm and beautiful environment. There are no heavy industries or urban sprawl; residents still make their living by harvesting the land and sea. The biggest change might be that when people scour Parrsboro's shores nowadays, they are just as likely to be looking for dinosaur fossils as for semi-precious gemstones. If this interests you, you might want to head directly to **Partridge Island,** 3km (1.7 miles) southwest of Parrsboro, to comb the shores for rare stones or fossil remains.

Fundy Geological Museum ⭐ (Kids)   It's not hard to find this museum—just follow the dinosaur signs. Children and adults alike will have a ball investigating the life-size models of ancient dinosaurs, or footprints (no larger than your fingernail) of some of the smallest dinosaurs in the world. There is a model of the prehistoric landscape that was home to the dinosaurs, plus some of the oldest dinosaur bones in Canada. Or you can watch paleontologists uncovering real prosauropod dinosaur bones in the Research Lab. For rock hounds, there is a collection of amethyst and agate gemstones that have been uncovered when the Fundy tides wash away the cliffs along the shore.

In July and August, museum staff conduct geological walks Saturdays at 9:30am. There is no charge; children 12 and under must be accompanied by an adult.

162 Two Islands Rd. ℭ **902/254-3814**. www.fundygeo.museum.gov.ns.ca. Admission C$5 (US$3.35) adults, C$4.25 (US$2.85) seniors & students, C$3 (US$2) children 6–17, free for children 5 and under, C$12 (US$8) families (two adults and two or more school-age children). June 1–Oct 15 daily 9:30am–5:30pm. Oct 16–May 31 Tues–Sat 9am–5pm. Closed Sun–Mon. Travel west from Truro on Highway 104 to Glenholm, exit 12. Follow this exit and look for signs for Highway 2 North to Parrsboro. Once in town, follow the dinosaur signs.

Parrsboro Rock & Mineral Shop & Museum   This museum was founded (and is still owned) by internationally known fossil collector Eldon George. George is passionate about rocks and fossils, and this passion led him to find the world's smallest dinosaur footprints (about the size of your thumbnail) along these shores. You will see samples of the footprints at his shop, along with gem-stones and minerals, prospectors' supplies, books, and maps. George also conducts tours daily from May to October.

39 Whitehall Rd. © **902/254-2981**. Admission free. May 1–Oct 31 Tue–Sun 9am–6pm. Closed Mon. Closed Nov 1–April 30. Follow route 2 into Parrsboro where it becomes Eastern Ave., turn left onto Main St.

6 The Unspoiled Eastern Shore

Visit Nova Scotia's Eastern Shore if you're looking for fun outdoors or time away from crowds, as this area isn't as touristy or commercially oriented as, say, Peggy's Cove. The winding coastal drive on the two-lane route from Halifax to **Sherbrooke** is lined with deep inlets, unsullied sandy beaches, and villages with interesting names like Chezzetcook, Mushaboom, and Ecum Secum.

Beaches such as **Martinique Beach Provincial Park** and **Clam Harbour Beach Park,** have fine silver sand and waves suitable for surfing—if you can handle the water temperature: cold as ice, except during the first two weeks of September. Then, on a sunny, warm day reminiscent of summer, head to Clam Harbour and you'll find the water in the shallow coves as warm as bathwater. See the sidebar "Sandy Beaches" later in this section. *Note:* Most destinations discussed in this section are located on route 7 unless otherwise noted.

ESSENTIALS

GETTING THERE   Take the A. Murray MacKay Bridge across the Halifax Harbor to Dartmouth, then follow Highway 107 until you reach **Musquodoboit Harbour,** where the highway ends. Take route 7 for the rest of the trip.

There are no regular bus services or railways along the Eastern Shore, but **Atlantic Canada Yourway Tours,** 6256 Windcrest Terrace, (© **902/453-1411;** www.globalserve.net/~alaing) offers tours in an air-conditioned minivan that seats 1 to 6, from May 1 to October 31, for C$35 (US$23.35) per hour. Plan for at least eight hours for this tour.

VISITOR INFORMATION   Stop into the **International Visitor's Centre** at 1595 Barrington St. (© **902/490-5946**) for information and maps about the Eastern Shore, or Marine Drive. Or you can pick up information at the **Sheet Harbour Visitor Information Centre** (© **902/885-2595**) on route 7, or at **Sherbrooke Village** (© **902/522-2400**) (see "Exploring the Area" below).

WHERE TO STAY & DINE

Liscombe Lodge ⋆   This spot has some of the most modern and well-equipped accommodations on the Eastern Shore, yet the surrounding area remains pristine—a nature lover's dream, with opportunities to explore trails, bird-watch, canoe, or kayak along the peaceful Liscombe River nearby. For those more land-inclined, there are free bicycles for guests' use, tennis, and shuffleboard. Accommodations consist of tree-shrouded, private chalets, each with a sitting area, fireplace, and verandah, or cottages with four bedrooms, a common living room, and stone fireplace. Your third option is to stay in the main lodge building; all guest rooms here have private balconies overlooking the river.

When you're ready to eat, ask for a window table in the **Riverside Room.** While you eat, watch the activity on the river, and at the bird feeding stations just outside. The restaurant's specialty is planked salmon cooked the traditional way, over an open pit. Breakfasts are hearty, with maritime treats including fish cakes, baked beans, and oatcakes.

Note that the lodge has become a popular spot for corporate meetings and conferences, so it's a good idea to check whether there's one booked for the same time you plan to be here—that is, assuming you want to count on peace and quiet.

Route 7, Liscombe Mills, NS B0J 2A0. ℂ **800/665-6343** or 902/779-2307. Fax 902/779-2700. www. signatureresorts.com. 65 units. C$145–C$199 (US$98–$132). Packages available. Extra person C$20 (US$13.35). Children 16 and under stay free in parents' room. AE, DISC, MC, V. Free parking. Closed late Oct–early May. Cross the A. Murray MacKay Bridge toward Dartmouth and proceed along the Highway and take the Main St./Eastern Shore ramp. Proceed on Main St., which eventually becomes Highway 107 toward Musquodoboit Harbour (Highway 107 ends here). Turn right on Highway 7 and proceed along Highway 7 through Musquodoboit Harbour then Sheet Harbour and on to Liscombe Mills. The entrance is located on the right side of the road prior to the Liscombe River. Pets accepted with some restrictions. **Amenities:** Restaurant (Canadian); heated indoor pool; outdoor tennis court; exercise room; sauna; complimentary bike rental; coin-op washers and dryers. *In room:* TV, coffeemaker, hair dryer.

EXPLORING THE AREA

Route 7 is the road that takes you from Halifax to **Sherbrooke,** and there will be glimpses of rocky shoreline along the way, but you'll also travel through a lot of strictly forested areas. If you have the opportunity and time to go exploring along the sideroads to the ocean, do so, as the coastline is often wild and rugged along this shore.

Fisherman's Life Museum   The museum represents the life of inshore fishermen and their families in the early 1900s. Stop here and try to imagine how a fisherman and his wife raised 13 daughters in this tiny abode, and what their everyday lives were like. You'll see them cooking on the wood stove, hooking rugs, and, if you're lucky, they may be taking molasses cake fresh out of the oven to serve with tea.

58 Navy Pool Loop, Jeddore. ℂ **902/889-2053**. www.fishermanslife.museum.gov.ns.ca. Admission C$2 (US$1.35) adults, C$1 (US$0.75) seniors, students & children all ages, C$5 (US$3.35) families. Jun 1– Oct 15 Mon–Sat 9:30am–5:30pm; Sun 1–5:30pm. Closed Oct 16–May 31. Look for signs on route 7.

Memory Lane Heritage Village ⭐   This museum re-creates village life in Nova Scotia during the 1940s and 50s. Everything from the clothing worn by the museum staff, to the baked beans served at the cookhouse, to the 1949 cub tractor by the barn, is authentically presented. The complex is made up of 13 buildings, most of them rescued from the surrounding communities, including a country general store, one-room schoolhouse, church, farmhouse and barn, and a fisherman's house and store, to name just a few.

The museum is run by the Lake Charlotte Area Heritage Society, and it is committed to bringing visitors a faithful depiction of the period, whether through furniture, food, or atmosphere. This was one of the reasons the museum won the Attractions Canada Award for the province of Nova Scotia in 2002. (These are fairly high-profile awards within the Canadian tourism industry, awarded by the federal government.)

Make sure you stop into the cookhouse before you leave to enjoy a homemade meal of baked beans, soup, fresh-baked bread, and dessert, served buffet-style daily between 11am and 5pm. It costs C$6 (US$4) per person, including beverages.

Route 7, Lake Charlotte. ℂ **902/845-1927**. www.heritagevillage.ca. Admission C$6 (US$4) adults, C$4 (US$2.70) seniors, students & children all ages. Jun 1–Oct 15 daily 10am–5pm. Closed Oct 16–May 31.

Sandy Beaches

When you reach Musquodoboit Harbour, look for the East Petpeswick Road and **Martinique Beach Provincial Park**. This 5-km (3-mile) long crescent beach is a great place for beachcombing, especially after a storm, and birdwatching for waterfowl. There's a picnic area behind the dunes, if you bring lunch, plus change houses and pit toilets. *Note:* Visitors are encouraged to use the boardwalks and paths so as not to disturb the ecology of the area.

About 100km (60 miles) east of Halifax is our personal favorite, **Clam Harbour Beach Park**. Except for during the sand sculpture contest held annually in August (see the Halifax Calendar of Events in chapter 2), this beach is rarely crowded. For an extra special treat, once you reach the water, head east for about 20 minutes and you'll come to the first of three small, secluded, crescent beaches where you can pretend the world is yours alone. Granted, it's often foggy and except for the first two weeks in September the water is frigid, but it's still beautiful and worth a visit. Once you reach **Lake Charlotte** on the drive out from Halifax, start watching for the signs directing you to the beach. There's a 10-km (6-mile) drive to the large parking area, where you'll also find picnic tables, boardwalks, change rooms, and flush toilets.

Sherbrooke Village ⭐⭐ *(Kids)*   You can spend a fast 4 or 5 hours here exploring this living history village depicting life in the 19th century, with its businesses, houses, and costumed guides. Climb into a horse-drawn carriage to travel around the village, or explore the various buildings to see how people lived from 1860 to pre–World War I.

There are approximately 80 buildings in the village, some of which are still used as contemporary homes. Over 25 buildings are open to the public, including the jail—an attractive enough white house, from the outside. The jail was built in 1862, and was used for 100 years to house the jailer and his family, not to mention the legal offenders. There are cells upstairs and down, as well as a typical parlor, kitchen, and bedroom. The Nature Centre is popular with children and contains a selection of plant and animal life native to the area. Children also enjoy learning how to work the turn-of-the-century telephone system used in the village. Once a lumber company store dating from the late 1860s, the Company Store today houses traditional art, crafts, and gifts. For a quick snack, choose a sandwich, salad, or seafood dish at the **What Cheer Tearoom** in the village.

Sherbrooke. ℂ **902/522-2400.** www.sherbrookevillage.museum.gov.ns.ca. Admission C$8.25 (US$5.50) adults, C$6.75 (US$4.50) seniors, C$3.75 (US$2.50) children 17 and under, C$23 (US$15.35) families. Jun 1–Oct 15 daily 9:30am–5:30pm. Closed Oct 16–May 31. Follow route 7 to Sherbrooke; once you arrive in Sherbrooke, follow the signs to Sherbrooke Village.

7 Cape Breton

Alexander Graham Bell, inventor of the telephone, said of Cape Breton Island, "I have traveled around the globe. I have seen the Canadian and American Rockies, the Andes, the Alps and the Highlands of Scotland, but for simple beauty, Cape Breton outrivals them all." Indeed, the island of Cape Breton is known all over the world for its beauty, music, and friendliness. People from Alaska to Australia have visited and photographed the famous **Cabot Trail.**

ESSENTIALS

GETTING THERE   If you're planning to drive from Halifax directly to Cape Breton, it's 282km (169 miles) and will take you approximately 3.5 hours. You travel along routes 102 and 104 in order to reach the **Canso Causeway,** which connects Cape Breton Island to the mainland. Just across the causeway, in **Port Hastings,** is where you need to make a decision: Do you want to drive through the mountains on the inside or outside lane of the highway? The inside lane hugs the passing rocks and trees; the outside lane takes you close to vertical drop-offs and pretty amazing views. Your choice will determine which way you follow the Cabot Trail. I recommend the inside—a safer lane from which to savor the view—and will describe the route from that sequence.

There are numerous 2- and 3-day bus tours that take you along the Cabot Trail, including one offered by **Atlantic Tours Gray Line,** 211-1660 Hollis St. (© **800/565-7173** or 902/423-6242; www.atlantictours.com). Tours operate from June 2 to October 13. The air-conditioned coach with guide leaves the **Citadel Halifax Hotel,** 1960 Brunswick St. (© **800/565-7162** or 902/422-1391; www.citadelhalifax.com) Mondays at 7:30am. Reservations are required; tickets cost C$518 (US$345.35) per person. This includes overnight accommodation and meals. **Atlantic Canada Yourway Tours,** 6256 Windcrest Terrace, (© **902/453-1411;** www.globalserve.net/~alaing) offers tours in an air-conditioned minivan that seats 1 to 6, from May 1 to October 31, for C$35 (US$23.35) per hour.

VISITOR INFORMATION   It's a good idea to pick up a road map of Cape Breton Island at the **Port Hastings Visitor Information Centre** (© **902/625-4201**), located on your right immediately after you cross the Canso Causeway. Purchase passes for entry into **Cape Breton Highlands National Park,** as well as permits for camping, backpacking, and fishing, at the **Cheticamp Information Centre.** There are free maps of the park's hiking trails available, and a bookstore with a good collection of nature books for sale. Park passes are also available at the **Ingonish Visitor Information Centre** (© **902/285-2535**).

WHERE TO STAY & DINE

Auberge Gisele's Inn ★   The inn overlooks the beautiful Bras d'Or Lakes and is surrounded by landscaped gardens. Guest rooms are spacious and attractively decorated, and 25 out of the 75 units have fireplaces. Two units have a Jacuzzi. The award-winning dining room is popular with local residents and visitors alike; the cuisine has a definite French flair. If the day is fine, choose to dine outside on the lovely patio. Breakfast is served from 7:30 to 9:30am, lunch is by reservation only, and dinner, from 5:30 to 10pm. The staff speaks French, Ukrainian, and German.

387 Shore Rd. © **800/304-0466** or 902/295-2849. Fax 902/295-2033. www.giseles.com. 75 units. July 1–Oct 12 C$135 (US$90) double; C$175 (US$117) deluxe; C$185 (US$124) executive. May 1–June 30 & Oct 13–Oct 31 C$105 (US$70) double; C$145 (US$97) deluxe; C$150 (US$100) executive. Closed Nov 1–April 30. Packages available. Extra person C$15 (US$10). AE, DISC, MC, V. Free parking. Take exit 8 to route 205. **Amenities:** Restaurant (French), lounge; sauna; bike rental; coin-op washers and dryers. *In room:* AC, TV, dataport, coffeemaker, hair dryer, iron.

Castle Rock Country Inn This is a modern Georgian-style inn overlooking the mountains and the ocean, and close to the Highlands Links golf course, rated 57th in the world. The rooms are spacious, but sparsely decorated in a contemporary country style, furnished with the requisite bed, writing desk, and armoire with satellite TV. The guest rooms do have wonderful views, however. When you're ready to socialize, chat in the upstairs sitting room, or on the large patio (did I mention, while you enjoy the breathtaking view?). There's a chance you may see a moose or a couple of soaring eagles. The dining room menu is limited, but the food is excellent. The inn is close to hiking trails and sea kayaking facilities.

39339 Cabot Trail, Ingonish Ferry. ℂ **888/884-7625** or 902/285-2700. Fax 902/285-2525. www.ingonish. com/castlerock. 17 units. May 1–June 14 C$94 (US$63) double non-ocean view; C$115 (US$77) double upper level ocean view. June 15–Oct 31 C$110 (US$67) double non-ocean view; C$138 (US$92) double upper level ocean view. Packages available. Extra person C$15 (US$10). MC, V. Free parking. Closed Nov 1–Apr 30. From the Canso Causeway follow route 19 to the Cabot Trail Route. **Amenities:** Restaurant, bar; golf course nearby; laundry service. *In room:* TV, hair dryer, iron, no phone.

Glenora Inn & Distillery ⚔ Set off the highway, the Glenora Inn & Distillery is picture perfect. There are six rustic log chalets on the mountainside with one, two, or three bedrooms, full kitchens and living areas with freestanding fireplaces and satellite TV. The view is sublime, but the drive up is challenging. The nine rooms in the distillery complex overlook a courtyard with flowerbeds. The inn's dining room is open for breakfast daily from 7am to 10am, lunch from 11am to 3pm, and serves high tea from 3pm to 4:30pm. Dinner is served Monday through Saturday from 5pm to 10pm. On Sundays, dinner is available all day.

Don't forget to take advantage of the fact that the Glenora Inn & Distillery is North America's only single-malt distillery (as if you would!). Tours of the distillery take place daily on the hour from 9am to 5pm and last approximately 25 minutes. The tour costs C$5 (US$3.35) per person, and samples are available at the end. The Glenora Pub has live entertainment nightly from 8pm to 10pm.

Glenville. ℂ **800/839-0491** or 902/258-2662. Fax 902/258-3572. www.glenoradistillery.com. 15 units. C$100 (US$67) double; C$147 (US$98) 1-bedroom chalet; C$185 (US$124) 2-bedroom chalet; C$210 (US$140) 3-bedroom chalet. Packages available. Extra person C$10 (US$7). Free parking. Follow route 19 from the Canso Causeway. **Amenities:** Restaurant (North American), pub. *In room:* TV.

EXPLORING THE AREA

Cape Breton Island was settled primarily by Scottish immigrants, who found the highlands reminded them of home. Today, the Scottish culture is still strong, and the Gaelic language is being preserved through speech and music.

Ideally, it's best to explore the **Cabot Trail** with your own vehicle, because there are so many places you'll want to stop and explore, and it's a 300-km (186-mile) road trip from beginning to end. There's a variety of museums, unique craft shops, hiking trails, and views, so be sure to allow yourself time to take it all in.

Celtic Music Interpretive Centre The mission statement of this organization is to collect, preserve, and promote the traditional music of Cape Breton Island through education, research, and performance. A tour of the facility proves it's fulfilling this mandate successfully. Do take the forty-minute tour, **"Adventure into Celtic Culture and Music."** It includes an introduction to Buddy MacMaster, the famed Cape Breton fiddler, an explanation of the tartan legacy of the area, the evolution of Celtic music throughout the past century, and culminates with a mini ceilidh, pronounced "kay-lee" (Gaelic for "a gathering," which always includes music). The cost of this tour is C$3 (US$2) per person.

Judique. On route 19. ℂ **902/787-2708**. www.celticmusicsite.com. Admission C$3 (US$2) for tour. Jun 1– Aug 30, Mon–Fri 9am–5pm. Closed Sat–Sun. Closed Sept 1–May 31. 18km (11 miles) from the Canso Cause- way on route 19.

The Inverness Miners' Museum   This museum is housed in a 1901 railway station and explains the importance of coal mining in the history of the region. It includes displays illustrating the underground miner, artifacts, paintings, and photographs. There's also an audio/visual collection and a small archive. Field trips to fossil and mine sites can be arranged. A tea room is located in a nearby railway caboose.

62 Lower Railway St. ℂ **902/258-3822**. Admission C$1 (US$0.75). June 15–Sept 3 Mon–Fri 9am–5pm; Sat–Sun noon–5pm. Closed Sept 4–June 14. Turn onto Lower Railway St. from route 19.

CHETICAMP

Scottish heritage gives way to a pocket of French Acadian culture in this busy fishing village. You'll see the Acadian flag flying and hear the unique Acadian language spoken everywhere you visit. Instead of Scottish oatcakes and breakfast kippers on the menu, you'll find Chicken Fricot and meat pies. Here, you will also find world-famous hooked rugs, a craft perfected by the early settlers in the 1600s. At the **Co-operative Artisanale de Cheticamp,** 15067 Cabot Trail (ℂ **902/224-2170;** www.co-opartisanale.com), choose from a selection of rugs and other hooked items for purchase. There's often hooking, spinning, or weav- ing demonstrations going on. Downstairs, there's a small museum detailing the history of early Acadian settlers in the area.

BADDECK

This is a lovely town overlooking Bras d'Or Lake, with lots to see and do, in- cluding golf, hiking, and boat tours for outdoor types, and shopping, museums to visit, and good restaurants for those who wish to take it a little easier.

Baddeck is considered both the beginning and the end of the Cabot Trail, for although it isn't even on the trail, it is the largest center within a close proxim- ity. It's an easy town to explore on foot; pick up a walking tour map from the **Baddeck Welcome Centre,** at the intersection of route 105 and route 205 (ℂ **902/295-1991**).

If you have the time, take the opportunity to experience a relaxing sail on the lake. **Amoeba Sailing Tours** (ℂ **902/295-2481** or 902/295-1426) offers cruises on a 15-m (50-foot) sailboat. The cruise costs C$17.25 (US$11.50) per person.

Alexander Graham Bell Historic Site ★★ (Kids)   It's hard to believe that one man could create so many of the inventions that affect our everyday lives. In this museum, there are hands-on activities that help to explain the theories behind the inventions; original artifacts from Bell's collections, and photographs of Bell at work. There are also replicas of airplanes, kites, and telephones— enough to keep parents and children busy for 2 hours or more. The museum is located on 25 acres of land that overlooks the Bras d'Or Lakes, as well as the mountains.

Chebucto St. (Highway 205.) ℂ **902/295-2069**. www.parkscanada.gc.ca. Admission C$4.25 (US$2.85) adults, C$3.25 (US$2.20) seniors, C$2.25 (US$1.50) children 17 and under, C$10.75 (US$7) families. June daily 9am–6pm; July–Aug daily 8:30am–7:30pm; Sept 1–Oct 15 daily 8:30am–6pm; Oct 16–May 31 daily 9am–5pm.

Cape Breton Highlands National Park ★★

Cape Breton Highlands National Park is an abundant 950 sq. km (366 sq. miles) of beautiful highlands and rugged shores. Activities include hiking, fishing, camping, bird-watching, and golfing. If you hike only one of the 26 hiking trails in the park, make it the **Skyline trail.** It's a relatively easy 7-km (4.3-mile) loop, partially on dirt and partially on boardwalk, with a breathtaking view of the ocean from a headland cliff. The trail has good bird-watching oppportunities; if you lower your gaze, you might even spot a bear or moose. *Note:* Bring a warm jacket, as the winds on the crest of the mountain can be brisk and cool.

The entrance to the park is just beyond Cheticamp. To obtain information, call ✆ **888/773-8888** or 902/285-2691, or log on to **www.parkscanada. gc.ca.** The park is open year-round, subject to weather. You will be charged admission to the park from mid May to mid October, high season. The cost is C$3.50 (US$2.35) for adults, C$2.50 (US$1.70) for seniors, C$1.50 (US$1) for children 6 to 16, free for children 5 and under. A family pass costs C$8 (US$5.35). To get to Cape Breton Highlands National Park, follow Route 19 (the Ceilidh Trail) from the Canso Causeway along the west coast of Cape Breton Island to Margaree Forks, then follow the Cabot Trail to Cheticamp.

8 Yarmouth, A Forgotten Treasure

Yarmouth is a vibrant fishing community, the cultural and business center of western Nova Scotia, and the docking site for two international ferry runs from the United States. Historic buildings, decent shopping, and fresh delicious seafood await you.

ESSENTIALS

GETTING THERE   You can either hop in your vehicle in Halifax and travel for 3 hours down Highway 103 to Yarmouth (don't be shocked by the 50-kmph (30-mph) speed limit through Barrington), or hop aboard one of the two minivan shuttle services that run between Halifax and Yarmouth. **Campbell's Shuttle Service** (✆ **800/742-6101** or 902/742-6101) travels from Halifax to Yarmouth daily, leaving Halifax at 4:30pm and arriving in Yarmouth by 8pm. The return trip to Halifax leaves Monday to Friday 8am, arriving in Halifax at approximately 11:30am, and Saturday and Sunday at 8:30am, arriving in Halifax at approximately noon. One-way tickets cost C$45 (US$30) per person; C$80 (US$53.50) per person return.

The **Cloud Nine Shuttle** (✆ **888/805-3335** or 902/749-3137) also travels to Yarmouth daily. The shuttle picks you up at your location in Halifax between 3pm and 4pm and arrives in Yarmouth between 6:30pm and 7:30pm. The return trip leaves Yarmouth by 8am and arrives in Halifax at approximately 11:30am. One-way tickets cost C$48 (US$32) per person; C$87 (US$58) per person return.

VISITOR INFORMATION   The **Yarmouth Visitor Information Centre** is located at 228 Main St. (✆ **902/742-6639**), on the corner of Main and Forest streets toward the south end of town.

WHERE TO STAY & DINE

Harbour's Edge Bed & Breakfast ⓐ   This lovely home is located at the innermost point of the Yarmouth Harbour, which provides a lovely view from the south-side rooms. The Italianate-style house was built in 1864 for Stayley Brown, a member of the Provincial Legislature, and is a registered Heritage property. All of the rooms are named after women who have lived there in the past. The combined sitting and breakfast room, named after a woman called Lucy Jarvis, also has an outdoor sitting area with a view of the harbor. (This outdoor area is also a great spot to do some bird-watching.) The Audrey Kenney Room is the largest guest room, with a queen size bed and a very large attached bathroom with a chaise lounge. The Clara Caie Room has a view of the harbor and a private bath down the hall. The Ellen Brown room is spacious, with a queen size bed and an attached bath. All rooms are tastefully decorated, with period furniture. The breakfast is hearty and delicious.

12 Vancouver St. ⓒ **902/742-2387**. Fax 902/472-4471. www.harboursedge.ns.ca. 3 units. C$100–$125 (US$66.70–$83.35) double. Rates include full breakfast. MC, V. Free parking. From Highway 103 turn left at the stop sign and continue to the street lights. Turn right onto Starrs Rd. and follow to the end. Turn right onto Main St. until you reach the horse fountain statue, where you turn left onto Vancouver St. *In room:* No phone.

Quick-n-Tasty Express   A satellite of Harris Quick-n-Tasty located in Dayton, this take-out restaurant is a converted railcar with a drive-through and picnic tables out front. Seafood is the specialty, of course; Harris' famous seafood chowder is some of the best in Nova Scotia. But you can also order sandwiches and burgers, including a veggie burger as well as a ginger and black bean burger.

75 Water St. ⓒ **902/742-8078**. Main courses C$7–$15 (US$5–$10). Jun 1–Oct 15 daily 8:30am–10pm; Oct 16–Dec 18 & Feb 1–May 31 daily 9:30am–8pm. Closed Dec 19–Jan 31. From Highway 103 turn left at the stop sign and continue to the street lights. Turn right onto Starrs Rd. and follow to the end. Turn left onto Main St, and continue to Forest St. Turn right and continue to the end, turn right onto Water St.

The Rodd Grand Hotel   This is located in the middle of town across from shady Frost Park. Guest rooms are standard, but many have a good view of the main street and the harborfront. The **Ship's Bell restaurant** has a full menu and serves a tender hip of beef, or, if you're craving seafood, choose a full lobster dinner. You can also enjoy dinner theater from June to October in **Hayley's Lounge.** Minivan tours of Yarmouth depart from the hotel June through October several times a day; the guides are particularly informative.

417 Main St. ⓒ **800/565-7633** or 902/742-2446. Fax 902/742-4645. www.rodd-hotels.ca. 138 units. May 1– Oct 31 C$169 (US$113) double; C$180 (US$120) executive. Nov 1–April 30 C$139 (US$93) double; C$165 (US$110) executive. Packages available. Extra person C$10 (US$7). Children 15 and under stay free in parents' room. AE, DISC, MC, V. Free parking. From Highway 103, turn left at the stop sign and continue to the street lights. Turn right onto Starrs Rd. and follow to the end. Turn left onto Main St. **Amenities:** Restaurant (North American), lounge; indoor pool; exercise room; bike rental; secretarial services; limited room service. *In room:* TV w/ pay movies, coffeemaker, hair dryer.

⌐ *Fun Fact* **Rumor Has It . . .**

There's a local legend that the seasonal song "It's Beginning to Look a Lot Like Christmas" was penned in the original Grand Hotel. The line "There's a tree in the Grand Hotel, one in the park as well," convinces Yarmouth residents that it has to refer to the local area.

Rudder's Seafood & Brew Pub Yarmouth's only brew pub is located in an old warehouse erected in the mid 1800s, and named after a 19th-century sailor who saved his ship by repairing the rudder on one of its transatlantic voyages. It's a popular spot for travelers and locals, and during the summer gets really busy, especially whenever a festival is taking place on the waterfront. The menu is more varied than regular pub fare, and the fishcakes can't be beat. If you want to indulge in some cultural eating, try the Rappie Pie, an Acadian treat made from chicken stock, strained potatoes, and seasonings, roasted in the oven, and served with ketchup or molasses. There's a choice of several beers brewed on-site; our favorite is called "Ruff." From May to October, the outdoor deck overlooking the harbor is the best spot in town to enjoy a brew and watch the sunset.

96 Water St. ✆ **902/742-7050**. Main courses C$7–$15 (US$4.70–$10). June–Oct Mon–Thurs 11am–10pm; Fri–Sun 11am–midnight or later. Nov–March Tues–Sat 11am–9pm; closed Sun–Mon. April–June daily 11am–10pm. From Highway 103 turn left at the stop sign and continue to the street lights. Turn right onto Starrs Rd. and follow to the end. Turn left onto Main St. and continue to Forest St. Turn right and continue to the end, turn right onto Water St.

EXPLORING THE AREA

Yarmouth was settled in 1761 and experienced prosperity early, through lucrative trade with the West Indies and New England. Evidence of this still stands in the form of stately captains' homes and merchants' mansions, many of which are seen in the HERITAGE DISTRICT. You can pick up a walking tour of this district and other heritage homes at the visitors center, or at the Yarmouth County Museum (see below).

The ferry terminal is located on Water Street. This is where **The Cat,** a high-speed catamaran that travels between Yarmouth and Bar Harbor, Maine, docks. Call ✆ **888/249-7245** for information, or log on to www.catferry.com. It's also the docking location for the **Scotia Prince,** a car ferry that travels between Yarmouth and Portland, Maine. Call ✆ **800/845-4073** or 902/742-6460 for information, or visit www.scotiaprince.com. See "Getting There" in chapter 2 for more on traveling to Nova Scotia by ferry from locations in Canada and the United States.

Cape Forchu Yarmouth Lighthouse & Museum ★ (Kids) Cape Forchu's rocky point juts out into the ocean, with the opening to Yarmouth Harbour on one side and False Harbour on the other. The **Yarmouth Lighthouse** sits atop the rocks, with a very small parking area nearby for bus tours and handicapped parking, and a larger one at the bottom. Climb the cheery red and white stairs to the main building, which houses a small museum of photos and information on the lighthouse's history. Outside, explore the rocks out to the point or walk the grassy hills behind. Remember that rogue ocean waves are always possible, so stay within safe boundaries.

Route 304. ✆ **902/742-1433**. Admission free. Site open year-round. Museum open May 15–Oct 15 daily 9am–5pm. Closed Oct 16–May 14. From Yarmouth, follow route 304 for 11km (7 miles) to the lighthouse.

Firefighters Museum of Nova Scotia ★ (Kids) Considered one of the best of its kind in North America, the museum's two floors are filled with antique fire trucks and equipment, including an 1863 Amoskeag. The walls are lined with photos of firefighters and fires fought, and there are also displays of firefighting artifacts including uniforms, helmets, and medals. The museum is worth a visit for everyone, and children will especially enjoy the antique toy fire engines.

451 Main St. ✆ **902/742-5525**. www.firefighters.museum.gov.ns.ca. Admission C$2.50 (US$1.70) adults, C$2 (US$1.35) seniors, C$1 (US$0.75) children 17 and under, C$5 (US$3.35) families. Jun 1–Jun 30 & Sept 1–Oct 15 Mon–Sat 9am–5pm. July 1–Aug 31 Mon–Sat 9am–9pm. Oct 16–May 31 Mon–Fri 9am–4pm; Sat noon–4pm. From Highway 103 turn left at the stop sign and continue to the street lights. Turn right onto Starrs Rd. and follow to the end. Turn left onto Main St.

Sweeney Museum ⍟   An amazing recreation of a working fishing dock developed from a collection of artifacts saved by the late Lawrence Sweeney throughout the years. It consists of five buildings, an 18.5-m (60-foot) trawler, and a 30-m (100-foot) wharf, all housed inside.

120 Water St. ✆ **902/742-3457**. www.agns.gov.ns.ca. Admission C$3 (US$2) adults & seniors, C$2.50 (US$1.70) children 5–17, free for children 4 and under, C$7.50 (US$5) families. May–Oct daily 10am–5pm. Closed Nov–April. From Highway 103 turn left at the stop sign and continue to the street lights. Turn right onto Starrs Rd. and follow to the end. Turn left onto Main St, and continue to Forest St. Turn right and continue to the end, turn right onto Water St.

Western Branch of the Art Gallery of Nova Scotia ⍟   The gallery is slated to open in June 2003, and along with nationally acclaimed art shows, local artists' work will be on display, and a permanent collection of **Maud Lewis** and other folk art will be displayed on the second floor. Although the gallery is new, the impressive, sandstone building has been around for almost 100 years.

341 Main St. ✆ **902/742-7279**. www.agns.gov.ns.ca. Admission C$5 (US$3.35) adults, C$4 (US$2.65) seniors, C$2 (US$1.35) students, free for children 12 and under. July 1–Sept 1 Tue–Fri 10am–6pm; Sat–Mon noon–5pm. Sept 2–June 30 Tue–Fri 10am–6pm; Sat–Sun noon–5pm. Closed Mon. From Highway 103 turn left at the stop sign and continue to the street lights. Turn right onto Starrs Rd. and follow to the end. Turn left onto Main St.

Yarmouth County Museum & Archives/Pelton Fuller House ⍟⍟   This award-winning museum contains treasures from Yarmouth's seafaring past, the original light from the Cape Forchu lighthouse, a stagecoach used on an old Yarmouth route, and an electric car, among others. There are pianos and organs, a large display of Nova Scotia glassware, an impressive collection of clothing from the last two centuries, dolls and other toys, and one of the largest collections of ship portraits in Canada. Lifestyles from Yarmouth's past are displayed downstairs in authentically decorated rooms, including a kitchen, bedroom, and blacksmith's forge.

Originally housed in an old stone church, recent additions to the museum have included a climate-controlled storage area for artifacts and a larger area for the archives. The archives contain the largest non-institutional collection outside of Halifax, and many people with links to the area visit from all over Canada and the United States to trace their genealogy. The museum's gift shop carries a good selection of books associated with the county and province.

Next door is the **Pelton Fuller House,** former summer home of the Fuller Brush man, Alfred Fuller, and his wife Mary Primrose, known around town as Prim. Mrs. Fuller donated the house to the museum before her death, and it is maintained in the same manner as when she lived there, complete with grand piano and a host of antiques. One of the upstairs rooms is full of Fuller Brush memorabilia. The house is open in July and August. If you want to visit both the museum and the Pelton Fuller House, ask about the combination discount.

22 Collins St. ✆ **902/742-5539**. http://yarmouthcountymuseum.ednet.ns.ca. Admission C$3 (US$2) adults, C$2.50 (US$1.70) seniors, C$1 (US$0.70) children 6–17, free for children 5 and under, C$6 (US$4) families. From Highway 103 turn left at the stop sign and continue to the street lights. Turn right onto Starrs Rd. and follow to the end. Turn left onto Main St. Continue on Main St. until you reach Collins St. Turn left.

SHOPPING **C. E. Dyke's**, 344 Main St. (② **902/742-4214**), is a china, jewelry, and gift store with 100 years of history. Stop in to see the wonderfully carved wooden display units—especially the carved heads at the top—even if you don't want to shop. **R. H. Davis Ltd.,** 361 Main St. (② **902/742-3557**) is the second of two family businesses on Main Street that have been active for over 100 years (the other being C. E. Dyke's). The Davis store carries a quality selection of gifts, stationery, and office supplies. The same family owns **Samuel B's,** 355 Main St. (② **902/742-3557**), two doors farther along. You have to hike up a steep set of stairs to reach the goodies, but once you're up there, you'll be met by nearly a dozen themed Christmas trees and beautiful Christmas collectibles.

Sapphire Sea, 268 Main St. (② **902-742-1036**) carries gifts, decor, and personal items associated with the sea. Whether it's lobster antipasto, a beautiful seashore-themed sweater, or simply a seabreeze-scented soap, you'll find it here.

Appendix: Halifax in Depth

Halifax has evolved from a one-time summer hunting ground for Native peoples to a vibrant city on Canada's east coast, and its history, culture, and architecture bear witness to this development. A walk through the city streets is a lesson in architectural styles. Buildings reflect a bevy of schools, including the formal stone Georgian and Federalist styles; the fussy, wooden, Victorian and Queen Anne fashions; and the Greek Revival and Italianate styles. They take their place beside more contemporary 20th-century designs.

Well into the 1900s, Halifax remained predominantly British in its culture and feel. Today, however, it's the most cosmopolitan city in the Atlantic region. This is partly because it draws international professionals to work and live here, and partly because of the students from around the world who attend university in Halifax—they lend it a certain air of freshness, vitality, and, yes, youth. The information in this Appendix endeavors to give you a little more insight into Halifax, and into Haligonians, too.

1 History 101

Halifax's recorded history goes back 400 years, but the harbor was used for summer fishing by Native peoples for centuries before that. The story of how this rough and ready garrison town became one of Canada's "smart cities" is a legend of war and disaster, of politics and education.

THE MI'KMAQ

Halifax's harbor—natural, deep, and protected—was a gathering place for Native peoples long before the Vikings and Europeans discovered its value. The Mi'kmaq first appeared approximately 10,000 years ago. They called the Atlantic region Mi'kma'ki, and the harbor area that is now Halifax Chebucto, meaning "the biggest harbor." There is archaeological evidence indicating that these first inhabitants were hunters and gatherers who migrated from the west, moving about as the seasonal resources changed. During the summer months they hunted and fished along the ocean shores, and built seagoing vessels so they could hunt whales and porpoises. In the winter they camped inland where the forest provided protection

Dateline

- 11,000 – 9,000 BC Paleo-Indian Period in Nova Scotia.
- 956 Norsemen make first contact with Native peoples in the New World.
- 1534 First recorded trade between Native peoples and Europeans.
- 1604 Samuel de Champlain explores the coastline and identifies Chebucto as a good, safe bay.
- 1711 France plans for a fort to be built at Chebucto.
- 1749 British Governor Cornwallis commences building Halifax, the first permanent English settlement. He brings approximately 2,500 British immigrants to help colonize the area.
- 1750 Halifax Farmers Market opens and is still in operation today. St. Paul's Anglican Church, the first protestant church in Canada, is built in Halifax.
- 1752 The first English newspaper, *The Halifax Gazette,* is published. North America's first Board of Trade is established in Halifax. Postal service is established between Halifax and New York City. Ferry service between Halifax and Dartmouth begins, making it the longest continually run saltwater ferry service in North America.

Continues

from storms, and allowed winter hunting. They also speared and trapped eels, beaver, and other water animals.

The Mi'kmaqs' first contact with Europeans did not alter their worldview. They had a legend that told of one of their spiritual beings traveling across the ocean to discover Europe. This legend also taught that blue-eyed people would arrive from the east to disrupt their lives. So the Mi'kmaq were prepared for the appearance of early explorers in sailing ships. They greeted them, set up trade with them, and incorporated the Europeans' new technologies into their own culture.

Most of the early trade took place with ships from France. The French brought Catholic missionary priests to the new land, and in 1610 the Mi'kmaq Grand Chief Membertou converted to Catholicism. This resulted in the first Mi'kmaq treaty with a European nation—an agreement with the Vatican and the Holy See. The treaty was symbolized by a wampum belt decorated with a black-robed priest, a cross, and a Mi'kmaq figure holding a pouch, representing the incorporation of Mi'kmaq spirituality into Roman Catholicism.

In 1621, when Britain began to make claims on this part of the new world, the Mi'kmaq found them to be ruthless, and often sided with the French when it came to land wars. The first of a series of treaties between the British Crown and the Mi'kmaq Nation was signed in 1725. All were reaffirmed in 1752, and culminated in the Treaty and Royal Proclamation of 1763. The treaties formalized the exchange of Mi'kmaq loyalty for a guarantee that they would be able to continue hunting and fishing in their territory. The Supreme Court of Canada has subsequently recognized these treaties as legal and binding. Under the terms of a 1959 act of the Canadian Parliament, all aboriginal

A Lutheran church is built in Halifax. A peace treaty is signed between the British and the Mi'kmaq, part of which allows them "free liberty of hunting and fishing as usual."

- **1758** Halifax enacts an Elective Assembly.
  British warships and transports stop in Halifax before attacking French Louisburg in what is now Cape Breton.
- **1764** Halifax's population reaches 3,000.
- **1776** Halifax harbors British troops before they move to the front in the American Revolution.
  Letters of Marque from the British government allow British vessels to attack enemy shipping. This becomes known as legalized piracy.
- **1782** Black Loyalists from the United States leave Halifax for Africa.
- **1789** King's College, a post-secondary institution, opens in Halifax.
- **1796** Maroons in Jamaica rebelled against British rule resulting in 543 men, women, and children being shipped to Halifax.
- **1800** Under Prince Edward, the Duke of Kent, Halifax becomes the strongest fortress outside of Europe.
- **1813** The first Sunday school in North America for people of color is organized.
- **1818** Plans for a new citadel fort in Halifax are designed.
- **1819** Province House is built in Halifax, and becomes home to the provincial Legislature. Charles Dickens, during a later visit, called the building "a gem of Georgian architecture."
- **1820** Alexander Keith opens a brewery.
- **1825** The Halifax Banking Company is founded (now the Canadian Imperial Bank of Commerce).
- **1832** The Bank of Nova Scotia is founded.
- **1837** The Royal Nova Scotian Yacht Squadron opens. It still operates today.
- **1840** The Cunard Steamship Line is founded. Samuel Cunard's steamship *The Brittania* completes its first transatlantic voyage from Liverpool, England to Halifax in 14 days.

people of Canada are Canadian citizens and have the right to vote in federal and provincial elections.

THE EUROPEANS

In the 1500s, European fishing boats made use of the shores and islands of Halifax, then known as Chebucto, to dry their fish before heading home to Portugal, France, Spain, and England. By the 1600s, France had a settlement at Port Royal, on the western coast of what is now Nova Scotia, and the soldiers and settlers traveled to and from Chebucto using an overland route of rivers and lakes shown to them by the Mi'kmaq.

While politics kept France and England at odds in Europe, the land of the Mi'kmaq was being used as booty whenever a war was won or lost. In 1711, during a period when France had control of Acadia (the territory included what is now Nova Scotia, New Brunswick, Prince Edward Island, and part of Maine), the French commissioned one of their engineers to draw up plans for a fort on an island in the harbor at Chebucto. France hoped this would help it establish a stronghold in Acadia. However, the Treaty of Utrecht, signed in 1713, limited France's military ambitions to the region now known as Cape Breton. Acadia enjoyed a long period of peace from 1713 to 1744. France used this time to complete its fortress at Louisburg in Cape Breton in anticipation of renewed hostilities with Britain, both in Europe and the new world. When the War of the Austrian Succession (1744–1748) spread to Acadia, the British captured the Louisbourg fortress, though it was later returned to France under the Treaty of Aix-la-Chapelle, signed in 1748.

The British wanted to counter France's position of power at the mouth of the St. Lawrence River, considered the gateway to the interior of

- **1842** Halifax is incorporated as a city. Charles Dickens visits Halifax. Cool!
- **1844** Charles Fenerty, a successful local lumberman, is one of the first people to use wood pulp to make paper.
- **1846** Kerosene is tested for use. Second recorded use of a Christmas tree in Canada is in Halifax. The first was in Quebec in 1781.
- **1847** The Halifax Zoo opens. (It would be sold to New York City in 1863.)
- **1848** Responsible Government is enacted in Halifax on February 1.
- **1849** The Pony Express carries news from the Cunard ships in Halifax to Digby, then by boat to Saint John, so that it can be sent to New York and appear in the paper the following day.
- **1850** The first official ice hockey game, using rules and a net, is played in Halifax. Abraham Gesner incorporates the Kerosene Gaslight Company, which revolutionizes streetlights and lighting in homes.
- **1864** Free public schools open. The Merchant Bank is founded in Halifax and later becomes the Royal Bank of Canada.
- **1867** Confederation. Nova Scotia is the richest province at this time. Many people wear black armbands to protest Confederation. The Halifax Public Gardens open.
- **1874** Halifax Stock Exchange begins operation.
- **1876** Halifax is linked to the rest of the continent via the Intercolonial Railway.
- **1881** Halifax Electrical Company begins generating power and servicing the area.
- **1884** The Dalhousie Law School opens.
- **1885** A steel, swing bridge is erected across the harbor between Halifax and Dartmouth. It only lasts a few months before it is carried out to sea in a storm.
- **1887** The Halifax Victoria School of Art & Design opens. The school is founded and run by Anna Leonowens, whose teaching is immortalized in the Broadway show and film *The King and I.*

Continues

the North American continent. So they decided to establish both a military base at the harbor of Chebucto and a civil government in Nova Scotia—the name the British had chosen for the present-day region of Nova Scotia and New Brunswick. In June 1749, Nova Scotia's new governor, Edward Cornwallis, arrived at Chebucto with 13 transport ships carrying approximately 2,500 British settlers to populate the new town. Governor Cornwallis named the settlement Halifax, after Lord Halifax (George Montagu Dunk), president of the British Board of Trade at that time. Under the direction of Cornwallis, settlers established an organized fishery and imported manufactured materials from Boston, and engineers mapped out the town's first streets. But during that first winter of 1749, many of the settlers, not used to the harsh climate and subsisting on a diet of salt meat and hard bread, succumbed to disease. Cornwallis imported a group of colonists from New England, already acclimatized to pioneer life, to take their place.

Halifax soon became a critical base for British war operations. General James Wolfe launched from the port when he captured Louisburg in 1758, and again in the following year when he conquered the French capital at Quebec, consolidating British North America. For the next 50 years, Halifax was home to numerous British armies as Britain fought the Seven Years War, the American Revolution, the Napoleonic Wars, and the War of 1812. Halifax played a strategic role in all of these engagements.

When the American Revolution began in 1776, English armies were dispatched from Halifax to Boston to fight the rebels, and retreated to Halifax at its conclusion in 1783. The War of 1812 brought British activity to Halifax as well. British Major General

- 1890 Halifax is the first city in North America to have electric streetlights.
- 1899 The Halifax Armouries is built on the corner of Cunard and North Park streets, and is used as the headquarters and training area for volunteers to the Boer War in South Africa.
- 1906 Britain bequeaths the Citadel to Canada, and the British soldiers leave.
- 1912 The *Titanic* sinks. The ships that left Halifax to retrieve survivors instead brought back 190 bodies. They are buried in cemeteries throughout the city.
- 1914 World War I begins. Most of the half-million Canadians who go to the front pass through Halifax.
- 1916 On July 1, the beginning of prohibition puts no less than 150 liquor wholesalers and retailers out of business. Halifax is left with hundreds of people jobless, and gallons of illegal booze. Bootlegging soon solves both problems.
- 1917 On December 6, Halifax experiences the largest man-made explosion before the atomic bomb. Two munitions ships collide in the harbor. Blocks of city dwellings are flattened, hundreds of lives are lost, thousands are injured.
- 1917 World War I Russian activist Leon Trotsky is brought to Halifax as a prisoner of war.
- 1918 Servicemen riot as tensions build up over war, and prohibition continues. When a charge of shoplifting is brought against a sailor, the servicemen break into City Hall and wreck everything in sight.
- 1928 The Halifax Harbour Commission is created and work is renewed on upgrading harbor facilities.
- 1930s Effects of the Great Depression are felt in Halifax.
- 1939 World War II begins. Halifax is the main training center for the Royal Canadian Navy.
- 1945 An ammunition barge explodes in the harbor and the Halifax Ammunition Dumps catch fire.
- 1945 On May 8, servicemen and civilians loot Halifax department stores and businesses, in what would

Robert Ross succeeded in razing Washington, D.C., during the war. Later, when he was killed in action, his regiment brought him to Halifax to be buried. British Captain Philip Bowes Vere Broke, of the HMS *Shannon,* gave Haligonians something to talk about on a quiet Sunday morning in 1813, when he entered Halifax Harbour with the American frigate *Chesapeake* in tow. During the American Revolution and again during the War of 1812, Britain issued Letters of Marque to seafaring vessels. Ships were "given license" to prey on enemy shipping and commerce in time of war, and were entitled to a portion of any profit taken. The sailors were known as privateers, and this is where the Privateers Wharf in Halifax gained its name. The difference between a pirate and a privateer could sometimes become blurred: Outlaws in peace soon became patriots and heroes in times of war. The same heroes who declined to give up their activities after a peace treaty was signed in far-off Europe again became bandits and criminals.

Daring exploits by the privateers enabled the local merchants who owned the privateering ships to amass great fortunes in a short period of time. While most of these riches passed into the hands of a few individuals, Halifax as a whole seemed to benefit from the prizes of plundering.

But more was happening in Halifax than housing British armies and privateering. Halifax's first royal guest, Prince William, arrived in Halifax in 1786 aboard his ship, *Pegasus.* The prince enjoyed the garrison town (and its drinking establishments) so much that he returned regularly for the next three years.

In 1794, Prince Edward, Duke of Kent, arrived in Halifax aboard the frigate *Blanche,* for a six-year stint as Commander in Chief of His Majesty's

become known as the V-E Day Riot. They even manage to break into Alexander Keith's Brewery and steal, destroy (and drink) 120,000 bottles of beer.
- 1955 The Angus L. Macdonald Bridge opens, linking the cities of Halifax and Dartmouth. Construction begins on the Halifax International Airport.
- 1962 The Bedford Institute of Oceanography opens as Canada's largest federal research center for oceanography.
- 1969 Africville land is expropriated and residents are relocated to other parts of Halifax.
- 1970 The A. Murray MacKay Bridge opens, linking Halifax and Dartmouth. The suspension bridge is approximately 1 kilometer (⅔ mile) long and located over "The Narrows," site of the where the 1917 explosion occurred.
- 1971 Pier 21 closes. Known as Canada's "front door," the pier had welcomed immigrants for over 50 years, and had witnessed the arrival of more than one million refugees, war brides, and troops.
- 1988 The Art Gallery of Nova Scotia moves into its permanent home, a historic building built in 1867 on Hollis Street.
- 1991 The population is 114,455.
- 1995 Halifax hosts the 21st Summit of the G–7 countries.
- 1996 Halifax, Dartmouth, Bedford, and Halifax County amalgamate to form the Halifax Regional Municipality (HRM).
- 1998 Swissair Flight 111 crashes into the ocean near Peggy's Cove.
- 2000 Halifax celebrates its 250th anniversary. 120 "Tall Ships" from around the world enter Halifax Harbour.
- 2001 HRM hosts hundreds of stranded air travelers whose planes are grounded due to the September 11, 2001 terrorist attacks in the U.S.
- 2002 Population of the Halifax Regional Municipality is 360,000.

forces in Nova Scotia. Prince Edward began immediately to strengthen the defenses of the harbor, including the fortifications at Citadel Hill, Point Pleasant, McNab's Island, and York Redoubt at the western entrance to the harbor. But, interestingly, he may be best remembered for his intense love affair with his French mistress, Julie St. Laurent, who accompanied him to Halifax. During his tenure in Nova Scotia, the prince was invited to stay at the estate of Sir John Wentworth, the Lieutenant Governor of Nova Scotia. Prince Edward renovated the residence and brought in landscapers from England to design the gardens around the estate. The result is today's Hemlock Ravine Park—185 acres of winding paths, trails, and vistas. Most poignant of all is the heart-shaped pond built by the prince in honor of Mademoiselle St. Laurent. Not surprisingly, it was named Julie's Pond, and still goes by that name today.

GROWTH AND DEVELOPMENT IN THE NINETEENTH CENTURY: ALEXANDER KEITH, JOSEPH HOWE & SAMUEL CUNARD

Throughout the 19th century, Halifax was a city of firsts. It was here that citizens opened the first Sunday school in North America for people of color, established the first Canadian bank, and played Canada's first official game of ice hockey. (Why was it the first "official" game? Because players used an actual net, and the whole game was governed by a set of rules. Play was apparently pretty lawless before then.) North America's first zoo and botanical gardens were in Halifax (later sold to New York City). The Halifax Public Gardens, the first public gardens in Canada, opened, along with the Dalhousie Law School and the Institute of Science.

While the development of Halifax can be attributed to a variety of influences, including the military, the harbor, and the institutions of higher learning, there were independent citizens who left their mark as well. From merchants to politicians, pirates to religious leaders, Halifax had its share of colorful people.

Joseph Howe (1804–1873) was one of Nova Scotia's most dynamic and popular politicians, and a statue in his honor stands outside of Province House in the city's downtown. He is known best for his fight for responsible government and against Confederation. Prior to 1847, the colonial governors appointed administrators in the British North American colonies. The elected assemblies had no control over these appointments and little influence on their decisions. Howe fought to convince Britain that the colonial governors should take their advice from an executive that the politicians—elected by the people—trusted. The governors would retain decision-making power on only a few important matters, including external relations and constitutional change. This became known as responsible government.

Howe purchased a provincial newspaper, the *Novascotian,* in 1827. The paper was published in Halifax, and Howe traveled the province by foot, horseback, and boat to collect subscriptions and promote his publication. Under his leadership, it soon became the most influential newspaper in the province. Howe used the newspaper to educate the citizens of Halifax by reporting on debates in the Legislative Assembly and writing about his travels throughout the province.

Howe's involvement with the *Novascotian* propelled him into the political arena. His editorials accused the government of being corrupt, and resulted in a libel charge in 1835. Howe chose to defend himself, and with some background study of law and six hours of impassioned oratory on the day of the trial, he won an acquittal. Following the trial, his editorials became even more concerned with political issues. Eventually, he decided that running for office was the best way to accomplish the changes he wanted. He was first elected in 1836, campaigning on a platform of support for responsible government. He held the offices of Speaker of the Assembly in 1841, and collector of excise for Halifax in 1842. To promote his desire for responsible government, he assumed the editorship of both the *Novascotian* and the *Morning Chronicle* from 1844 to 1846, making them a rallying point for Liberal principles. His efforts were rewarded with a seven-seat Liberal majority in the 1847 election, leading to the formation of the first responsible government in Canada in January 1848.

Howe was given the post of provincial secretary so that he could work to adapt existing institutions to the new system of government. He also began a campaign of railway construction. In 1854, he resigned as the provincial secretary in order to head the railway commission, which eventually succeeded in completing lines from Halifax to Windsor and Truro.

In the 1860s, Howe became active in the anti-Confederation movement in Nova Scotia. He felt that in a confederation, Nova Scotia, as a smaller union member, would be ignored. Howe also believed that Upper Canada was too absorbed in its own affairs to concern itself with Nova Scotia. In Howe's opinion, Confederation would ultimately lead to the ruin of Nova Scotia's economy and a loss of independence. When the British North America Act was passed in 1867, making Confederation official, Howe actually led a delegation to England to repeal it, to no avail. Howe was later elected to the federal government in 1869, where Canada's first prime minister, Sir John A. Macdonald, convinced Howe he could continue his work as secretary of state for the provinces. In 1873, Howe became lieutenant governor of Nova Scotia, but served only a few weeks before his death.

A contemporary of Howe's, Alexander Keith (1795–1873) contributed to the growth of Halifax via politics and other ways as well. Keith left Scotland for Halifax in 1820. He became brewer and business manager for a Charles Boggs, who owned a brewery on Argyle Street. Keith soon bought out the brewery, and in 1822 he moved his brewery and premises to larger facilities on Lower Water Street. Keith expanded again in 1836, when he built a new brewery on Hollis Street. In 1863, he built Keith Hall, his private residence, which was connected by a tunnel to the brewery. Keith's appointment as director of the Bank of Nova Scotia in 1837 is an indication of his importance in the Halifax business community. In 1838, he helped found the Halifax Marine Insurance Association, and during the 1840s, he was on the board of management of the Colonial Life Assurance Company. He was director of the Halifax Gas, Light, and Water Company, incorporated in 1840, and in 1844 he helped incorporate the Halifax Water Company, becoming a director in 1856. By 1864, Keith was a director of the Provincial Permanent Building and Investment Society.

Keith's interest in utilities and insurance was only a part of his involvement in the public life of Halifax, though. He was elected to the first Halifax city council in 1841 and was selected by the council to sit as mayor in 1843. Keith stayed on the city council and was elected mayor by the general population of the city in 1853 and 1854. In 1843 he was also appointed to the Nova Scotia Legislative Assembly, the governing body of the province, and in June 1867 he accepted the appointment of president of the council, declining a seat in the newly formed Canadian Senate.

Another influential Haligonian was Samuel Cunard (1787–1865). Born and raised in Halifax, Cunard had a gift for business. At age 17 he managed his own general store, and later he joined his father, Abraham, in the lumber business and expanded into coal, iron, and shipping.

Fascinated by the development of the steamship and its ability to run on a set schedule, Cunard dreamed of creating a transatlantic steamship service. In 1839, Cunard won a contract with the British Admiralty to carry the mail between England and Halifax twice a month; he would then distribute the mail to Boston and Quebec. Named the British and North America Mail Steam Packet Company (it soon became known simply as the Cunard Shipping Line, or Cunard Line), the company built four steamships: the *Britannia, Acadia, Caledonia,* and *Columbia.* In July 1840, the *Britannia* completed the firm's first transatlantic voyage from Liverpool to Halifax, and then on to Boston. The entire trip took 14 days. After this groundbreaking crossing, Cunard committed to nothing but the best ships, the best officers, and the best men. He made the motto of his company "Speed, Comfort, Safety." During the Crimean War (1854–1856), Cunard allowed his ships to be used as troop carriers or converted hospital ships. For this endeavor, he was knighted. It was also Cunard who initiated the system of sailing with green lights to starboard, red to port, and white on the masthead. This soon became the standard for the entire maritime world. When Samuel Cunard died in 1865, he left behind a prosperous company that had changed the very nature of transatlantic transport. As an interesting footnote to Cunard, it's worth noting that not a single life was lost on a Cunard ship in the first 65 years of the company's history—an amazing and unparalleled record, especially when you consider that most other transatlantic services were dazzled by the notion of speed, often at the expense of many lives. The sinking of the *Titanic,* in 1912, is only the most visible of these. The first disaster the Cunard Shipping Line experienced wasn't until 50 years after Cunard's death, with the sinking of the *Lusitania* in 1915, at the beginning of World War I. It was torpedoed by a German submarine.

HALIFAX IN THE WORLD WARS

After more than 50 years of peace, Halifax once again became a strategic location during World War I. At that time, Halifax's prominent role as a naval port invited the attention of German submarines. While the threat of attack was real, the enemy did not cause the disaster that actually occurred, one that became known as the Halifax Explosion

On December 6, 1917, a French ship loaded with munitions for the war collided with a Belgian relief vessel near "The Narrows" between the outer Halifax Harbour and the Bedford Basin. A fire broke out, followed by what has become known as the Halifax Explosion, which flattened over 5 sq. km (2 sq. miles) of homes and businesses. Thousands of people were killed or injured, and more were left homeless.

Halifax eventually rebuilt and the war ended. But the city was still had problems. Financial difficulties emerged in the Maritimes long before what became known in North America as the "Dirty Thirties." In 1922, provincial politicians formed the Maritime Rights Movement to try to rectify what those living in Nova Scotia, New Brunswick, and Prince Edward Island perceived as the federal government's neglect of the Maritime provinces. In 1925, a delegation traveled from Halifax to Ottawa, calling attention to the increasingly desperate conditions in the Maritime region. Prime Minister Mackenzie King appointed Sir Andrew Rae Duncan to study the problem and find solutions. The resulting Duncan Commission made numerous recommendations, some of which affected Halifax.

The most important was an infusion of federal money to create the Halifax Harbour Commission and to complete dockyard renovations that were begun in 1913 but abandoned in 1921 due to lack of funds. The neglected dockyards were transformed into a world-class port, with a cold storage plant, a new quay wall, grain elevators, and refurbished piers. With these enhancements Halifax was able to improve its economic stability.

When World War II began in 1939, Halifax once again mobilized. Thomas Raddall writes in his book *Warden of the North*: "By the summer of 1940 Britain like a diver in deep waters was dependent for life upon a slender and fragile line stretching across the sea, and that line began at Halifax." The majority of the Allied "fast convoys," ships that sailed at faster than 15 knots, assembled at and departed from Halifax. The harbor's entrance was protected by the city's defenses and by submarine nets stretched across the harbor mouth. There was ample room for more than 100 ships to assemble in the large inner part of the harbor.

The dockyard was active in ship repair throughout the war; Halifax Harbour became known as "Cripple Creek," as over 7,000 vessels received repairs there between 1939 and 1945.

The city became a part-time home to the huge liners *Queen Mary, Queen Elizabeth*, and *Aquitania,* and such famous smaller liners as the *Empress of Britain, Empress of Australia, Monarch of Bermuda,* and the *Duchess of York.* Before the fall of France to Germany in the summer of 1940, units of the French fleet visited Halifax frequently for fuel and supplies.

Winston Churchill visited Halifax on his way back from the Washington Conference in 1943. He spent several hours touring the city, strolling through the Public Gardens, and inspecting the port from the top of Citadel Hill. A year later, in September 1944, he was back again, as he made his way to the Quebec Conference, this time with a large staff and accompanied by Mrs. Churchill. Hundreds of servicemen and citizens recognized the British prime minister and his trademark cigar.

THE TWENTY-FIRST CENTURY AND BEYOND

Today, Halifax's harbor is home to the Canadian Navy's Maritime Command as well as Canada's Atlantic fleet, and is the main Atlantic base for the Canadian Coast Guard. Halifax also hosts the North Atlantic Treaty Organization (NATO) Standing Naval Force Atlantic. This rapid-reaction task force is composed of ships from NATO member countries, including Canada, the United States, Great Britain, France, the Netherlands, and Germany. Halifax is also a significant port of call for many shipping companies and passenger cruise lines.

Although there's been much ink spilled about Halifax's rich history, it's working hard to be a city of the future—not just one of the past. It is well positioned to take advantage of the oil and gas finds off the Atlantic coast. It has one of the highest per-capita Internet usages in Canada (68%), and it has all the elements in place, including training and technological expertise and equipment, to become a world leader in the Information and Communications Technology (ICT) industry. Year after year, surveys consistently rank Halifax as one of the top places to do business in North America.

2 Halifax Architecture

As one of the oldest cities in Canada, Halifax displays a cross-section of architectural styles. Combine the architectural periods with the tastes of people who were influential in having public buildings designed, and the variety is greater still.

St. Paul's Anglican Church, built in 1750, is considered the oldest Protestant Church in Canada, and the oldest building in Halifax. The church was framed in Boston and erected in Halifax, and the original building incorporated a unique blending of the styles of celebrated British architects Sir Christopher Wren and James Gibbs.

McLean House on Hollis Street was built in 1797 and is probably the earliest example of a house with Scottish dormers in Halifax. The five-sided dormers were popular with those of Scottish ancestry, and you will notice them on houses throughout the city.

One of Halifax's four round buildings, St. George's Round Church, was built in 1800. Its circular Palladian design is reminiscent of early Roman architecture. Prince Edward, Duke of Kent, commander of the forces in Nova Scotia at the time, played an active role in planning this church. Originally perfectly round, a porch and chancel were added between 1822 and 1827. Another project instigated by Prince Edward was the Town Clock, finished in 1803. It is also Palladian, with four clock faces and bells that ring every 15 minutes. The third round building in Halifax is also associated with Prince Edward and is located on the shore of the Bedford Basin. It is known as The Rotunda, or music room, and the Prince had it built for his mistress, Julie St. Laurent. A completely round building with 20 exterior pillars and 8 windows, it is the only building that remains of the Prince's estate. Point Pleasant Park is home to the last round building associated with the Prince. The round, stone Martello Tower was built as part of the fortifications added by Prince Edward during his tenure.

Canada's first Georgian building is Halifax's Province House. It was designed and built by Richard Scott between 1811 and 1818. The exterior is of sandstone, and inside there is a large oak table originally used by Colonel Edward Cornwallis (the city's founder) on his flagship HMS *Beaufort*. It is now used by the Cabinet of the government of Nova Scotia.

The buildings known as the Historic Properties form Canada's oldest surviving group of waterfront warehouses. The oldest building in the group, called Privateers Warehouse, was built in 1813. The surrounding docks hold 200-year-old secrets from Halifax's sea trade, including her pirates and smugglers. Halifax is famous for its star-shaped Citadel, completed in 1856. This is the fourth in a series of forts built on the hill since 1749, and it is an excellent example of a 19th-century bastion fortification, complete with defensive ditch, ramparts, musketry gallery, powder magazine, and signal masts. The fort was never attacked, but was garrisoned by the British Army until 1906 and by Canadian Forces during both World Wars.

The Granville Mall, which presents some of the finest Victorian-Italianate facades in Canada, was erected after the original ones were destroyed by fire in 1859. Bishop Street in the downtown area appears much the same as it would have in the 1860s. One of the buildings, a four-unit town house, was built in 1862, and represents a typical residence for the upper-middle-class city dweller of that time.

South Park Street and Young Avenue are lined with beautiful Victorian homes, and you will find excellent examples of Halifax's ornate storm porches.

The new home of the Art Gallery of Nova Scotia is the old Dominion Building, built in 1864. The Victorian-Italianate facade of this building originally looked down on an outdoor farmers' market, active on the site for more than 100 years.

Twentieth-century architecture is represented by the CBC buildings on South Park Street and by the Bank of Nova Scotia, a registered historic building in the Art Deco style of the 1930s. Contemporary architecture is represented by the two office towers of Purdy's Wharf, which were completed in 1986 and are located on the waterfront. The buildings' foundation supports are built into the harbor floor and salt water is used for the indoor air-conditioning.

3 Recommended Reading & Viewing

FURTHER HALIFAX READING

Halifax boasts a plethora of books about its history, but for a real feel for the military role, try Thomas Raddall's *Halifax, Warden of the North* (republished by Nimbus Publishing, 1993). Raddall also talks about the Mi'kmaq and the city's first settlers, right up to the wartime booms in the 20th century. At 348 pages, it's a quick intro to the historic city. For people interested in Halifax's association with the sinking of the *Titanic,* there's *Titanic Halifax* by Alan Jeffers and Rob Gordon (Nimbus Publishing, 1998). The 108-page book is filled with information about the graveyards, ghosts, and historic buildings in Halifax that are a part of this tragic story. A new book that gives a more anecdotal history is *Halifax Street Names: An Illustrated Guide* (Formac Publishing Ltd., 2002). The book is edited by Shelagh Mackenzie and offers fascinating contributions from more than 60 local historians, heritage activists, and longtime residents of the city. Street names are often a clue to the entertaining history of a community, and those in this book are no exception. There are also numerous sketches and photographs that give an insight into everyday life during the first two centuries of the city's existence. In *Halifax, The Smart City,* by Graham Walker, you'll find a contemporary overview of what makes Halifax tick. Photographer Jocelin d'Entremont supplements the text with scenes from present-day Halifax.

I DIDN'T KNOW THAT WAS FILMED IN HALIFAX!

In recent years, Hollywood has filmed a number of movies, or parts of movies, in Halifax. This is a result of the lower Canadian dollar, the availability of skilled film crews, and the appealing Halifax architecture and coastline. Halifax has accommodated film crews from *Titanic, The Shipping News, The Real Howard Spitz, A Glimpse of Hell,* and *K-19: The Widowmaker*. Haligonians have been thrilled to catch glimpses of actors Kelsey Grammer, Harrison Ford, and James Caan. For the best view of Halifax on film, choose *Titanic*—all the modern-day scenes were filmed in the city.

Index

See also Accommodations and Restaurant indexes, below.

ACCOMMODATIONS

FROMMER'S® COMPLETE TRAVEL GUIDES

Alaska
Amsterdam
Argentina & Chile
Arizona
Atlanta
Australia
Austria
Bahamas
Barcelona, Madrid & Seville
Beijing
Belgium, Holland &
 Luxembourg
Bermuda
Boston
British Columbia & the
 Canadian Rockies
Budapest & the Best of Hungary
California
Canada
Cancún, Cozumel & the
 Yucatán
Cape Cod, Nantucket &
 Martha's Vineyard
Caribbean
Caribbean Cruises & Ports
 of Call
Caribbean Ports of Call
Carolinas & Georgia
Chicago
China
Colorado
Costa Rica
Denmark
Denver, Boulder & Colorado
 Springs
England
Europe

European Cruises & Ports of Call
Florida
France
Germany
Greece
Greek Islands
Hawaii
Hong Kong
Honolulu, Waikiki & Oahu
Ireland
Israel
Italy
Jamaica
Japan
Las Vegas
London
Los Angeles
Maryland & Delaware
Maui
Mexico
Montana & Wyoming
Montréal & Québec City
Munich & the Bavarian Alps
Nashville & Memphis
Nepal
New England
New Mexico
New Orleans
New York City
New Zealand
Nova Scotia, New Brunswick &
 Prince Edward Island
Oregon
Paris
Philadelphia & the Amish
 Country
Portugal

Prague & the Best of the Czech
 Republic
Provence & the Riviera
Puerto Rico
Rome
San Antonio & Austin
San Diego
San Francisco
Santa Fe, Taos & Albuquerque
Scandinavia
Scotland
Seattle & Portland
Shanghai
Singapore & Malaysia
South Africa
Southeast Asia
South Florida
South Pacific
Spain
Sweden
Switzerland
Texas
Thailand
Tokyo
Toronto
Tuscany & Umbria
USA
Utah
Vancouver & Victoria
Vermont, New Hampshire
 & Maine
Vienna & the Danube Valley
Virgin Islands
Virginia
Walt Disney World & Orlando
Washington, D.C.
Washington State

FROMMER'S® DOLLAR-A-DAY GUIDES

Australia from $50 a Day
California from $70 a Day
Caribbean from $70 a Day
England from $70 a Day
Europe from $70 a Day

Florida from $70 a Day
Hawaii from $70 a Day
Ireland from $60 a Day
Italy from $70 a Day
London from $85 a Day

New York from $80 a Day
Paris from $80 a Day
San Francisco from $60 a Day
Washington, D.C.,
 from $70 a Day

FROMMER'S® PORTABLE GUIDES

Acapulco, Ixtapa &
 Zihuatanejo
Alaska Cruises & Ports
 of Call
Amsterdam
Australia's Great Barrier Reef
Bahamas
Baja & Los Cabos
Berlin
Boston
California Wine Country
Charleston & Savannah
Chicago

Dublin
Hawaii: The Big Island
Hong Kong
Houston
Las Vegas
London
Los Angeles
Maine Coast
Maui
Miami
New Orleans
New York City
Paris

Phoenix & Scottsdale
Portland
Puerto Rico
Puerto Vallarta, Manzanillo &
 Guadalajara
San Diego
San Francisco
Seattle
Sydney
Tampa & St. Petersburg
Vancouver
Venice
Washington, D.C.

FROMMER'S® NATIONAL PARK GUIDES

Family Vacations in the
 National Parks
Grand Canyon

National Parks of the American
 West
Rocky Mountain
Yellowstone & Grand Teton

Yosemite & Sequoia/
 Kings Canyon
Zion & Bryce Canyon

FROMMER'S® MEMORABLE WALKS

Chicago	New York	San Francisco
London	Paris	Washington, D.C.

FROMMER'S® GREAT OUTDOOR GUIDES

Arizona & New Mexico	Northern California	Southern New England
New England	Southern California & Baja	Vermont & New Hampshire

FROMMER'S® BORN TO SHOP GUIDES

Born to Shop: France	Born to Shop: Italy	Born to Shop: New York
Born to Shop: Hong Kong,	Born to Shop: London	Born to Shop: Paris
Shanghai & Beijing		

FROMMER'S® IRREVERENT GUIDES

Amsterdam	Los Angeles	Seattle & Portland
Boston	Manhattan	Vancouver
Chicago	New Orleans	Walt Disney World
Las Vegas	Paris	Washington, D.C.
London	San Francisco	

FROMMER'S® BEST-LOVED DRIVING TOURS

America	France	New England
Britain	Germany	Scotland
California	Ireland	Spain
Florida	Italy	Western Europe

THE UNOFFICIAL GUIDES®

Bed & Breakfasts in California	Golf Vacations in the	New Orleans
Bed & Breakfasts in	Eastern U.S.	New York City
New England	The Great Smoky &	Paris
Bed & Breakfasts in the North-	Blue Ridge Mountains	San Francisco
west	Inside Disney	Skiing in the West
Bed & Breakfasts in Southeast	Hawaii	Southeast with Kids
Beyond Disney	Las Vegas	Walt Disney World
Branson, Missouri	London	Walt Disney World for
California with Kids	Mid-Atlantic with Kids	Grown-ups
Chicago	Mini Las Vegas	Walt Disney World for Kids
Cruises	Mini-Mickey	Washington, D.C.
Disneyland	New England with Kids	World's Best Diving Vacations
Florida with Kids		

SPECIAL-INTEREST TITLES

Frommer's Britain's Best Bed & Breakfasts and
Country Inns
Frommer's France's Best Bed & Breakfasts and
Country Inns
Frommer's Italy's Best Bed & Breakfasts and
Country Inns
Frommer's Caribbean Hideaways
Frommer's Adventure Guide to Australia &
New Zealand
Frommer's Adventure Guide to Central America
Frommer's Adventure Guide to India & Pakistan
Frommer's Adventure Guide to South America
Frommer's Adventure Guide to Southeast Asia
Frommer's Adventure Guide to Southern Africa
Frommer's Gay & Lesbian Europe
Frommer's Exploring America by RV
Hanging Out in England

Hanging Out in Europe
Hanging Out in France
Hanging Out in Ireland
Hanging Out in Italy
Hanging Out in Spain
Israel Past & Present
Frommer's The Moon
Frommer's New York City with Kids
The New York Times' Guide to Unforgettable
Weekends
Places Rated Almanac
Retirement Places Rated
Frommer's Road Atlas Britain
Frommer's Road Atlas Europe
Frommer's Washington, D.C., with Kids
Frommer's What the Airlines Never Tell You